Great St Mary's has been the church of the University of Cambridge since the first students arrived in the town in around 1240. The medieval church was the home of lectures and disputations, as well as of church worship – and even the occasional riot.

Cambridge became a centre of the English Reformation, and the early German theologian Martin Bucer was buried, exhumed, burnt and then commemorated in the church. It became a home of the classic Anglican sermon, preached, in theory, before the whole university. After the Second World War a new young vicar, Mervyn Stockwood, made the church into the centre of a remarkable religious revival, with a succession of well-known speakers preaching to large student congregations, sometimes leading to long queues stretching around Market Place or down King's Parade. As well as sharing in the intellectual and religious history of the land, Great St Mary's is also a parish church in the market of an East Anglian town, much loved by generations of local people.

Great St Mary's long, distinguished and sometimes turbulent history is described in this affectionate portrait of the church, from its earliest beginnings to its present life. The contributors include leading academics in the University – Christopher Brooke, Patrick Collinson and David Thompson – a former vicar of the church, Hugh Montefiore, and past and present members of the congregation including David Owen (Lord Owen, CH).

JOHN BINNS is Vicar of Great St Mary's.
PETER MEADOWS is Archivist of the Diocese of Ely

Great St Mary's

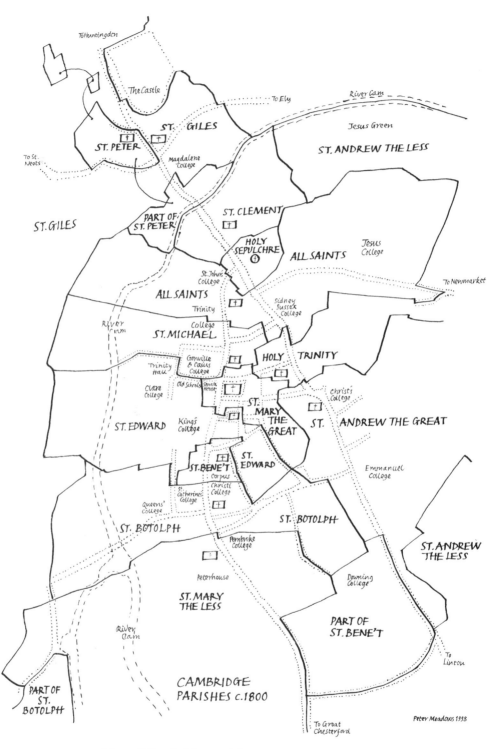

1. Map of Cambridge parishes

Great St Mary's

Cambridge's University Church

Edited by
JOHN BINNS
Vicar of Great St Mary's

and PETER MEADOWS
Archivist of the Diocese of Ely

GREAT ST MARY'S
THE UNIVERSITY CHURCH

Published for Great St Mary's, the University Church, Cambridge, United Kingdom

First published 2000

Printed in the United Kingdom at the University Press, Cambridge

Typeface Ehrhardt (*The Monotype Corporation*) 11.5/13.5pt   *System* QuarkXPress® [SE]

A catalogue record for this book is available from the British Library

ISBN 0 521 775027 paperback

Copies of this book are available for purchase
both from Great St Mary's Church, Cambridge CB2 3PQ,
and from Cambridge University Press Bookshop,
1 Trinity Street, Cambridge CB2 1SZ.

Contents

vii

Illustrations

Figures

Contributors

JOHN BINNS (St John's) is Vicar of Great St Mary's.

JASON BRAY (Fitzwilliam) is a Minor Canon of St Woolos' Cathedral, Newport.

LYNNE BROUGHTON (Clare Hall) is Associate Lecturer in the Faculty of Divinity.

CHRISTOPHER BROOKE was Dixie Professor of Ecclesiastical History in the University and is a Fellow of Gonville and Caius College.

PATRICK COLLINSON was Regius Professor of Modern History in the University and is a Fellow of Trinity College.

GARETH DAVIES (Homerton) is a member of the Society of Cambridge Youths bell-ringers.

PETER MEADOWS (Pembroke) is Under Librarian in the Department of Manuscripts and University Archives and Archivist of the Diocese of Ely.

HUGHE MONTEFIORE was Dean of Gonville and Caius College, Vicar of Great St Mary's and Bishop of Birmingham.

DAVID OWEN, Baron Owen of Plymouth (Sidney Sussex) was Secretary of State for Foreign and Commonwealth Affairs, founder and leader of the Social Democratic Party, and Co-Chairman of the International Conference on the former Yugoslavia.

GRAHAM SUDBURY (Magdalene) was Director of Music at Great St Mary's and the Perse School.

DAVID THOMPSON is Lecturer in the Faculty of Divinity, Director of the Centre for Advanced Religious and Theological Studies in the University, and is a Fellow of Fitzwilliam College.

GRIM ST MARYS MAY BALL

Featuring in Church:

The Black & Blacker Minstrels

PLUS **Adam Mombassa Ph.D. and**
The Frelimo Steel Band

Free Sparkling Cocoa!

In the Clay Cross Chapel:

Encounter Groups — "Eyeball to Eyeball"

10.00 p.m. - 2.00 a.m. "Christ and Turbo-Engineering".

2.00 a.m. - 4.00 a.m. "The Human Face of John Robinson".

Chair Cleric — Revd. Moses Wildebeeste Ph. D. (Strathclyde)

In the Kier Hardie Garden of Rest.

6.00 a.m. Non Verbal Communication
6.30 a.m. Small Arms Demonstration by Mothers' Union (Volunteer Reserve)
8.30 a.m. Festal Picket of Peterhouse (Bring the Kiddies!)

Tickets: Apply G.S.M., G.H.Q.

Price 15 Roubles, double.
(reduction for tribes)

2. Grim St Mary's May Ball poster (see page 83)

Introduction

The idea for this book arose out of an uneasy sense that a golden period in the history of Great St Mary's was coming to an end. The decision to discontinue the famous Sunday evening university services may have been inevitable but was difficult to take. It was as if we were deliberately reducing the stature of the church and diminishing its ministry. Then we were saddened to hear of the death of greatly respected and much-loved figures who had helped to shape the modern Great St Mary's and influenced many of us in deep and diverse ways. Mervyn Stockwood died in 1995 and Stanley Booth-Clibborn a year later. The memories of clergy, events, sermons were still vivid but were inevitably slipping into forgetfulness. It was time – people felt – to remember and celebrate the ministry of Great St Mary's, the university church of Cambridge, to generations of post-war students and residents of the city. It was time to pay an affectionate tribute to its vicars and other clergy, especially as the church found itself organising two memorial services.

So Desmond Perkins, churchwarden from 1969 to 1976 and a long-standing member of the congregation, set about uncovering and collating documents, press-cuttings, newsletters and minutes of meetings. A series of interviews was also held with a variety of members of the congregation – past and present. The result of all this industry was loaded into a set of files, which became known as the 'archives'. I was told about these when I arrived as a new incumbent in 1994. They were kept on the piano of a member of the congregation because they were too precious to be kept in the church building. Not knowing what they were I imagined a unique set of medieval pipe rolls and churchwardens' records from Tudor times and felt that I should take them into a more secure environment. On receipt of the plastic carrier bags I discovered the true nature of the collection.

The 'archives' suitably edited are the raw material from which some of the later chapters of this volume were written. Without them – and without the generous labours of Desmond Perkins – this history would not have been written.

About this time – in fact in early 1996 – a series of lectures was arranged. These aroused much interest in the university and city and gave further indication of the extent of the influence of the church. They form five of the chapters of this book – numbered 1, 2, 3, 5 and 6.

The strand that runs through all the material collected here is the double life of Great St Mary's Church. It is the church of the University of Cambridge – and has been since the university was founded. This has ensured that it has been in close contact with the intellectual, religious and political life of the church – and even nation. It was at the centre of the events of the Reformation, and new trends in theological thinking have been presented and debated within its walls. In addition it is a parish church. This needs a little explanation, since its location in the middle of the town and its large size has, at least in recent years, resulted in the fact that it has not had an intimate connection with any one area of the city. But it has enabled it to develop strong local roots. All sorts and conditions of the residents of the East Anglian market town of Cambridge have felt at home in it and have clearly considered that they have an almost proprietorial ownership of it.

As a result of this double life, theological debates and controversies have been articulated in the midst of a local congregation and of a town church. Academics and artisans rubbed shoulders in Great St Mary's and their interaction has given the church its distinctive character. It is from this that the interest of this story comes. It could be seen as a history of the theology and liturgy of the Church of England, enacted and experienced in a parochial context.

The volume is divided into three parts. The first traces the history of the church from its earliest days until the Second World War. This includes the five hundred or so years from the church's beginnings until the present building was constructed. This rebuilding took place in the early part of the Reformation, and the church was closely involved in the bitter and protracted controversies of this period. The last of the three chapters in the first part explores the lengthy period between the end of the Reformation and the middle of the present century.

The second part contains four chapters which look more closely at the contemporary ministry of Great St Mary's. These include the nature of its place within the university and city of Cambridge. More specifically, the extraordinary revival of Christianity in Cambridge in the 1950s and 1960s in which Great St Mary's played such an important part is analysed and the causes of it discussed. For many people Great St Mary's evokes immediate memories of a glittering succession of the influential and colourful priests who were its vicars. These are the subject of the two chapters which conclude Part Two.

The final part concerns the building – and some of the activities which have gone on inside it. The fabric and the furnishings have a complex history, and successive ages have transformed the appearance of the building. Among the parts of the Great St Mary's tradition which have become especially celebrated are the music and the bells. These are much more than a postscript, but a reminder that the life of Great St Mary's cannot be reduced to theological or liturgical dimensions. The bells, organs and choirs have not only contributed to the life of the church but to the life of the city, and indeed – through the Cambridge chimes which were reproduced at Westminster – have become known throughout the world.

We are grateful to many members of the congregation who have given interest, ideas and encouragement in the preparation of this book, especially Ruth Bridgen, John Lonsdale, Mike Hobart, Walter Mitchell and Mary Turner.

PART ONE

Great St Mary's in history

1 Urban church and university church: Great St Mary's from its origin to 1523

CHRISTOPHER BROOKE

Great St Mary's lay, and lies, in the very heart of medieval Cambrdge. For it is there that the University of Cambridge began – and there was a church on the site long before the university was thought of; it may even be that the oldest truly urban church of Cambridge lay there.

Let me start with two contrasts. Within the grim Victorian shell of St Giles on Castle Hill lies the remnant of the first church on the site, a charming eleventh-century chancel arch in a church whose foundation can be dated with some precision to 1092 or thereabouts. The early history of Great St Mary's cannot be documented, nor its foundation dated – not within six hundred years, to put it at its most extreme.

The other contrast can best be observed by walking in imagination on the path by the north-west corner of King's Chapel. There one can contemplate two noble churches, one built, the other rebuilt, in the fifteenth and early sixteenth centuries, two of the central buildings of the University of Cambridge, the nave of Great St Mary's and the chapel of King's College; both probably completed under the direction and to the design of the same architect, John Wastell. The church is splendid – but dwarfed by the chapel; and there one can see in the mind's eye an almost incredible contrast between what a succession of megalomaniac kings thought appropriate for the chapel of one college and what the university authorities and their allies among the citizens thought a fitting home for the place where the whole university and the town were to meet. For that is the significance of the nave of Great St Mary's. We hear much of the squabbles of town and gown, and of the friction which marked their relations on many occasions. But in a very real sense city and university created each other – and of this the nave of Great St Mary's is the symbol. The two communities met and mingled here, as town and gown met in St Michael's and Little St Mary's and elsewhere.

The city of Cambridge is the mother of us all: before there were colleges there was a university, and before the university – a relatively parvenu institution no older than 1209 at the earliest – there was a town, with market place and churches and streets and houses. If we want to search out its footprints we cannot do better than walk along the Roman road into Cambridge, the Huntingdon Road, past the castle – past the site of All Saints by the Castle, long since demolished – past St Peter and St Giles, across Magdalene Bridge, which gave its name to our shire, past St Clement and Holy Sepulchre (and its neighbour St George, which was lost perhaps by 1200), then right down the old High Street – St John's Street, Trinity Street, King's Parade, Trumpington Street, call it what you will: but the High Street I shall call it as it was till the nineteenth century. We pass the ghost of the other All Saints beside the Divinity School, and St Michael's and Great St Mary's; and as we go south along the High Street we pass near St Edward, the Saxon king, and St Benet, the Italian monk with his Saxon tower, past St Botolph and (in imagination) out through the Trumpington Gate to the church of St Peter commonly known, since it was rebuilt in the middle of the fourteenth century, as the church of Little St Mary's. These are the true footprints of the first Cambridge, the late Saxon town; and the saints clustered so thick on the ground are an astonishing reminder of the shape and pattern of early English towns, with a church every hundred yards or so.

As we marched down Castle Hill and along the High Street we passed twelve churches – not a bad score for a modest market town. But we have not seen them all. If we had gone along the Roman road till it becomes St Andrew's Street we should have passed Holy Trinity and St Andrew the Great, now happily restored.

If we were to dig in the ample lawns of King's to the west of the chapel we should find the lost church of St John the Baptist – St John Zachary. There were fifteen parish churches in medieval Cambridge, sixteen if we include St Andrew the Less, alias Barnwell Priory – and though they have been altered many times, they are the principal monuments of its early days, most of them first built, we may reckon, between the tenth and the twelfth centuries, though some may be older. In the twelfth and thirteenth centuries they were joined by a group of churches of monks and nuns and regular canons and friars – conventual churches, most of which have come and gone; and in the late Middle Ages by college chapels – sometimes united to parish churches, sometimes separate and apart. By the 1530s, when the axe fell on the conventual churches, and the 1540s, when the colleges came near to following them into oblivion, Cambridge was teeming with churches. But the most remarkable feature in this proliferation of places of worship is the growth of the parish churches in the early Middle Ages.

Cambridge sits where the old Roman road crossed the river. Beside it on Castle Hill there had been the Roman fort and some settlement may have survived in this region; and it was clearly populous in Norman times when part of it was built up into the Norman castle. But Cambridge as a town lay south and east of the river and is evidently a new creation of mid- or late Saxon times. The shape and pattern of the town makes this abundantly clear. We know the shape of early Cambridge by three major tokens. First of all, the great open fields to east and west – which formed the fields of Cambridge till the enclosures of the early nineteenth century – impinge upon a town whose centre lies about the Roman road, the High Street and the river. We do not know when the fields were so defined; but they identify the town that lies between. North Cambridge, the suburb on Castle Hill, has no fields impinging on it but those of Chesterton, the royal manor to the north-east.

The second token of the shape of Cambridge is its streets: the Roman road and the High Street are familiar enough today — the former still remarkably straight except where it evaded the castle and where it dodged, by Christ's, to go through the Barnwell Gate; the High Street a characteristic medieval meander. But there was a third street now largely hidden by the growth of the academic quarter in the fifteenth and sixteenth centuries. The great beauty of Cambridge today lies in this academic quarter, in the group of college and university buildings which runs from St John's in the north, between the High Street and the river – with the Backs beyond, south to Queens', with Peterhouse lying out to the south. It is this above all which gives Cambridge its incomparable beauty as a modern city. But all this obscures and obliterates a third of the medieval town. For the third main street of Cambridge, Mill Street, ran from the south of Trinity along Trinity Lane and through King's to Queens' Lane, and about it were houses and lanes, forming a little grid of streets near the river. It seems likely that this was the region which felt first the contraction which came to many English towns in the fourteenth and fifteenth centuries; and that it was in part the falling rents and poverty of the region which attracted the attention of King Henry VI. Whatever the grounds, King Henry had the whole centre of this region swept clear; but he never enjoyed the resources to build the college of his dreams: he was soon bereft of money, senses and throne; and although Henry VII and Henry VIII finished his chapel a generation later, and much later generations built stately buildings here and there, the greater part of this region of Cambridge is now grass. And the whole quarter has lost its civic aspect and become a line of colleges. Thus the grid of streets with its three main roads marks the core of Saxon Cambridge, with the Market Place at its heart.

The third token of its early shape are the churches, which point so eloquently to a time when the High Street was its most flourishing artery and groups of tiny, prosperous communities could afford each to enjoy their own place of worship.

If we ask how it all began we enter a world of mystery and guesswork. Many English towns owed their foundation or revival to King Alfred at the end of the ninth century; but not Cambridge. It is a reasonable presumption that it was already forming, however modestly, before his day. A few years ago Jeremy Haslam wrote an interesting paper in the *Proceedings of the Cambridge Antiquarian Society*, arguing that it was a Mercian town founded by King Offa in the mid-eighth century, and that is likely enough; but it remains a guess. It is rather more than a guess that the recovery of Cambridge from the Danes in 917 by Edward the Elder marks the beginning of a major development – that the heart of Cambridge, south of the river, is of the tenth century. Haslam also conjectured that the original mother church of Cambridge, under whose wings the others grew up, was St Giles on the edge of Castle Hill; and that is extremely unlikely. He had the misfortune to light on the one church which is closely dated – and there is no good ground for doubting that St Giles was built for a small house of canons founded in or about 1092. If I had to look for a mother church of Cambridge, I should look rather in the centre of the Saxon town and the region of the market place; I would look at the church which lies between the High Street and the Market Place overlooking the Market, much as the greatest of all the churches of medieval Germany, Mainz Cathedral, still looks over its ancient market place. My choice would be Great St Mary's. But this is only a conjecture: there seems nothing but the site to identify it firmly as such.

In our search for the meaning of these tiny parishes and their place in the life of early Cambridge, let us look first at the saints themselves – who they were, and why they should have been honoured. It used to be said that when a church was dedicated to a saint some relics of that saint – preferably large or small pieces of the saint's bones – were an essential part of the dedication; and that they were planted in the altars at the service. This simply cannot be true, since many churches were dedicated to archangels like St Michael who had no bones, or to the deity, or to Mary, whose body (as was universally assumed in the Middle Ages) went up to heaven whole and entire; and if it had been so, local saints whose relics might be readily provided would have enjoyed an immense advantage. In the seventh and eighth centuries St Peter came first with a handsome lead – though most commonly accompanied by the other great apostle whose shrine was in Rome, St Paul. Second came the blessed Virgin, with Paul a close third; then Andrew, Martin, Michael and Lawrence. Little bits of Peter and Paul (or bits alleged to be theirs) undoubtedly strayed into English relic collections, and perhaps of Andrew and Lawrence too. Even Mary is represented in the more bizarre collections of relics, which might contain fragments of her veil, even drops of her milk – and on the continent, here and there, cults gathered round statues of her. Peterborough Abbey, which had one of the most esoteric collections, reckoned among them pieces of Jesus' manger, swaddling clothes, cross and sepulchre – and of the loaves with which he fed the five thousand; elsewhere some of his milk teeth were alleged. The cult of relics was powerful, but not in Cambridge: relics were above all for pilgrims, that is, for those who wanted to travel in search of their saints, whether by boat to Ely to call on St Etheldreda or by horse to Peterborough (well stocked with Anglo-Saxon saints) or Bury (for St Edmund) – where were the nearest notable shrines. By the twelfth century the Blessed Virgin had swept Peter off his feet – she outnumbers him fivefold or so. In all discussion of dedications we have to recall that churches can change their dedications – as St Peter without Trumpington Gate became Little St Mary's; but such evidence as has been sifted (and a great deal has not) suggests that this – though it may have been common in country churches – was relatively unusual in urban churches, in the mid- or late Middle Ages.

Every church is and was God's home, and it seems a little strange to have churches specifically dedicated to the Holy Trinity. It prompts the question, what was the meaning of dedication to a saint? To this, strangely, there is no easy answer. Broadly speaking, some special association with a saint or with the Holy Trinity or with Christ – as in Christ Church, Canterbury Cathedral – seems to be particularly attached to the high altar of a church; in some cases multiple dedications relate to a group of altars. But in the dedication rituals of the early and central Middle Ages in this country there is no special place for the invocation of a patron saint – though in some parts of the service his or her presence seems taken for granted. The dedication service, however, is specially designed to emphasise that the church is God's church. None the less, these dedications were very real; and the saint – or the Trinity – were regarded as the proprietors of their church.

Let us retrace our steps and revisit a few among the Cambridge churches. St Peter had five churches in London and remained exceedingly popular. St Peter on Castle Hill may well be on the site of the first church in the modest early settlement in north Cambridge – St Peter outside Trumpington Gate shows that he had not lost his popularity in the late eleventh or early twelfth century. So one might expect of the prince of the apostles; but most of the apostles in truth will not appear on any of our lists.

After the Blessed Virgin Mary and the apostles come a noble array of English, French and universal saints who can be most clearly viewed in a rough chronological sequence. St Michael flourished at all times, never more than in the ninth and tenth centuries, which was the first heyday of his shrine on Monte Gargano in Italy and which also saw the rise of the Mont Saint-Michel in Normandy and the Sagra di San Michele near Turin. If we deduce from these examples that he was a saint who liked hilly places we shall learn little of the reason why he had a church in Cambridge – or a church with a Saxon tower in Oxford or seven churches wthin the walls of the city of London. Clearly he had many adherents who were prepared to foster his cult in flat places. When the Vikings became Christian in the tenth and eleventh centuries they adopted Clement, the early pope and Roman martyr, as one of their chief patrons. St Clement's in Cambridge lies near the wharves on the river to which Viking traders might have come. The link is conjectural, but is a very likely conjecture.

Whatever else the proliferation of tiny parishes and small churches reflects, it represents the outward and visible sign of a popular religious movement, recorded in every part of Europe in the tenth, and especially in the eleventh and twelfth centuries. Behind it, and in some relation to it not easily defined, lay the monastic revivals of the tenth century. From the tenth century onwards every monastic community (with a few partial exceptions) was subjected to the Rule of St Benedict. It seems fairly clear that the height of his fame among builders of parish churches lay in the tenth and eleventh centuries; and we may attribute our own St Benet's to the tenth century – for its tower, even if it cannot be closely dated, is not likely to be much later than about the year 1000.

St Edward and St Botolph are native English saints, a reminder that English cults flourished in the century before the Conquest and – especially in the towns, where well-to-do English survived after the Norman Conquest more successfully than in the countryside – in the century after the Conquest. Edward, king and so-called martyr, was King Edgar's eldest son, who was murdered in 978 at Corfe while still little more than a boy, and succeeded by his younger brother Aethelred II. In later years Aethelred was to foster the cult of his murdered brother; but the cult had little staying power, so far as we know, and churches dedicated to the martyr are not numerous; we may suppose that ours represents the age of Aethelred or soon after, that is to say the first half of the eleventh century or thereabouts. St Botolph was a seventh-century East Anglian abbot of whom little is known but who was much admired. His cult among the ordinary folk of parishes came later. Botolph seems sometimes to have appeared in new suburbs by town gates when these were forming in the eleventh and early twelfth centuries – London is a very striking example, with three of his churches by three gates. It seems likely to be significant that St Botolph in Cambridge lies just within the Trumpington Gate. In the present state of knowledge the date of the gate, and indeed of the King's Ditch or dyke or rampart which formed the main defensive system round Cambridge, is a matter of guesswork; the guess currently favoured places it in the eleventh century and it was surely not later. We may think that St Botolph represents the community around the Trumpington Gate of the late eleventh century, asserting its devotion to a native English, East Anglian saint. Of St Peter without Trumpington Gate we have an early record of 1207. Throughout its early years St Peter seems to have been served (as were many parish churches in the twelfth century) by a dynasty of hereditary parsons, the first of whom must have flourished about 1100.

St Giles and the Holy Sepulchre begin to shift our attention from parish churches to conventual churches at the turn of the eleventh and twelfth centuries. A little later the nuns of St Radegund – an eminent Gallic abbess from Poitiers whose order is rarely to be found in England – were settled about 1150 in their magnificent urban park (as we would regard it today), which is now the precinct of Jesus College. At much the same time the leper hospital of St Mary Magdalene was built – as leper hospitals were wont to be – outside the city boundaries, along the Newmarket Road. Its church is an enchanting survival from the mid-twelfth century. About 1200 the hospital of St John the Evangelist was founded where the college now stands. In the thirteenth century we move into the world of the friars, and later of the colleges – and also to a new roll-call of saints.

The parish boundaries of Cambridge are first fully recorded in a map of the early nineteenth century, though we have many indications of their shape from medieval documents. In Cambridge, as in London, the earliest parishes in the centre look like pieces of a very intricate jigsaw puzzle;

roads and crossroads and above all markets lie in their heart, not at their boundaries; the jagged edges strongly suggest ancient property boundaries rather haphazardly gathered together. On the map the tiny ancient parish of Great St Mary's looks like a dagger embedded in the heart of Cambridge. Shifting property boundaries could modify the details of the picture; but the basic story in London is of almost unbelievable conservatism over the centuries – so that the parishes there survived the disappearance of most of the churches in the Great Fire of 1666 by nearly 250 years. We cannot assume anything quite so dramatic in Cambridge; but it is reasonable to think that the parishes, here as in London, were originally formed by groups of neighbours who built and worshipped in the church at the centre of their community. But the churches were constantly being altered and rebuilt, so that none of those in the centre of Cambridge now looks the least like its twelfth-century predecessor, save only the Round Church, which was largely rebuilt by the Cambridge Camden Society in the 1840s precisely to represent once again the church of the early twelfth century – of which indeed it incorporates large genuine fragments. If one wants to know what they originally looked like, one can visit St Giles and contemplate its original chancel arch, and in imagination build round it a small church of two cells – a nave and chancel, joined by the arch. Better still one can go along the Newmarket Road and over the railway bridge, and there, on the left, is the mid-twelfth century leper chapel, perfectly preserved. In form it is just such a two-celled church as I have described, and identical with innumerable twelfth-century parish churches elsewhere, and we may suppose that many of our churches much resembled it. But just as it had been the natural aspiration of citizens who had any means, and any hope of entering a heavenly city hereafter, to share in building the original church, so every generation reckoned to leave its mark by adding a porch or an aisle, or by rebuilding this or that part of it. This aspiration lasted right through the Middle Ages, and though it flagged somewhat after the Reformation, it survived more than is commonly allowed – to be substantially revived in the nineteenth century.

Three of the churches of Cambridge were entirely rebuilt each in a single campaign as part of the growth of academic Cambridge in the late Middle Ages. St Michael's was rebuilt by the wealthy civil servant Hervey de Stanton so as to form, as to one third, a parish church as before, and as to two-thirds, a college chapel for his new foundation of Michaelhouse, a hundred yards away along what is now Trinity Lane. Little St Mary's was rebuilt in the mid-fourteenth century to be

Peterhouse Chapel and a parish church combined. The third is Great St Mary's.

To understand the cooperation between citizens and academics to which these churches so visibly bear witness, we need to go back to the origin of the university itself, in the thirteenth century. No one now doubts that academic Cambridge was a child of Oxford; but it is curious that the most specific link between the two has never been fully explored. Both universities were founded under the shadow of a St Mary's Church. In Oxford, the meeting place of the university in the late Middle Ages was St Mary the Virgin, and although the link cannot be documented before the late thirteenth century, everything points to its antiquity; not least the growth of the earliest schools in the streets running away from the High Street, by its side. Similarly, in Cambridge: the earliest grace (or proposal for legislation) known to have been passed by the Regent Masters within Great St Mary's Church is of 1275; but there is copious evidence by the late thirteenth century of the link between church and university – and it is abundantly clear in the fourteenth century, when the university began to build the Old Schools, that this site, so near Great St Mary's, was already well established. It seems probable indeed that the first masters, fleeing from Oxford in or about 1209, abandoning the protection of the Blessed Virgin in Oxford, sought out her church in Cambridge as their first refuge. By the late thirteenth century – and probably long before – the old nave of the old church was the Senate House and meeting place of the university, as it remained till the present Senate House was built early in the eighteenth century. It was here in 1381 that the insurgent townsfolk in the so-called Peasants' Revolt (so-called, because in Cambridge it was essentially the citizens' revolt) found and looted the principal university chest. The church itself was the first home of the university archives – not, as Catherine Hall has pointed out to me (and has sometimes been said) – the tower. It was here, a hundred years later, that their successors joined the leading figures of the university in rebuilding the nave.

Riot is perhaps the more familiar feature of the legend of Cambridge's past; and it is all the more worth exploring the other side of the coin, of coexistence and collaboration, a little further. Like the university itself, the idea of bringing town and gown together in church was inspired by Oxford. The pattern and model of Oxford colleges was Merton. Even if one or two others had an earlier prehistory, Merton set the pattern in combining fine buildings, endowment for poor (or moderately poor) students with prayers and masses for the dead. But Walter de Merton, when choosing his site in Oxford, had deliberately laid his hand on the parish church of St John the Baptist: and his fellows, carrying out his intentions after his death, rebuilt the chancel of the church in the 1290s on a grand scale to provide a college chapel. The parishioners had to make do with the rest – that is, with the crossing of a cruciform church; they were promised a nave by and by – and in the fifteenth century they were given that splendid tower which is one of the beauties of the Oxford skyline; a nave would follow in due course, the parishioners' very own. Then in the early sixteenth century a rascally warden of Merton (the phrase came to me from Merton's own historian, Dr Roger Highfield) allowed the site of the nave to pass to Bishop Fox for a negligible rent as part of the site for Corpus Christi College, Oxford – and the parishioners never had their nave; in the nineteenth century they even lost their church. There are striking parallels and differences in the story of Little St Mary's. The old church of St Peter outside Trumpington Gate, which gave its name to Peterhouse in 1284, was rebuilt in the 1340s or so by the fellows of Peterhouse – though we do not know how they got the money. They built a stately chancel, very closely modelled on Merton's, though flowing curvilinear tracery has replaced the geometry of the 1290s. They left stray bits of the old church for the parishioners – and, once again, the hope of a nave was never realised. But in the case of Little St Mary's the parishioners won in the end: first, they left St Peter to the fellows and did homage to Our Lady, thus becoming the parishioners of Little St Mary's; and later, when the seventeenth-century fellows sought peace and seclusion of a kind more common in college chapels, the parishioners were left in possession of the whole church.

The moral of this story is perhaps that the fine ideal of collaboration between town and gown in regular worship lay in the world of dreams – or anyway was never realised as the early benefactors had intended. Put another way, it became a marriage of convenience, which in due course became in some ways a marriage of great inconvenience to one or other party. That is probably too pessimistic a view: it is more likely that in these instances college and parish found there were both benefits and disadvantages in their coexistence. It is certain that Great St Mary's – as well as giving hospitality to university ceremonies and commencements and sermons – housed flourishing chapels and guilds, and that the children of the parish were baptised – and wedded and buried – under its wing. For me, Great St Mary's is first and foremost a baptismal church, in which three of my grandchildren have been christened in recent years. To its medieval parishioners it was even more than that: it was the centre of their community life – where they met to be baptised, to marry and to be mourned – and for many other occasions, religious and not so religious, in between. They continued to support it by offerings voluntary and involuntary – especially by paying the tithe, originally an income tax amounting to a tenth of every kind of income, intended to support the poor and all who needed help; but later converted into a tax on agrarian income, mainly for the support of one kind of poor only, namely the clergy.

It seems clear meanwhile that in St Michael's, Little St Mary's and Merton Chapel the colleges were the dominant partners; and that is hardly surprising, given the tiny areas and the modest populations which formed the parishes. In due course Michaelhouse was to be absorbed in Trinity; but long before that, in the late fourteenth century, a close link had been forged between Trinity's principal precursor, the King's Hall, and Great St Mary's. The King's Hall was a much older foundation than King's College and for most of its history entirely distinct. It had been founded in 1317 by King Edward II, and greatly enlarged by his son, Edward III, to provide higher education for the members of the chapel royal. The chapel royal was (and partly still is) a curious institution dedicated to the Holy Trinity and providing a great panoply of services to the royal court – services indeed in more senses than one, since its younger members often grew up to be civil servants. Since it was part of the chapel royal it was wholly under royal control – in token of which the Master of Trinity is still appointed by the crown – though since it was enlarged and refounded by Henry VIII it has achieved a certain measure of independence in other respects. As part of his process of endowment of the King's Hall, Edward III arranged for the appropriation of Great St Mary's to his college – that is to say, he arranged for the major tithes, roughly two-thirds of its tithe income, to be transferred to the college – a common process in medieval church finance, and one very satisfactory to Edward, since he could not benefit from the tithes himself. The corollary in this custom of the English church is that the rector – the person or body who receives the major tithes – was also responsible for the upkeep of the chancel; and it quite often happens therefore that the chancel of a medieval English parish church was last rebuilt shortly before it was appropriated – and that the rectors have only kept it in repair since then. The lien with the King's Hall explains why the chancel of Great St Mary's – though often restored – is in essence older than the nave. The tithes have long since disappeared, but in the singularly untidy clearing up in the Tithe Act of 1935 the Cambridge colleges remained (in the odd phrase of the church lawyers) lay rectors, responsible for the upkeep of the chancels. This is a very obscure branch of ecclesiastical law; but no matter – so long as the college pays.

With the grant of tithes Edward III also granted the advowson, the right to present or choose the vicar; and this double gift has brought a close link between church and college ever since – a link which is wholly independent of the older and closer link of church and university. Needless to say the two have often intertwined – as in the person of the Reverend Henry Richards Luard, Fellow of Trinity and University Registrary in the late nineteenth century, who was also Vicar of Great St Mary's and was the moving spirit behind the late nineteenth-century restoration which has given so much of the church its present character.

Equally decisive was an earlier link; for it was a former fellow of the King's Hall, Dr Thomas Barowe, whose gift to the building fund in 1495 was the decisive event in the fund-raising for a new nave. Concerning the rebuilding of this church we have some contemporary sources – proctors' accounts, fund-raising accounts, churchwardens' accounts, and the great indenture between Thomas Barowe and the university – and notes made by or for two eminent sixteenth-century antiquaries who were close friends and accomplices in quack history, Matthew Parker, Master of Corpus and Archbishop of Canterbury, and John Caius, third founder and Master of Gonville and Caius College. Most modern narratives have started from the antiquaries, and fitted the contemporary sources in as best they could – not always realising that it was an antiquarian reconstruction they were using, nor compensating for the biases the antiquaries allowed themselves. Parker and Caius were zealous historians according to their lights, but their lights were dim – and they were good subjects of Tudor sovereigns, not inclined to put the works of King Richard III on a pedestal, and devoted to the university, which they wished to have all the credit for rebuilding the nave: 'at the University's cost and by its efforts, and so truly to be called the University's Church', as Dr Caius tendentiously observed.

What the indenture of 21 January 1495 tells us is that Thomas Barowe, Archdeacon of Colchester, eminent Doctor of Laws (that is, both of canon and civil or Roman law) of the University of Cambridge, and onetime Fellow of the King's Hall – 'for the honour of God almighty and of the most blessed Mary, mother of Our Lord Jesus Christ and glorious virgin, and his protector and most special patron' – has given £240 (a mighty sum in coin of the fifteenth century) 'for the restoration of the university chest and the building of the church of the blessed Virgin of our university aforesaid'. Part of the gift was for an elaborate obit –

masses and prayers and ceremonies in honour of King Richard III and Dr Thomas Barowe – who were to be enrolled in the list of the university's benefactors. It is interesting to observe that Richard modestly disappeared from the university's benefactors' services for a considerable period, but in recent generations has been restored, evidently by a modern antiquary who had read the indenture.

What the proctors' accounts tell us is that Richard Duke of Gloucester (the future Richard III) gave twenty marks – £13. 6s. 8d. – in 1475–6 for no specified purpose: and they record other occasional collections and disbursements which more clearly relate to Great St Mary's. In 1478–9 £20 was handed over towards the new work at Great St Mary's; then silence falls. In the 1490s a major effort at fund-raising, only scantily noted in the proctors' accounts, evidently set the work going effectively at last. It is to be noted that the senior proctor in 1478–9 was William Stockdale, Fellow of Peterhouse; and Stockdale was vice-chancellor between 1493 and 1498, when the major fund-raising was undertaken – from bishops, abbots, priors and doctors and masters of the university. Modern fund-raisers may complain that bishops are now impoverished and abbots few and far between; but the truth is that this splendid nave was built in a land infinitely poorer than modern Britain – and that the university sources only tell us half the story: I am sure the parishioners and the people of Cambridge paid handsomely too. That said, William Stockdale may be regarded as the prime agent in the rebuilding of this nave, and the 1490s rather than the 1470s the era when it truly got under way.

Apart from William Stockdale as vice-chancellor the proctors have been the chief fund-raisers, the development officers as we should call them, in the university's affairs. Now the senior proctor in 1494–5 was John Fisher, Fellow of Michaelhouse and future vice-chancellor, chancellor and martyr. In his own hand he made the famous entry, 'I had lunch with the lady mother of the king' – an event which opened the collaboration between Fisher and the Lady Margaret Beaufort from which sprang Christ's and St John's and very much else besides, and entitles Fisher to the highest rank among Cambridge fund-raisers and benefactors. It is interesting, and very likely significant, that the great benefaction of January 1495 fell within Fisher's term of office as Senior Proctor too – as well as in the vice-chancellorship of Stockdale – but any link between them and Dr Barowe, and Dr Barowe's patron King Richard, was hardly likely to be mentioned over the lunch table of the lady mother of the king.

Dr Caius tells us that the first stone of the new nave was laid in 1478, and on the authority of William Gage, a Fellow of Peterhouse who died in 1500 (ten years before Caius was born), the first stone of the tower in 1491, on 16 May at 6.45 p.m.; that King Henry VII gave some fine oak trees in Great Chesterford which did not belong to him, and this is confirmed by the draft of a tear-stained letter of apology to the Abbot of Westminster (who apparently did own them), and the fine oak timbers over our heads; that the nave was finished in 1519 and the tower very much later – outside my period altogether. Now this general scheme of dates cannot be far wrong, though it would be rash to assert it is exactly right. Behind it lies another scheme of chronology, strongly suggested by the bold – even rash – way that Thomas Barowe associated King Richard III with his own benefaction ten years after the battle of Bosworth Field. It is interesting to observe the contrast between the antechapel of King's, filled to bursting with Beaufort–Tudor emblems, and the nave of Great St Mary's which Barowe turned (in intention at least) into a monument to Richard III.

Some years before the start of the present nave, in 1470, King Henry VI had been momentarily hoisted back on to the throne and Edward IV sent into exile. When Edward returned in 1471 and resumed the throne, the principal beneficiary from the ensuing forfeitures was Edward's brother, Richard Duke of Gloucester; and among many other improvements to his lot he became a principal landowner in Cambridgeshire. The fund-raisers and beggars of Cambridge took due note: the founder of Queens', Andrew Doket – equally at home with royalty of every faction – won Richard's ear and a mighty benefaction which melted away on Bosworth Field – but Doket, lucky man, had died the year before. Meanwhile Thomas Barowe had flourished exceedingly in the service of Richard as duke and king: he had become a mighty pluralist, canon (at the height) of seven cathedrals and collegiate churches, and rector here and there besides. He was Richard's chancellor as duke, Master of the Rolls in 1483, Keeper of the Great Seal on the eve of Bosworth Field. There he doubtless lost the mitre which must have been his had Richard survived; but he lost nothing else; he was a survivor, as Great St Mary's bears witness to this day. He lived to make his princely benefaction in 1495 and to die in peace in 1499. He was a devout Cambridge man who no doubt had a hand, with the university authorities, in interesting Richard III in Great St Mary's – and Barowe's gift replaces whatever the university and the church had lost in 1485. It is indeed possible that the twenty marks of 1475–6 were a first token of support, lubricating an appeal which took many years to mature.

The churchwardens' accounts only start in 1504 and so they tell us the end of our story: of stalls for the chancel in 1518–19, of the roodloft in 1521–2 and a tiny payment for some mysterious process which seems to pertain to the figures of Mary and John on either side of the great rood or crucifix above the rood loft in 1522–3.

The most certain fact is the church itself. By whatever means, vice-chancellors, proctors and churchwardens succeeded in raising the money and organising a great building enterprise – starting perhaps in the late 1470s, rising to a climax in the 1490s. It was a bold stroke to invoke the memory of Richard III in this enterprise; but entirely successful – for in spite of it (or perhaps even because of it) Henry VII and his lady mother joined more modestly among the donors.

The Blessed Virgin has never been so honoured in Cambridge as in the generations which preceded the Reformation. For the turn of the fifteenth and sixteenth centuries saw John Wastell and his colleagues at work here, shaping this nave, and in the chapel of St Mary and St Nicholas, King's College chapel over the road, he completed what his predecessors had begun. The great fan vault, the decoration of the stone-work in the antechapel especially, are his. The lofty nave of Great St Mary's, and the celestial geometry of the stonework are very character-istic of this notable architect. It is difficult for us today, as we contemplate grey stonework on a grey Cambridge day, to appreciate the effect he intended. But modern electricity recreates something of the play of light and the deep shadows he created – and can give us a sense of the excite-ment his geometry would originally have conveyed. Imagine stonework and roof adorned with the colours of the rainbow and lit by a thousand candles, and you will gain some impression of the offering Wastell and his fellow masons – and Barowe and all the benefactors rounded up by the vice-chancellor and the proctors – laid before God and his Mother.

Meanwhile, in King's Chapel, the vault was going up, the windows were given their tracery – and then their glass. The glazing of King's Chapel went on long after the rood beam and the rood were in place in Great St Mary's – long after Wastell was dead. Right into the late 1540s the glaziers paid by King Henry VIII were completing the glass of King's Chapel. They form in sum the most dramatic late medieval biography of Our Lady – a life cycle in whose central scenes, naturally enough, are enacted the birth, life and death of her Son. But it is strange to reflect that Henry was completing a supreme work of medieval devotion with one hand while ordering the Henrician Reformation with the other. Very soon after the carpenters' hammers had set the rood in place it was to be taken down – to the profit of the carpenters no doubt – but to the bewilderment of those of us who view this dramatic change from afar.

Bibliographical note

In preparing this chapter I am much indebted to Dr John Binns, Dr Rosalind Brooke, Dr Elisabeth Leedham-Green and Mrs Catherine Hall. The earlier pages are partly based on a lecture I gave in celebration of Little St Mary's in 1990.

There are full accounts of the churches in Cambridge by Helen Cam in *Victoria History of Cambridgeshire* (henceforth vol. *VCH*), III (London, 1959), pp. 123–33, for Great St Mary's, esp. 129–31; and in *Royal Commission on Historical Monuments, City of Cambridge*, 2 parts (London, 1959), esp. part II, pp. 275–80. I have discussed them in 'The Churches of Medieval Cambridge', in *History, Society and the Churches: Essays in Honour of Owen Chadwick*, ed. D. Beales and G. Best (Cambridge, 1985), pp. 49–76, esp. p.71; see also my 'The Missionary at Home: the Church in the Towns 1000–1250', *Studies in Church History*, 6 (1970), 59–83; J. Campbell, 'The Church in Anglo-Saxon Towns', *Studies in Church History*, 16 (1979), 119–35; and his 'Norwich' in *Atlas of Historic Towns*, vol. II, ed. M. D. Lobel and W. H. Johns (London, 1975). For a general survey see Richard Morris, *Churches in the Landscape* (London, 1989); and for background, R. and C. Brooke, *Popular Religion in the Middle Ages* (London, 1984). On early Cambridge, see M. D. Lobel in *Atlas of Historic Towns*, vol. II, 'Cambridge'; on origins, J. Haslam, 'The Development and Topography of Saxon Cambridge', *Proceedings of the Cambridge Antiquarian Society*, 72 (1982–3), 13–29 (to be used with caution). Our knowledge of the topography of medieval Cambridge, including the parish boundaries, will be enormously enhanced when Rosemary Horrox has completed her *Survey of Medieval Cambridge*. For the fields, see esp. C. P. Hall and J. R. Ravensdale, *The West Fields of Cambridge* (Cambridge Antiquarian Records Society, 1976 for 1974–5). For the hospitals, M. Rubin, *Charity and Community in Medieval Cambridge* (Cambridge, 1987); for the leper hospital, see photograph by Wim Swaan in C. Brooke, R. Highfield and W. Swaan, *Oxford and Cambridge* (Cambridge, 1988), plate 10. For London, see C. Brooke and G. Keir, *London 800–1216; the Shaping of a City* (London, 1975), chap. 6. For Mercian towns, A. Pearn, 'Origin and Development of Churches and

Parishes: a Comparative Study of Hereford, Shrewsbury and Chester', PhD thesis, University of Cambridge, 1988. For dedications, Alison Binns, *Dedications of Monastic Houses in England and Wales* (Woodbridge, 1989); W. Levison, *England and the Continent in the Eighth Century* (Oxford, 1946), pp. 259–65; R. Clark, 'The Dedications of Medieval Churches in Derbyshire', *Derbyshire Archaeological Journal*, 112 (1992), 48–61.

The *VCH* (vol. III, 129–31) gives references to many of the sources for Great St Mary's. For my purpose, especially important are the indenture between the university and Thomas Barowe, Cambridge University Library, University Archives, Luard 136, the proctors' accounts in *Grace Book A*, ed. S. M. Leathes, and *Grace Book B*, ed. M. Bateson, 2 vols. (Cambridge Antiquarian Society, Luard Memorial Series vols. I–III, Cambridge, 1897, 1903–5), esp. A, vol. I, p. 111 (1475–6), 129–31 (1478–9), 210, 213 (1487–8) and B, vol. I, pp. 11 (1488), 111 (1497–8), 192 (1503–4), 236–7 (1508–9), 248 (1509–10); vol. II, pp. 60, 69 (1517–19, for glazing); and *The Churchwardens' Accounts of St Mary the Great*, 1504–1635, ed. J. E. Foster (Cambridge Antiquarian Society 35, 1905), esp. pp. 41, 46, 53 (1518–19, 1521–2, 1522–3). The proctors' account for 1497–8 (*Grace Book B*, vol. I, p. 111) has an entry for payment to a carpenter 'pro ligatura tabule in qua scripsit nomina benefactorum ad fabricam ecclesie beate Marie', which was probably the source of the list copied by or for Matthew Stokes in the 1560s in Cambridge University Library, University Archives Grace Book (Delta), fos. 327r–329r. The antiquarian sources are: Matthew Parker, Corpus Christi College MS 106, pp. 14–15 (fair copy of extracts from proctors' accounts with notes by Parker) copied by Matthew Stokes in 1564 in Grace Book A (Delta), fos. 329v–330r; J. Caius, *Historiae Cantebrigiensis Academiae Liberi* (London, 1574), pp. 89–91, partly based on, and published by, Parker (Parker's own copy is in the Caius Library, F.4.24, but has no significant marginalia). Parker's extracts etc. were copied, probably from Stokes, by nineteenth- and twentieth-century antiquaries in Cambridge University Archives, CUR 18.1 (1) and 1(4); also by S. Sandars, *Historical and Architectural Notes on Great St Mary's Church, Cambridge* (Cambridge Antiquarian Society, 1869) and W. D. Bushell, *The Church of St Mary the Great* (Cambridge, 1948) – both of which have much other useful information which needs to be used with caution.

On Thomas Barowe, William Gage and William Stockdale, see A. B. Emden, *A Biographical Register of the University of Cambridge to 1500* (Cambridge, 1963), pp. 40–1, 255, 557. On John Fisher and his lunch with the Lady Margaret Beaufort, see *Humanism, Reform and the Reformation, the Career of Bishop John Fisher*, ed. B. Bradshaw and E. Duffy (Cambridge, 1989), esp. pp. 57, 65 n.56. For John Wastell and his role at Great St Mary's see John Harvey, *English Mediaeval Architects*: *A Biographical Dictionary Down to 1550* (2nd edn, Gloucester, 1984), pp. 316–25, esp. p. 319; and *ibid.* pp. 18–19, 60 on the role of Simon Clerk, Wastell's colleague or predecessor, and John Bell, who seems likely to have been Wastell's assistant in executing the work; F. Woodman, *The Architectural History of King's College Chapel* (London, 1986), pp. 155, 157, 178, 200, 203, and F. Woodman in *Cambridge Review* C (1978), 104–7, who was rightly sceptical of the importance of 1478 as a centenary, but did not at that time penetrate behind the printed sources.

2 Reformation or deformation? The reformed church and the university

PATRICK COLLINSON

In 1633, William Laud, Archbishop of Canterbury, was being shown Dunblane Cathedral in Scotland. Somebody remarked that the somewhat dilapidated building he was looking at had once been 'a brave kirk', before the Reformation. The archbishop exploded. 'What fellow! Deformation not Reformation!'

Reformation/Deformation is so neatly obvious a formulation that Laud cannot have been the first to have said it. In 1558, the Puritan Antony Gilby wrote that 'there was no reformation but a deformation in the time of that tyrant and lecherous monster', meaning Henry VIII. Gilby, of course, wanted more reformation, Laud less, which made his remark in 1633 scandalous, especially in Scotland. But one of the latest to have said it, at somewhat greater length than Archbishop Laud's three words, is my friend and colleague Eamon Duffy in a book of 654 pages, *The Stripping of the Altars*. Dr Duffy first celebrates the richness of traditional religious devotion in pre-Reformation England; and then tells what for him is the deplorable story of its repudiation, betrayal and systematic, efficient destruction. He tells us how one of the most Catholic countries in Europe became one of the least, without adequately explaining why: the subject, perhaps, of another book.

I do not know of a more vivid demonstration of the theme of reformation/deformation than the accounts and inventories of this parish church of Great St Mary's throughout the years of religious transmogrification which are the subject of this chapter. (The OED, I see, defines 'transmogrify' as to transform utterly, grotesquely or strangely, words I think Dr Duffy would happily endorse.) The Great St Mary's inventories are especially telling evidence of deformation. In the published text of these accounts, the list of 'jewells, goods and cattels' for which the churchwardens were responsible in 1504 runs to thirteen closely packed pages. By the reign of Elizabeth, the inventory of church goods occupies less than half a page, a list of bare essentials. In the 1630s, little had changed. An old man in his seventies would have been looking at the same blue velvet cloth on the communion table since he was a small child. If he wanted something to read, there were the works of Bishop Jewel against the Catholics, published and purchased in about 1610, but written in the 1560s.

Going back to 1504, how did they cram it all in? Of eight altars besides the high altar, four answered for their furnishings to the churchwardens. Each was supplied with its own vestments (ten for St Andrew, eleven for the Holy Trinity), its own altar cloths, mass books and much else. The great cope case contained six copes for the high altar alone. There were crosses and candlesticks galore, and the many images with their lights perpetually burning before them were appropriately adorned and equipped. There was an arrow for St Edmund, a cross staff for St Nicholas, a wheel for St Catherine. One particularly numinous object was a silver reliquary containing some of the oil of St Nicholas, oil thought to exude miraculously from the saint's tomb at Bari. That was an object of devotion and may have drawn pilgrims, as perhaps did the image of the Virgin, for this, as Professor Brooke reminds us in chapter 1, was the most widely popular cult of the early sixteenth century, celebrated over the road on a scale to make Cecil B. De Mille green with envy The image of St Mary in this church was more intimate, clad in a charming costume complete with silver shoes and a old chain of nine links around her neck.

The church which contained all this was spanking new. Let me add one or two details to what Christopher Brooke has told us about the great rebuilding. The story that many of the begging letters to pay for this large project were written by the poet Skelton, supposedly Curate of Trumpington, is, I fear, too good to be true. What is more certain is that the crowning touches were the magnificent and richly carved roodloft, with all its niches and pedestals and images, 'crests, vaults, orbs, lyntells', completed in 1523 at a cost of £92.6s.8d; and the great west window, glazed in 1530 and costing £61.8s.10d. To understand the iconoclasm of the Reformation, we have to appreciate that what was destroyed was not some charming relic of a quaint medieval past, 'things I have loved long since and lost awhile' (Philip Larkin's 'England Gone'), but a building put up and richly embellished the day before yesterday. It was contemporary religion, and religious art, on which violent hands were laid. The image of the Trinity in the roodloft was brightly gilded in 1526. It would last for only twenty years or so.

A few years after the inventory of 1504 was made, a civil lawyer from Trinity Hall whose name was Thomas Bilney preached a sermon at

Willesden, which at that time (however improbable it may seem now) was a notable centre of the Marian cult. He told his congregation: 'Put away your golden gods, your silver gods, your stony gods, and leave your offerings.' Going on pilgrimage was 'naught'. There was worse to come. Bilney told the good people gathered at Willesden some of the facts of religious life. Priests were known to take the jewels off the church images and to hang them around the necks of their women, 'the vilest of women', abandoned women. Then they put them back again. Bilney would have known that Our Lady of Willesden herself had been called by some 'a common bawd' and 'a sturdy whore'. To speak of defamation rather than deformation, sexual defamation was an important element in Reformation polemic. Catholicism itself was denounced as a kind of spiritual whoredom. But let Bilney continue. As King Hezekiah destroyed the brazen serpent in the Temple, so should kings and princes nowadays destroy and burn the images of saints set up in the churches. That must have gone down well in Willesden! So well that in 1531 it was Thomas Bilney himself who was burned as a heretic in his native Norwich, although most people there believed him to be no such thing, only an outspoken critic of clerical extravagance. Presently Henry VIII, in fair imitation of Hezekiah, would order the destruction of some of those gaudy images, 'feigned images', said the Royal Injunction of 1538. The Reformation had begun. So it was that within ten years of Bilney's burning, the churchwardens of Great St Mary's made their way in September to Stourbridge Fair, outside the town, and sold St Mary's chain of nine links and with it the precious box of St Nicholas and his oil. Reformation or deformation?

There is a structural problem for this chapter which we had better confront before we proceed any further. We are dealing with an ambivalent building, the ambivalence of town and gown: at once the Church of St Mary by, or at, the Market, 'juxta Forum', or, not later than the early seventeenth century, 'Mary Major'; and the Public Church of the University, in the words of the martyrologist John Foxe, 'the place of resort, when there is any common assembly or meeting of the university'. This was a parish church, a civic church with places of honour for the mayor and aldermen, a diocesan church where the bishop's consistory court met for many centuries and episcopal synods and visitations were held, a place of university business. Church, university and teeming market town were hugger mugger on this site, sharing a space which had not been subjected to any kind of town planning, or even sanitisation. There was no view from the church to the Schools of the University until, in 1574, Archbishop Parker paid for a little street to be cut through, which he called 'University Street' but which became known as Regents' Walk, running across what is now the grass separating the Senate House from King's Chapel. The street outside the church, the King's High Street, was only twenty-five feet wide, and you must imagine a row of shops and tenements opposite, including two pubs, the New Angel and the Green Dragon. First one shop and then (from 1587) two were built against the west wall of the church itself, either side of the door, in Dutch style. In 1636 it was said that the church was 'blinded up' by these shops, which obscured the windows, and they projected twenty-four feet out from the church. For some decades of the mid-sixteenth century, the tenant was a fletcher, Thomas Jackson. A fletcher sold, and, I suppose made, bows and arrows. But presently the shops were taken over by the book trade, binding, showing and selling books, with the stock-in-trade, 'fats' or barrels of books, spilling over into the church. From 1589, the premises were leased to John Legate, the founding father of the university press. So here was the beginning of a tradition now continued on the other side of Market Street. Not until the 1760s were these hovels (aediculae) removed, the walls made good and the railings which you see today erected, the parish having demised the property to the university for a thousand years for a yearly rent of a penny. (Is it still paid?)

Every year it was necessary to cart away quantities of dung; in 1575 'eight loads of mire', in 1576 'the filthe about the churche'. Was this inside or out, of animal or human origin? The liberal use of straw to cope with nastiness may explain the eight loads. Frankincense was regularly purchased, not for any liturgical purpose but to drown the stench. When Queen Elizabeth came to Cambridge in 1564, twenty loads of sand were spread over the churchyard. What horrors was this sand meant to conceal? Would you care to have been a parishioner of Great St Mary's in 1564?

One may speak of a kind of symbiosis of parish and university within this building. The university's own premises (the Schools) were too cramped to house the most public of ceremonies, and especially the annual graduation proceedings, known as 'Commencements'. Congregations had been held in this church long before there were any Schools, which were built only in the fourteenth century. During the rebuilding of the nave, they were moved to the houses of the Austin Friars and Franciscans. With the Dissolution of the Monasteries, there was some talk of appropriating the Franciscan church as a permanent academic theatre. But then, some time after 1540, everything came back to St Mary's, which would remain the assembly hall of the university until Gibbs' Senate House was completed in 1730.

It can never have been a wholly satisfactory arrangement. In 1636 we are told that between congregations, the church served as a 'lumber-house' for university gear, mainly the staging or 'scaffolds'. From, at the latest, the early seventeenth century when Bodley's building at Oxford threw down a challenge, the university was intermittently looking for funds and space for what was variously called a theatre, commencement house, or *musaeum*. In the late 1620s, George Villiers, Duke of Buckingham, a controversial chancellor, promised £7,000 for the purpose, but then got himself assassinated. Dr John Cosin of Peterhouse, a future Bishop of Durham, had his own design and even his own development office. Cosin was particularly unhappy about the antics of the satirical *praevaricator* whose function it was to make a mockery of some parts of the proceedings at the major commencement, for doctors and masters. (The presiding officer at the BA ceremony was known as 'Mr Tripos', from the three-legged stool on which he sat.) But then the Civil War happened. And so the inconvenience of what was now seen by some, like Cosin, as a profane use of the church, was continued into the eighteenth century. Commencements apart, the church was used with great frequency for a variety of other academic exercises, such as the sermons *ad clerum,* preached by an incepting Bachelor or Doctor of Divinity. In 1616 James I required all students to attend sermons at Great St Mary's. How did they all fit in?

But to read the churchwardens' accounts you would not know how much use the university made of the church. One is reminded of Hong Kong, where Chinese and expatriates occupy the same space while having almost nothing to do with each other. However, from the 1550s, the churchwardens began to collect money from the graduands, and by 1565 this was a regular going rate for both Masters and Bachelors. In 1610, 192 BAs took their degrees: this brought in 'at 4d a bachelor' (the exact words of the accounts), £3. 3s. With the steady expansion of the university, this source of revenue was far from insignificant. In 1629, there were 255 Bachelors, in 1640 206 MAs and 239 BAs. This brought in seven or eight pounds, or 10 to 15 per cent of the income of the parish.

I should like to learn from someone more learned, or differently learned, whether or on what terms this symbiotic relationship was formalised; that is to say, what the legally defined interest of the university, as distinct from the rectorial interest of the King's Hall, and, later, Trinity College, may have been. All that I know is that in 1639 when Dr

Cosin as vice-chancellor, pursuing an avant-garde ecclesiological agenda, presumed to change the internal arrangements of the church, the parish insisted that the use made of the church by the university was by its permission; and it prepared to fight, and pay for, a major legal battle in defence of its rights. This sentence occurs in the accounts for 1640: 'Payd for a coppy of an order where in the University claymeth the use of the church and the parishioners never would condescend to it.'

But back to the beginnings of the Reformation: which means, back to Thomas Bilney, our Trinity Hall lawyer who disliked sacred images, wanton women and shining gewgaws as much as he abhorred music. We are told that when Thomas Thirlby, a future Bishop of Ely and Westminster and a son of this parish, began to play his recorder in the chamber above Bilney's head, he would resort straight to his prayer. 'He could abide no singing', and coming away from this church 'he would lament to his scholars the curiosity of their dainty singing, which he called a mockery with God'. Dainty singing was under sentence too and soon would be heard here no more.

We should not mock 'little Bilney', who, according to the martyrologist and historian John Foxe was the taproot of the Protestant Reformation in Cambridge, which almost means, nationally; for as Gordon Rupp put it long ago, and with an implied reference to Charles Simeon and the Evangelical tradition of the nineteenth century, the Reformation was practically 'a Cambridge movement'. Cambridge supplied more than its fair share of early Protestant reformers, Marian martyrs, Marian exiles. And it all seems to have begun with Bilney who, says Foxe, was 'the first framer of this university in the faith of Christ': a faith which Bilney found out for himself, existentially, as he read, more for the sake of the good Latin than for any other reason, Erasmus' new version of the New Testament, based on the first printed Greek text, the *Novum Instrumentum*. 'At last I heard speak of Jesus, even when the New Testament was first set forth by Erasmus . . . And at the first reading . . . I chanced upon this sentence of St Paul . . . "It is a true saying, and worthy of all men to be embraced, that Christ Jesus came into the world to save sinners, of whom I am the chief and principal." This one sentence . . . did so exhilirate my heart, being before wounded with the guilt of my sins, and being almost in despair, that immediately I felt a marvellous comfort and quietness, insomuch that "my bruised bones leaped for joy".' These evangelical words are a reminder that the Protestant Reformation, which was about to happen, was not only about deformation. At its heart was the rediscovery of the sheer gratuitousness of God's grace, that we are made safe for all eternity by God's utterly free mercy, granted through Christ's sacrifice on the Cross, given in spite of our deeply innate sinfulness.

Bilney's converting experience, which replicated but was evidently quite independent of Martin Luther's apprehension of justification by faith alone, expressed itself in practical Christianity, much as with later generations of Cambridge men experiencing an intensification of their religious profession: Puritans later in the sixteenth century, 'Simeonites' in the early nineteenth century. Foxe tells us about Bilney's preaching at the 'lazars' cots' (lepers' cottages), wrapping them in sheets, helping them to what they wanted, if they would convert to Christ; how he was 'laborious and painful to the desperates, a preacher to the prisoners and comfortless, a great doer in Cambridge'. William Tyndale, who may have been a Cambridge man, was about to tell everyone who could read or listen to English, as part of the package which included his fresh, arresting, printed text of the New Testament, that such 'great doings' were the natural and even inevitable fruit of a true and lively faith, a powerful, effective thing. Archbishop Cranmer, a Jesus man, would soon tell the English church, in the Book of Homilies which was part of the basic furnishings of this church for centuries, that the justified man was bound to do good works, but not with this intent, to be made good by the doing of them. In Foxe's words, Bilney had in his heart an incredible desire to allure many to the love of true religion and godliness. His converts included some of the leaders of the early English Protestant movement, notably Robert Barnes, Luther's most faithful English disciple, and the greatest preacher of the early Reformation, Hugh Latimer. In this sense, if we trust Foxe, Bilney, though not quite a Protestant himself (he died believing in transubstantiation and the supremacy of the pope), began the Reformation, in Cambridge and beyond.

But in another sense, and dimension, the Reformation was begun by Henry VIII, and a complex series of negotiations and alliances of convenience, involving the religious imperative of Tyndale's Bible and the political agenda of the king and some of his ministers, began a process of public, legislated religious change which, with all its fits and starts, on looking back has the deceptive appearance of inexorability. Under Henry VIII, the process was erratic, inconsistent and subject to U-turns. But the monasteries went to the wall, the English Bible was officially adopted and promoted, and the cult of saints and their images and pilgrimages took a battering. In the reign of his young son, Edward VI, there was a Reformation as complete as the Church of England would ever see: a whitewashed *tabula rasa*, no more masses, no more purgatory, no more altars and crosses, the salvation faith of Bilney, Tyndale and Latimer perfectly if discreetly wrapped up in Cranmer's Prayer Book: not that dear old thing for which some Anglicans nostalgically yearn, but a new thing, far more shocking in 1549 and even more (the second more radically reformed Prayer Book) in 1552, than any Alternative Service Book. For one thing, it was in English, to be 'understanded of', and participated in, by the people, who for Cranmer were God's people, his elect, a new imagining of what Christianity was. Cranmer's communion service spoke memorably of the sacrifice of Christ, once offered, as a full, perfect and sufficient satisfaction for the sins of the whole world, the most full-blooded and uncompromising statement of that faith in any Protestant liturgy. The mass, the heart of Catholicism, was redundant and, as the more outspoken reformers would say, blasphemous. And then came Queen Mary, to whose reign we shall return in a moment, for it witnessed the most dramatic single event in the history of this church in the sixteenth century.

But, first, how were these swings and somersaults registered in the accounts of St Mary at the Market? The later years of Henry VIII saw the dismantling of shrines and the sale of some of the precious and pretty things which had adorned them. In 1548, the first year of Edward VI, 'certen old implements of the church' were sold, from painted cloths to a silver parcel-gilt cross weighing ninety two ounces at 4s.10d an ounce: realising the large sum of £46. 17s. 10d, some of which was given to the poor. In 1551 the altar stones were sold for nine shillings. Over the next two or three years, most of the church's stock of vestments and plate, even wax (240 pounds weight of wax) was sold off: £45 worth of plate to a London buyer, £28 worth of vestments, including ten copes, to one of the churchwardens. All this marketing was very prudent, for soon much of what was left (not much by the sound of it) was confiscated and handed over to the royal commissioners. Deformation! What, by way of Reformation, took the place of all that finery? The Great Bible above all, sponsored by Henry VIII and his ministers. In 1549 the English service was purchased for sixteen pence, the Book of Homilies for twenty pence. In 1551 money was spent on the 'wrythtynge of the church walles with scryptures'.

As with England as a whole, so it was in Cambridge. A radical reform of religion had taken place, legally and administratively, on paper and in church fabric and furnishings, which had yet to happen in any more authentic and real sense. Hearts and minds had not been touched, still less won and transformed: or, not very many hearts and minds. A certain fixation in traditional, Protestant historiography, focusing, for example, on the famous but very slenderly documented group of early reformers meeting at the White Horse Tavern, has tended to conceal the dominance of traditional, conservative belief which prevailed until at least the early years of Elizabeth. My own college, Trinity, was mistakenly represented by one of the most celebrated of our university historians as a reformed house, 100 per cent committed to the new ways, when it was nothing of the kind but rather a safe haven for conservative refugees from progressive St John's. John Redman, the first master and true founder of the college, was very far from being a 'new Christian', as Protestants were contemptuously known in Oxford. In principle, the university was reformed. The religious houses were no more. Canon law studies had been abolished (the abolition of one whole faculty when there were only five), theological study in the scholastic tradition was discouraged, and according to the royal injunctions of 1535, which Mullinger thought marked the watershed between the medieval and modern age, doctrine was to be taught according to 'the true sense' of Scripture. Now, what was that? No one in the 1540s was very sure. The minds and consciences of individuals, future bishops like Ridley and Grindal, and even Archbishop Cranmer himself, were stumbling uncertainly into an unknown landscape, like John Henry Newman in 'Lead Kindly Light'.

One great boost for the cause of Reformation was the arrival, in a Cambridge now experiencing the full blast of the official Edwardian reforms, of Martin Bucer, the great teacher and quasi-bishop of the Rhineland city of Strasbourg. Bucer ranked in the pecking order of Protestant reformers number three or number four, an outstanding theologian and a practical religious statesman who had made Strasbourg one of the great cities on a hill of Reformation Europe. Bucer was a tireless ecumenist, arbitrating between warring religious parties, and an influential if prolix writer. What he thought up, Calvin in Geneva expressed in better prose and implemented with superior political and managerial skills. But as Gordon Rupp used to say, Bucer was a great character. He left a permanent mark on the men he touched, who in Cambridge included several future bishops and leaders of the Elizabethan Church.

This great man now became Regius Professor of Divinity, one of the most distinguished holders of that office in the entire history of Cambridge. But within fourteen months of his first lecture, Cambridge and its deplorable climate had killed him at not much more than fifty. He had written to Calvin of a kind of paralysis in his legs, arms and hands. 'My stomach too is easily put out of order, and my bowells are in an obstinate state.' At this time, Bucer was stiffly opposed by Cambridge conservatism, and he made a pessimistic diagnosis of the entire religious landscape in Edwardian England: 'fallow ground' he called it, a country which had lost one religion but had still to discover its replacement. In the university, he found, or claimed to have found, that 'by far the greater part of the Fellows are either most bitter papists, or profligate epicureans'. More generally, he complained to Calvin of the 'desolation and betrayal of the churches, which with very few exceptions, are entrusted to those who neither know, nor care to know, anything about Christ'.

Perhaps Bucer exaggerated. When he died, in March 1551, there was one of those great Cambridge funerals, to be remembered for all time to come, with two future Archbishops of Canterbury playing a prominent part. Matthew Parker preached the sermon and his successor Edmund Grindal, a man deeply devoted to Bucer's memory in years to come, bore the coffin. Three thousand people attended. When everything was over, the churchwardens had to spend twopence 'for naylles to mend the seats in the chyrche when M. Doctor Bucer was buryed'. It seems that it was always necessary to mend the seats, after a big funeral.

But unfortunately everything was not over. When Catholic Mary succeeded her half-brother and the Cambridge Protestants scattered into their German and Swiss exile, or stayed behind to face the music, an interdict was slapped on St Mary's, and also on neighbouring St Michael's, where Bucer's offsider Paul Fagius, a Protestant German professor of Hebrew, had been buried. The presence of these heretical bodies made it impossible for the parishioners of St Mary's and St Michael's to receive the sacraments or, indeed, to bury their own dead. This was in January 1557. A prolonged and grotesque process followed and took all month. Ceremonies were held to condemn the two Germans, posthumously, of heresy, and to order the exhumation of their bodies. In early February, the deed was done, the bodies taken up out of their graves and burned in the market place on market day, 'a cart load of books with them'. John Foxe, the martyrologist, had a field day with these bizarre proceedings. The country people at their market stalls laughed when they saw the coffins securely tied to the stake. 'To what purpose serveth that chain?' 'It was not to be feared they would run away.' The next day, on a wet and dismal morning such as Bucer had known all too well, there was a great mud-spattered religious procession around the town. There was more expense for our long-suffering churchwardens: 'For the new

halloweing and Reconcyleng of our chyrch for being interdicted' – 'fran-
kinsens and swate perfumes for the sacrament and herbes etc. 8d'; oh,
and 22d for covering over Bucer's grave.

At the formal sentencing of Bucer and Fagius, the speeches and
sermons included an oration by Dr Andrew Perne, Master of
Peterhouse, currently vice-chancellor and deemed by some to be 'the
most Catholic' of the university's leading lights: though he had some
kind of Protestant past. It was a denunciation of Bucer, according to
Foxe's source, 'such a shameful railing that it is not possible to defame a
man more than he did'. Foxe's account goes on to report that these words
were uttered against Perne's own conscience, for his best friends claimed
to have seen him, either before or after the ceremony, striking himself on
the breast, weeping and wishing that his soul might depart to be with
Bucer's. Perne's own copy of Foxe's *Acts and Monuments*, or 'Book of
Martyrs', survives in his library at Peterhouse. The passage in question
has a hole burned in it, in the middle of the page, as if by someone
holding up a lighted candle. By one of history's supreme ironies, when
Protestant Elizabeth succeeded Mary and a new ceremony was held to
reinstate Bucer and Fagius in their honours and degrees, the Vice-
Chancellor who presided was, once again, Andrew Perne.

Consequently, Perne became the vicar of Bray of Elizabethan
England, his very name a byword for religious inconsistency. When the
queen came to Cambridge on a famous state visit in 1564, there was a
theological disputation staged for her benefit in Great St Mary's, in
which Perne argued that the church was of greater authority than
Scripture, identifying the Church of Rome as the authentic stock of tradition from which the English church was descended and derived its
liturgy and sacraments, a true if defective church. This caused offence
and probably cost Perne his bishopric, so that he remained at Peterhouse
for another twenty-five years. Perne, who was better at burning dead
Protestants than live ones, might nowadays be called pragmatic. It was a
pragmatism consistently exercised in the interests of his university, his
college, and this church. Nor was his capacity to conceal his own religious opinions, or his instinct to survive, protect and preserve, through all
the twists and turns of changes in government and doctrine, all that
unusual. Cambridge was full of learned doctors and heads of houses who
looked both ways and no doubt devoutly wished that there were not those
two ways between which they were forced to choose.

This was so far the case that the real tumult of the Reformation happened not in the 1530s and 1540s but in the sixties and seventies, as new

generations of students and young graduates, the regent masters who in principle governed the university, expressed their contempt for their conservative and prevaricating seniors. One small but telling symbol of protest was their refusal to wear, in chapel and church, the white linen surplice which was the standard ecclesiastical garment required by the terms of the Elizabethan religious settlement, but which in the perception of critics of the settlement soon to be called Puritans was a hated relic of the recent, popish past. Soon the authority by which these things were urged and imposed, the bishops themselves, was called in question, and Thomas Cartwright of Trinity, no obscure young radical but the Lady Margaret Professor, denounced hierarchy from the pulpit of this church as unscriptural, insisting that the ministry, discipline and constitution of the church must be validated from certain New Testament texts. This was the beginning of English Presbyterianism. According to pious legend, when Cartwright preached, 'the sexton was fain to take down the windows, by reason of the multitude that came to hear him'. The sexton may have been 'fain', but to take down the windows of Great St Mary's was not a light undertaking and I find no evidence in the accounts that this was ever done. However, money was often spent to repair the windows, possibly broken by stone-throwing. After the performance of college plays it was always necessary to mend windows. People, and perhaps especially the young, were not well-behaved in Elizabethan Cambridge.

From the evidence of near riotous scenes in college chapels and petitions in Cartwright's favour bearing scores of signatures, there is no reason to doubt that Cambridge towards 1570 was experiencing a kind of generational revolt and a mood of near hysteria: 1968, so to speak, in an Elizabethan context, and an academic pressure cooker; or that the incipient revolt was firmly suppressed, by Andrew Perne and his protégé, the newly installed Master of Trinity, John Whitgift. Whitgift and Perne drew up new statutes for the university which would last for three centuries, and which put an end to the turbulent democracy of the young graduates, placing government in the hands of the heads of houses. It was, said Perne, in a letter to the chancellor, William Cecil, time 'to bridle the untamed affections of younge Regentes'. This was not the end but the beginning of the story of Puritanism in Elizabethan Cambridge. But it was the end so far as Cambridge was concerned, of Thomas Cartwright, who was the first victim of the new statutes, losing his chair and his fellowship.

What was also only just beginning were many decades of heated religious controversy, a state of instability which we may trace to the drastic and precipitate changes of the Reformation itself, and to the failure of public authority to clarify and define certain crucial matters which the Reformation had thrown into uncertainty, such as the scope of scriptural authority for religious practice, matters which Whitgift and Cartwright would debate in hundreds, if not thousands, of pages of print, throughout the 1570s. The Elizabethan Settlement had in reality settled nothing, or had left much that was unsettled. Particular issues were the allegedly corrupt government of the church by archbishops and bishops and the whole system of church government which they represented: the list was endless – archdeacons, cathedral churches (the cathedrals were the strongholds of a conservative interpretation of the settlement), the church courts, unreformed church finance, the lack of effective pastoral discipline and the abuse of the church's ultimate pastoral sanction, excommunication. The failings of a clergy unable or unwilling to exercise a truly godly, converting, preaching ministry, was a running sore. In spite of the new and more rigorous Whitgiftian regime, these matters were still ventilated from the pulpit of Great St Mary's from time to time. The doctrine of saving grace was another powder keg. According to what most English churchmen in leading academic positions held to be orthodox Protestant doctrine, salvation was restricted to God's elect, chosen before the foundation of the world. Grace in respect of these elect persons was compelling and saving faith could not fail and could not be lost. But these doctrines were not securely protected by the Thirty-Nine Articles of Religion, and in the 1590s a series of challenges to Calvinism was mounted, again from the pulpit of Great St Mary's. Anti-Calvinism, or Arminianism as the contrary tendency came to be known, at first failed to make headway. But in the 1620s and 1630s it gathered political support and became aggressive and even dominant. Most of the provocative sermons of these seventy years or so were heard in Great St Mary's: Presbyterian sermons, hot Puritan sermons, anti-Calvinist sermons. And we know about them from the disciplinary proceedings in the vice-chancellor's court which followed and which also happened here.

But it would be quite wrong to suggest that the Elizabethan and early Stuart church was one great cockpit of theological conflict and acrimony. It was not. And when we consider this church not as a forum for academic debate but as a parish church we discover a norm which was much less exciting, and turbulent. So (remembering my earlier analogy) what of the Chinese inhabitants of this little ecclesiastical Hong Kong? The early Elizabethan accounts record the making of arrangements which would remain largely unaltered for the next 250 years. The restored Marian altar and the magnificent roodloft were removed. The only candles now in use were to light the church in winter and they cost no more than a shilling a year, which is what it cost in 1564 to whitewash the interior of the church, an operation regularly repeated. In place of the great rood, the eye was now caught by the Ten Commandments, painted on boards. All over Europe this was the great age of the Decalogue. The images on the windows were 'washed out' (whatever that may have meant), although the Virgin Mary remained to be blotted out in the even more iconoclastic 1640s. However, her embroidered image on an altar cloth was cut out and sold for six shillings. Quantities of candlesticks, crosses and vestments were disposed of in the London market, which probably means that they went overseas to Catholic Europe, where there was a great demand for English needlework. Towards 1570 all that was left were two or three surplices and a single cope, probably not used, and the cope was sold in 1609 for thirty shillings. There was a silver communion cup and a small quantity of velvet cloths, coverings and cushions for pulpit and altar: still called in the accounts the altar, although it was now in reality a communion table, carried down into the nave on the two or three Sundays in the year when the sacrament was administered. In the 1560s the service was still sung and the organs kept in repair. But by 1584 the organs were broken and the annual inventory speaks only of an organ case with some pipes. This was sold for a pound in 1613. The only music in Elizabethan and Jacobean Great St Mary's would have been the metrical psalms, sung unaccompanied.

It is necessary to explain what the internal arrangements of this church were, in the seventeenth and on into the eighteenth centuries. These matters are very poorly understood, mainly because the Victorian age was so thorough in the business of what was called church restoration. The result has been that the profoundly Protestant (you might say un-Anglican) character of what have been called 'Prayer Book churches' has been almost totally forgotten. In his book *Churches the Victorians Forgot*, Mark Chatfield was able to count only some 140 out of 8,000 pre-Victorian buildings which have remained more or less untouched. Appreciation of the old, dry, style, such as we find in a passage of Hardy's *Jude the Obscure*, is rare.

In Great St Mary's, the arrangements were unusually complex, given the dual and even multiple purposes to which the building was dedicated. Imagine the pulpit halfway down the nave and looking towards the tower. The pulpit was the focal point of interest in an early seventeenth-century church, and the chancel was full of seating facing in the pulpit's direction. Even the communion service, the so-called 'second service', was conducted from the pulpit. Preachers used prayers of their own composition before the sermon, not the Prayer Book, sometimes praying extempore. Praying for the queen, who was a French Roman Catholic, in the 1630s, a preacher said, 'very abruptly': 'And why do the people imagine a vain thing? Lord, thou knowest there is but one Religion, one Baptism, one Lord. How can there be two faiths?'

The area immediately around the pulpit in Great St Mary's was called the cockpit. It was railed in and reserved for Masters of Arts, who were entitled to sit uncovered during sermons, and who may or may not have been scandalised when many townsmen did the same. There was a short-lived gallery for doctors of the university, and special seats, probably in or towards the chancel, for the mayor, aldermen and bailiffs. On one occasion, the assize judges, who included Sir Edward Coke, came into Great St Mary's and one of them occupied the mayor's seat. The mayor 'offered them very kindly to sitt in the seate under hym', which was thought courageous on his part. Other special seats were reserved for the 'auncientest parishioners' that is, not the eldest but senior heavyweights. Around the cockpit were the children and servants, who seem to have stood. But there were forms for the poor to sit on. By an order of 1610, no seats were to be occupied by scholars under the degree of MA, which presumably means that the scholars were usurping seats to which they were not entitled. A hostile account of 1636 speaks of 'boys and townsmen' filling the chancel, 'all in a rude heap betwixt the Doctors and the Altar', while in the body of the church, men, women and scholars were 'thrust together promiscuously'.

This was a report drawn up for an abortive visitation by Archbishop Laud, who was an indignant critic of the slovenly state of the parish churches. Historians have been too ready to take at face value those Laudian polemics and jeremiads, and I would not want you to think that the Elizabethan and Jacobean story of Great St Mary's was one of unrelieved neglect and decay. We now appreciate that, generally in England, expenditure on repairs and maintenance revived and intensified around the turn of the sixteenth and seventeenth centuries, markedly so in London. Here, in Cambridge, the parishioners were 'cessed' or rated on an annual basis, at Easter, raising sums recorded in the 'Easter book' of as much as thirty pounds. These funds were applied to paying the minister's stipend (only £8. 13s. 4d, but increased in 1595 to £13. 6s. 8d), and to the cost of building works. As these wages indicate, the ministers were not men of any great distinction. Thanks to the university, Great St Mary's got its sermons on the cheap and had no need to pay for a learned and celebrated preacher of its own.

The accounts supply us with the names of all the rate-paying parishioners together with what they paid for most years in the seventeenth century. Even the parish poor, the almsfolks, were rated at threepence, which may have been resented, although the idea may have been to incorporate them fully into the parish community. In 1608, 142 parishioners, plus servants and almsfolks, paid a total of £16. 16s. 9d. But the parish was filling up. By 1623, the Easter book lists 184 parishioners paying £33. 16s. 11d, and in 1637 it was 214 parishioners and more than £28. But by the 1650s the population had fallen back to a little over a hundred. Why was that? Separate accounts were kept by the overseers of the poor, for which the parishioners 'of ability', as the seventeenth century put it, were separately rated. Surveying the accounts through the later sixteenth and seventeenth centuries, one observes the emergence of the parish, and to be precise its vestry, as the basic unit of local government. Some historians speak of the 'secularisation' of the parish.

Few years passed without some work on the fabric. But by far the greatest event for Great St Mary's in the entire period covered by this chapter was the completion of the tower, or steeple, as it is invariably called in the accounts. Work on the tower had begun in 1491, but by the mid-sixteenth century had been suspended. By then it stood only to the height of the nave, and little more was done for the next forty years. The bells were hung in a temporary structure, at first thatched and then roofed with tiles which came from the Austin Friars. But the 1590s saw another burst of strenuous building works, and even more strenuous fund-raising, which pushed the tower up another twenty-four feet, to accommodate a proper bell chamber. All this effort is recorded in the accounts in the greatest detail. When the country clergy turned up at the commencement in 1592, as they always did, they were found to be good for sixty pounds. Francis Bacon donated a pound, the Earl of Essex £10. 10s. £10 came from the estate of the now deceased Dr Perne, a great friend to the project. In the colleges, students paid two shillings, fellows ten, fellow commoners five shillings, 'or more as their tutors thought fitting'. In the two years 1593–4, the work cost £219. 3s. 4d., and it would go on until 1608. Great quantities of stone were carted along the High Street from the bridge. The work was directed by Robert Grumbold, who was paid nine shillings a week. The narrow pay differentials are interesting, for ordinary labourers earned four shillings, almost half the pay of the master mason. The Grumbold family would spend the next 150 years rebuilding Cambridge. It was the Grumbolds who built the library of St John's, the Wren Library, and the buildings on the river front at Clare. Their hallmark was the use of stone balls on parapets and gables, as still to be seen at Clare, and four stone balls would adorn the turrets of Great St Mary's until they were removed, some thought 'injudiciously', in 1841. The intention was to crown the tower with a spire eighty feet high, matching, and perhaps rivalling is the right word, the spire of Oxford's university church. But parishioners and fund-raisers had had enough, and the spire was never built.

Why all this effort? We now know that in many parts of England in the 1590s, and certainly in this region, church towers were being rebuilt or strengthened. This was in spite of a depressing economic climate, an even more depressing climate in the literal sense and wartime taxation. But perhaps low wages, the lowest in five hundred years, were a positive incentive. Look at those church towers when the weather improves and you next find yourselves out and about. Much work that you assume to be late medieval may in fact date from these years. But why? Because the towers were functionally bell-towers, and a new and improved mechanism had just been invented which made possible a technical advance in the art of bellringing. Bells had previously been tolled to advertise morning prayer or the sermon, or to announce a death, what were called in Great St Mary's 'the towls of distinction': for which the parish clerk was paid fourpence a time. But now the bells were rung, and especially on the dates which honoured the monarchy, a Protestant monarchy, and commemorated the victories and even more the providential deliverances of the Protestant nation. One such occasion was 'crownation day', 17 November, actually the anniversary of Queen Elizabeth's accession in 1558, sometimes called 'the birthday of the Gospel'. These triumphant bellringings, often accompanied by bonfires, were the essence of the public culture of Protestant England, replacing the old calendrical festivals and rituals of Merry England. 17 November, for example, took the place of the traditional ringing on All Souls night, a fortnight before.

Here the bells were hoisted up into their new bell-frame in 1596: 'given in money to drinke among those that did helpe to drawe up the belles into the steeple and place them in their several rooms, 8d'. Fifteen years later it was decided to recast the four bells as five. 116 parishioners forked out £41. 10s. 6d, and the new peal of bells cost £58. 13s. 7d, £18 of that for the bell founder. For the rest of the seventeenth century, the new bells would ring out for crownation day, for royal births, and on

5 November, the anniversary of the Gunpowder Plot, observed throughout the years of the English Republic, and beyond. When, in October 1623, Prince Charles returned from Madrid without a Spanish bride, the bells were rung for three consecutive days, which cost four shillings, plus 3s. 4d for the bonfire. On such occasions, the bells were rung by a company of scholar ringers.

Soon after that event, the religious climate of Cambridge began to change, leaving the bare, old-fashioned churchmanship of Great St Mary's far behind. We are speaking of a new fashion which some historians label Arminianism, others Laudianism, others still Carolinism, attributing the new policy to Charles I in person. But non-historians may find the most meaningful description for these innovations 'High Church', a term only mildly anachronistic for the period. What William Laud and some of his episcopal colleagues vigorously promoted was the famous 'beauty of holiness', a new value placed on the liturgy and on enrichment of worship, an unprecedented veneration for the place of worship itself and salient points within it. The altar was now to be elevated above the pulpit and set altar-wise in a permanent position against the east wall, guarded with rails at which communicants were to kneel to receive. Some of these things were required by the church's canons, now to be more strictly enforced, even enforced for the first time. Other ceremonies, such as bowing to the altar, went beyond the canons and were regarded by many as a total and unwarranted innovation. The underlying rationale was the repudiation of the Calvinist doctrine which was so prevalent in the early Stuart church as to be widely regarded as orthodoxy. To assert against the Calvinists the universal availability of saving grace, with an ever-present danger of falling from grace, was to underwrite an inclusive religion of prayer and sacraments, a religion to be worked at, especially in conformable participation in the ceremonies of the church. But all this was widely suspected and feared as covert popery, a denial of the Reformation itself. Here was dynamite, enough dynamite, through a complex process of ignition and combustion, to start a civil war.

The colleges and their heads were divided. Beale of St John's, Sterne of Jesus, and, above all, Cosin of Peterhouse, turned their chapels into liturgical theatres, with rich furnishings, pictures and music, drawing by their novelty and beauty curious and susceptible students from other, more conservative colleges. Great St Mary's, by contrast, was in a time warp, with its whitewashed walls, clear glass windows, old-fashioned impromptu prayers from the pulpit, old-fashioned communion drill.

There was a tiny old-fashioned library of books out of a rapidly receding past: the Paraphrases of Erasmus on the New Testament, the Works of Bishop Jewel, the sermons of the sixteenth-century Swiss reformer Bullunger known as the Decades, but not, incidentally, the *Acts and Monuments* or 'Book of Martyrs' of John Foxe. It is often said that all parish churches were required to purchase the Book of Martyrs. But this was not so, the book costing more than the annual income of most churches, and the order applied only to great churches such as cathedrals. The nearest thing to innovation at Great St Mary's was the purchase, in 1633, of a desk for Bishop Jewel to lie upon.

In 1639 Dr John Cosin of Peterhouse was vice-chancellor, and he seized the opportunity to reform the backward ways of what he considered to be, first and foremost, the university church. He began to make a total alteration in the seating plan, taking down the rails from the cockpit, clearing the aldermanic seats out of the chancel, indeed, excluding the parishioners from the chancel altogether, which was the standard Laudian programme in many cathedral churches. The communion table was now to be raised up, an altar of degrees, and railed in, with the chancel separated from the nave by a new and costly screen. None of this work is mentioned in the accounts and the screen and rails were probably a gift, perhaps from Cosin himself. Certainly none of this had been cleared with the 'auncientest' parishioners, who now put up a spirited resistance to Cosin and all his ways. What he had done and proposed 'the parishioners there will in noe wise assent unto or approve of'; insisting that they would enter both church and chancel 'to serve God as they have done time out of mind of man'. They envisaged a fighting fund to sustain the great legal battle which now seemed to be inevitable. But events would soon intervene to provide a political rather than a legal resolution to this contretemps. Cosin and the parishioners of Great St Mary's did not know it, but they were struggling, like Holmes and Moriarty, on the edge of a precipice and great waterfall, the English Revolution.

But meanwhile Cosin enjoyed his triumph. At the Commemoration of Benefactors in 1640 (yet another occasion when the university took over the church) the Te Deum and the psalms were sung by the Peterhouse choir 'after their own fashion'. We hear from a letter writer: 'Dr John stretched his throat, he never sung so in's life. There he held us from before 9 to almost 12 of the clock.' I recall that it was Cosin who gave us that great hymn, 'Come Holy Ghost our souls inspire!'

The triumph was short-lived. The Long Parliament would meet within days and the curtain was rising on the next chapter. Presently,

parliament would order a general removal of altar rails, which was carried
out in this church in 1641: 'Payd for takeinge down the rayles and level-
ling the chancell, £2.7s.' The rails had some defenders and the action
was resisted. Soon the crosses were removed from the tower and the
chancel. At this time the inventory lists two communion tables. Is it possible that the parish had left Cosin's altar at the east end unused and had
continued to carry another table of their own down into the nave in the
old 'time out of mind' fashion? These confrontations may help to explain
what is otherwise very mysterious: how Cambridge should have chosen
to elect as one of its MPs for the Long Parliament an obscure and impe-
cunious gentleman living in Ely called Oliver Cromwell.

To read the accounts through the 1640s and 1650s you would hardly
know there was a war on. It was business as usual. Of course the Prayer
Book disappears from the annual inventories. According to a good but
improbable story, contained in a collection of fictions called *Qurela
Cantabriiensis*, it was torn up by some of the 4,000 soldiers now quartered
in Cambridge, and in Cromwell's very presence. When Cosin's screen
was defaced by the soldiery, and it was an ornament to the church
without any imagery on it whatsoever, Dr Samuel Ward, Master of
Sidney Sussex and a leading Calvinist, no lover of Laudian innovations,
asked them to leave it alone. 'They returned him such language as we are
ashamed here to express.' Ward was about to die in custody, a suspected
malignant. These were hard and bitter times.

But at Great St Mary's the Puritan substitute for the Prayer Book, the
Directory of Public Worship, was not purchased, and one suspects that
the time-honoured rhythm of prayers and sermons went on without
much change, right through the years of war, regicide, republic and pro-
tectorate. Time will not allow us to take the story any further. But,
moving on swiftly to 1660, here are the last entries from the churchwardens' accounts of Great St Mary's with which I shall weary you: 'For the
takinge downe of the Rebells armes and setting up the King's. 6d.' 'Given
to the Ringers May 10th at the proclaiming of the King, 5 shillings.' 'To
the Ringers at the King's coming into England May 29th, 2s.6d.' Or
almost the last entries. In an inventory for 1696 (and we are now almost
into the eighteenth century whither Dr Thompson will conduct us) the
dear old books and only those books are still to be found: Erasmus'
Paraphrases and Bishop Jewel's *Works*. Nothing much had changed in
100 years.

Bibliographical note

I am indebted to Dr Kenneth Fincham of the University of Kent at Canterbury and to Mr Arnold Hunt of Trinity College Cambridge for several helpful comments and suggestions. I owe my knowledge of the religious complexion of Trinity College in its early years to Mr Colin Armstrong.

The principal source for this chapter are the churchwardens' accounts of Great St Mary's which are complete for the years 1504–1699 (Cambridgeshire Record Office, MS P 30/4/1 (1504–1635), P 30/4/2 (1635–1699)). The first volume has been published by J. E. Foster as *Churchwardens' Accounts of St Mary, the Great Cambridge from 1504 to 1635* (Cambridge Antiquarian Society Publications no. 35, 1905). Further information will be found in *An Inventory of the Historical Monuments in the City of Cambridge* (Royal Commission on Historical Monuments), vol. II, (1959), pp. 275–80; Samuel Sandars, *Historical and Architectural Notes on Great St Mary's Church Cambridge* (Cambridge, 1869) (the copy in Cambridge University Library, SSS.49.12, contains many additional handwritten notes by the author); W. D. Bushell, *The Church of St Mary the Great. The University Church at Cambridge* (Cambridge, 1948); and G. J. Gray, 'The Shops at the West End of Great St Mary's Church, Cambridge', *Proceedings of the Cambridge Antiquarian Society*, n.s. 7 (1909), 235–49.

Recent studies of the English parish, its finances and officers, include Beat Kumin, *The Shaping of a Community: The Rise and Reformation of the English Parish c.1400–1560* (Aldershot, 1996), and *The Parish in English Life 1400–1600*, ed. Katherine L. French, Gary G. Gibbs and Beat A. Kumin (Manchester and New York, 1997).

The history of Cambridge University in this period can be explored in the source materials collected by C. H. Cooper, *Annals of Cambridge from the Earliest Times to the Royal Injunctions of 1535*, 5 vols. (Cambridge ,1873) and *The University of Cambridge from the Royal Injunctions of 1535 to the Accession of Charles the First* (Cambridge, 1884) which can now be supplemented with D. R. Leader, *A History of the University of Cambridge, vol. I, The University to 1546* (Cambridge, 1988), and Elisabeth Leedham-Green, *A Concise History of the University of Cambridge* (Cambridge, 1996).

The story of 'little Bilney', copiously documented, is told by John Foxe in his *Acts and Monuments*, popularly known as 'The Book of Martyrs', and published, incrementally, in 1563, 1570, 1576 and 1583 (in the author's lifetime). Pending the critical edition at present in preparation, most readers will have little choice but to use the highly unsatisfactory nineteenth century edition by George Townsend and Stephen Reed Cattley, where the Bilney material appears in vol. IV (London, 1837), pp. 619–56. For Tyndale and

Cranmer, see David Daniell, *William Tyndale: A Biography* (New Haven and London, 1994) and Diarmaid MacCulloch, *Thomas Cranmer: A Life* (New Haven and London, 1996).

The very extensive recent literature on the English Reformation is reviewed by Patrick Collinson in 'The English Reformation, 1945–1995', *Companion to Historiography*, ed. Michael Bentley (London and New York, 1997), pp. 336–60. A. G. Dickens, *The English Reformation* (London, 1964; revised edn, London, 1989) was considered to be almost definitive when first published. It presented the Reformation as an idea whose moment had come. But it has since been overtaken by a wave of so-called 'revisionist' scholarship. Of particular significance for the early part of this chapter, and generally highly influential, is Eamon Duffy, *The Stripping of the Altars: Traditional Religion in England, c.1400–c.1580* (New Haven and London, 1992). See also J. J. Scarisbrick, *The Reformation and the English People* (Oxford, 1984), and Christopher Haigh, ed., *The English Reformation Revised* (Cambridge, 1987) (and especially the essay by Ronald Hutton on the reception of the Reformation in the parishes).

For Martin Bucer and Andrew Perne, see Patrick Collinson, 'The Reformer and the Archbishop: Martin Bucer and an English Bucerian', in *Godly People: Essays on English Protestantism and Puritanism*, ed. Collinson (London, 1983), pp. 19–44; and Patrick Collinson, 'Perne the Turncoat: An Elizabethan Reputation', in Collinson, *Elizabethan Essays* (London and Rio Grande, 1994), pp.179–217. The standard account of the Reformation in Cambridge is H. C. Porter, *Reformation and Reaction in Tudor Cambridge* (Cambridge, 1958).

On the subject of Puritanism, it will be convenient to consult the extensive bibliography appended to Patrick Collinson, *English Puritanism*, Historical Association General Series 106 (revised edn, London, 1987), as well as his *The Elizabethan Puritan Movement* (London and Berkeley, 1967; Oxford 1990). Of particular importance for Cambridge Puritanism is Peter Lake, *Moderate Puritans and the Elizabethan Church* (Cambridge, 1982). See also his *Anglicans and Puritans? Presbyterianism and English Conformist Thought from Whitgift to Hooker* (London, 1988).

The Laudian reaction which struck Great St Mary's in the person of John Cosin, Master of Peterhouse, is a much discussed and much controverted subject. See Nicholas Tyacke, *Anti-Calvinists: The Rise of Arminianism c. 1590–1640* (revised edn, Oxford 1990), and Anthony Milton, *Catholic and Reformed: the Roman and Protestant Churches in English Protestant Thought, 1600–1640* (Cambridge, 1995).

The general cultural background to the building of the tower of Great St Mary's and the ringing of its bells will be found in David Cressy, *Bonfires and Bells. National Memory and the Protestant Calendar in Elizabethan and Stuart England* (London, 1989). The technicalities of this subject are explored by Anthony Woodger, 'Post-Reformation Mixed Gothic in Huntingdonshire Church Towers and its Campanological Associations', *The Archaeological Journal*, 141 (1985), 269–308.

3 The decline and revival of university Christianity, 1750–1950

DAVID M. THOMPSON

The two hundred years from 1750 to 1950 constitute nearly half the history of the Church of England. How were the various movements in the church reflected in Cambridge in general, and at Great St Mary's in particular? In this period, perhaps more than before or since, the university dominated the history of the church. Thus the chapter opens with a discussion of the university sermon: its decline, its rise and then its further decline. This is followed by an explanation of the change in Cambridge religion in the nineteenth century, and in particular in the later part, through an examination of the work of two most notable vicars, Henry Richards Luard and William Cunningham. In conclusion, there are some general reflections on the changes that have taken place in the university, in the church and in the town in the twentieth century.

The university sermon

In 1750, a series of orders and regulations passed the Senate concerning undergraduate behaviour. Undergraduates were forbidden to keep servants, guns or horses; to leave the town or to stay out after 11.00 pm, to go to houses of ill fame 'in the precincts of the University or adjacent villages'. Tavern and coffee house keepers were forbidden to give undergraduates credit, or to serve them wine or strong drink. No one was allowed to visit 'coffee-houses, tennis courts, cricket grounds, or other places of publick diversion and entertainment twixt the hours of 9 and 12 in the morning on pain of a fine of 10 shillings', and there were similar penalties for breaking windows or playing dice. 'These orders and regulations', wrote W. Cooper in his *Annals of Cambridge*, 'caused great heats and animosities in the University.' Right in the middle of these regulations came no. 6, which read as follows:

49

> Every person *in statu pupillari* who does not attend St Mary's
> Church at the stated times of sermons shall forfeit the sum of six
> pence for every offence unless he can make it appear that he was
> excused by the Master or one of the deans of his College. And that
> such absentees may the more easily be found out and punished, dis-
> tinct places in the galleries shall be appointed for each college to sit
> in, and the sizars of each college in a monthly rotation shall make
> out lists of the names of all such as are comprehended within this
> order (as in their private chapels) and carry the names of the absen-
> tees to their respective tutors, who shall immediately pay the penalty
> incurred by their respective pupils to the sizar who pricked the bill
> that month and for his sole use.

What is the significance of this order? Conveniently for the title of this
chapter, it comes in 1750, right at the beginning of our period, and may
therefore be taken to indicate the importance attached by the university
authorities at this time to the university sermon as part of the disciplined
life of undergraduates. It also suggests that attendance at the sermons
was being neglected. We have no idea how rigorously this rule was
enforced, but the fact that various of the other prohibitions were
repeated at regular intervals suggests that the means of enforcement,
despite being elaborate, were not actually delivering the goods. But it is
also a reminder of the general significance of the sermon in eighteenth-
century religion, and Great St Mary's was the place where sermons were
preached. As is well known, mattins and evensong in the Book of
Common Prayer do not require a sermon to be preached, though they
indicate where it is to be preached if there is to be one. Sermons were, in
fact, rare in college chapels until the nineteenth century. In 1856, Joseph
Romilly, University Registrary and Fellow of Trinity, noted that there
was agitation to try a sermon in the college chapel (as they have at
Corpus, King's, Queens', Jesus and Clare), and continued, 'We tried the
experiment some years ago: it was a failure & broke down after 2 terms,
– we have agreed now to try again – on the reduced scale of 2 Sermons
per term, one on 1st Sunday at beg^g of term, the other on the Sunday
before Sacr^t' (which also suggests that the Sacrament was only celebrated once a term in Trinity Chapel). These sermons were to be separate from the usual morning service, and at 11.00. But only a day later he
noted that, under the influence of two fellows who had not been there the
day before, one being Adam Sedgwick, they decided to abandon the idea.
They tried again in Lent 1859, with sermons at the communion service
at 10.30, and he noted the attendances in considerable detail.

The importance attached to sermons in the study of theology generally is indicated in the advice drawn up for a young student by Daniel Waterland, the early eighteenth-century Anglican theologian. He was Dean and Tutor of Magdalene when he first drew it up in 1706; he subsequently became master in 1713. It was reprinted in 1730 and 1740. He advised his students to read and make abridgements of two sermons every Sunday and holy day; and he listed a four-year programme of reading, which included the sermons of Sharpe, Calamy, Spratt, Blackhall, Hoadley, South, Young, Scott, Tillotson (which took the entire second year), Clagget, Atterbury and Stillingfleet. It was, therefore, not surprising that in the eighteenth century Great St Mary's was adapted to make it more suitable for preaching. Part of the money came from the benefaction of William Worts of Landbeach, a graduate of St Catharine's College, who is perhaps best remembered for the building of Worts Causeway which originally ran from Emmanuel College to the Gog Magog Hills. His father was a Fellow of Caius and Esquire Bedell, who married the daughter of Thomas Daye, an apothecary in this parish, and it is thought that it was largely from his father-in-law's side that the money came for the great benefaction. Worts himself, who was only thirty-two when he died in 1709, is buried in the north aisle. He left £3,000 to be used for the building of galleries for the use of undergraduates and BAs, 'so that they might the more decently and conveniently hear the sermon'. The sum was to be spent when the interest on it had reached £1,500, in other words £4,500 in all. Mr Reneu of Jesus College, writing to a friend in October 1709 about the gift, said that no charity of that value could have been better disposed of:

> For as to ye Building of Galleries in St Mary's, y^t you know was as much wanted as anything could be; for besides ye undecency of seeing so many Gentlemen's sons *standing* in ye Isles; ye want of seats brought in y^t ill Custom of talking & walking about ye Church all ye service, so yt there's is [*sic*] often such a noise, one can hardly hear ye minister, let him have never so good a voice; but by this means, this will be regulated.

The galleries were not, in fact, built until 1735, when an agreement was made between the university and the parish that the university would have the sole use of them and be responsible for their upkeep. The destruction of the houses in front of the Old Schools, up to where the Senate House now stands, had reduced the rateable value of the parish and had increased the financial burdens on the remaining parishioners;

therefore they were grateful that the university took over the responsibility for the upkeep. The aisle galleries are made of oak; their erection was supervised by James Gibbs, who was also responsible for the Senate House; and they added 476 seats to the thousand or so on the ground floor, that is to say an increase of rather more than 40 per cent. At the same time the parishioners agreed to the erection of a new pulpit by the university in what was called 'the pit', that is the main floor of the nave, provided that the university gave £150 for new pews for the parishioners, presumably under the aisle galleries since 'the pit' was appropriated for the use of MAs. The new pulpit was a three-decker pulpit, that is to say the preacher stood at the top, with two lower seats, one for the minister when reading prayers, and one at the bottom for the parish clerk. It was situated in the middle of the nave, facing east.

In 1754 a new chancel gallery was built over the whole of the western half of the chancel. This was allotted to the doctors, professors and heads of houses, with an armchair for the vice-chancellor in the middle. There had been a doctors' gallery in the chancel between 1610 and 1617, but that was taken down on the instructions of James I while he was visiting Newmarket in 1616. The chancel gallery was called 'the throne', but it was known to the undergraduates as 'Golgotha'. This was an allusion to the meaning of that word given in Matthew 27:33, 'a place of a te skull', i.e. the place of the heads (of Houses). That gallery was built under the supervision of James Essex, the Cambridge architect who designed several late eighteenth-century buildings, for example at Queens' College, and who was also involved in restoration work at Lincoln Cathedral because of the strong links between the cathedral and Cambridge in that period.

Some disliked the chancel gallery at the time. The Reverend William Cole (of Clare and King's) was one such; in 1757 he wrote that it was not decent for those sitting there to have their backs to the altar, especially in a university. Others, however, described the galleries as spacious and convenient. Finally, in 1819 a western gallery was built to increase the accommodation available for BAs and undergraduates. This was designed by William Wilkins, who built Downing College, the New Court of Trinity, the New Court of Corpus and University College, London.

The layout of the church before the restoration of 1863 is illustrated in two nineteenth-century photographs (illustrations 12 and 13). At first it seems almost unrecognisable as the church which exists today. In the interior facing west (illustration 12) the organ remains the same, but the new west gallery of 1819 comes forward about as far as the first bay. In front of that is the three-decker pulpit, with pews facing sideways, as in so many college chapels, so as to give a good view. But the interior facing east (illustration 13) shows the most striking difference. The chancel gallery with a comfortable armchair for the vice-chancellor is clearly visible; the gallery is also supported by typical eighteenth-century classical round arches. The back wall of the gallery was panelled, and right at the top was the royal coat-of-arms, enjoined under the Reformation statutes. Even behind the gallery, though this is not visible from the engraving, there was a characteristic pedimented reredos behind the altar, rather than the open east window which can be seen now. Perhaps it should be noted that other Cambridge churches, like most Anglican churches in the eighteenth century, gave a similar centrality to the pulpit. Le Keux's engravings show that Little St Mary's also had an elegant central pulpit, though it did not obscure the east window.

The expansion of accommodation just described is to be explained largely by the church's function as the place for university sermons. In the eighteenth century, these sermons were preached every Sunday through the year, morning and afternoon, and on specified holy days, as well as the state festivals of the monarch's accession, the Gunpowder Plot (5 November), the execution of Charles I (29 January) and the Restoration of Charles II (29 May). Sermons were preached in English from Elizabeth I's reign, and the mayor and corporation often liked to attend. A grace of 5 June 1666 provided that sermons *ad clerum* should be preached in Latin, because of the danger to life from the plague, so that gownsmen should not mix with the townsfolk. It was obviously assumed that they would not come to a sermon which was in Latin. The Elizabethan statutes had required every MA of the university who was a regent, i.e. resident in Cambridge, to preach two sermons in the university church, one in English and one in Latin, though the latter requirement very quickly slipped away. By the eighteenth century, the rule was that all Bachelors of Divinity and then all MAs in holy orders, should preach in turn as called upon – the morning sermons being provided by a rota of colleges and those in the afternoon being delivered in the order of the seniority of graduates of the university. It was rather like the arrangement that existed in the cathedrals for the preaching of sermons by prebendaries and, as in the cathedrals, people increasingly paid someone else to preach in their place because it was inconvenient to come to Cambridge to do it. That was why, in 1802, it was agreed to draw up a list of select preachers in order that the substitute should be competent.

By the 1840s it was customary to leave the afternoon sermon to the select preacher, who was often appointed for a month at a time. Today all university sermons preached in Great St Mary's are by those appointed by the Select Preachers Syndicate.

The low point for attendance seems to have been the mid-eighteenth century, which probably explains the rule of 1750, cited at the beginning. In 1757, Thomas Gray, who was at Pembroke, wrote to a friend that the Duke of Bedford had brought his son up to Trinity with a friend, and 'Mr Sturgeon preached to them and the Heads, for no body else was present.' Gilbert Wakefield, who came up to Jesus in 1772 and was a Fellow from 1776 to 1778, noted that a friend of his once proposed that undergraduates should be compelled to attend the sermons or they should be abolished. He did not find more than six or seven backers, and commented, 'What can be conceived more disgraceful to the University than for strangers to go into the Church on a Saint's day and to see the preacher exhibiting only to the Vice-Chancellor, the beadle, Mr Blue-Coat [the university marshall] and the Walls.'

The Reverend James Scott, Fellow of Trinity, frequently occupied the university pulpit between 1761 and 1771, and whenever he did so, his biographer noted that 'St Mary's was crowded: the parts of the Church appropriated to the University were filled. Noblemen, bishops, heads of houses, professors, tutors, Masters of Arts, undergraduates, all attended St Mary's to hear this celebrated preacher.' The townspeople were also enthusiastic. It was noted that, whereas the university sermons were 'in general uninteresting, the matter studiously obstruse, and the delivery of it unimpassioned and lifeless', Mr Scott's preaching was quite different. But Scott was not always popular. The common method of expressing disapproval in those days was called 'scraping', i.e. scraping one's feet against the floor during the sermon. When Scott preached against gaming on 21 June 1767, he was scraped, so on the following Sunday he preached on Ecclesiastes 5:1, 'Keep thy foot, when thou goest to the House of God.' 'No sooner was the text pronounced than the galleries were in an uproar; but Mr Scott, so far from being either overcome by affright, or roused to indignation, calmly requested the Vice-Chancellor to preserve silence.' With the assistance of the proctors this was achieved, and he then preached an eloquent sermon.

Someone less lucky was John Wilgress, Fellow of Pembroke who, at the height of the controversy over subscription to the thirty-nine articles in November 1773, preached a sermon attacking latitudinarians, maintaining that liberty of private opinion rent the church of Christ and made as many creeds as persons. He was soundly scraped, and at the end of the sermon, the vice-chancellor called to the proctors to take the names of the gentlemen in the galleries. There was a general hissing, and a rush to get out before the doors were shut. The Bishop of Peterborough, the proctors and the vice-chancellor arrived at the foot of the staircase, whereupon the young men pushed, broke the door off its hinges, and many escaped. Although the names were taken of the rest, no action followed.

Cambridge evangelicals

Henry Gunning of Christ's College, Senior Esquire Bedell, noted of the 1780s that the sermon for Addenbrooke's Hospital preached on the Thursday before Commencement (the old name for what is now called General Admission to degrees) always secured a crowded church. Commencement was also usually crowded and doctors wore scarlet. In 1784 there was a notable sermon by the Master of Magdalene, Peter Peckard, against the slave trade, when, instead of the usual bidding prayer, he asked the prayers of the congregation for our brethren in the West Indies who were labouring under the most galling oppression. He then proposed a prize essay on whether it was permitted to give unwilling people into slavery. The winner was Thomas Clarkson of St John's College, whose investigation into the slave trade, stimulated by that sermon, was so influential in changing the popular mood, and eventually brought about the abolition of the slave trade in 1807. Indeed in 1814, just before the Congress of Vienna, there was a university sermon suggesting that Britain should press the case at the Congress of Vienna for the abolition of the slave trade throughout the whole of Europe. By this time the influence of evangelical opinions was making a definite mark upon the university.

Until the election of Isaac Milner as President of Queens' in 1778, evangelical opinions were mainly confined to Magdalene College. But, in 1779, Charles Simeon had come up to King's as an undergraduate, and he was ordained in 1782. The idea that undergraduates only attended St Mary's is belied by Simeon, who went both to Holy Trinity and to St Edward's. In 1782 he was appointed curate of Holy Trinity, though he had a twelve-year-long battle with the lecturer elected by the parishioners, before he was secured undisturbed possession of the church. On Advent Sunday 1786 Simeon preached for the first time in Great St

Mary's. The church was crowded with undergraduates, and there was great excitement. Simeon's own services at Holy Trinity had often been disrupted by undergraduates, and this continued until the early 1790s. There was obviously some expectation of scraping. But Simeon's style commanded the attention of the congregation.

> He was heard to the end to with the most respectful and riveted attention [wrote Simeon's biographer]. The vast congregation departed in a mood very different from that in which it had assembled; and it was evident from remarks which were overheard when going out, and the subdued tone in which they were made, that many were seriously affected by, as well as surprised at, what they had heard. Of two young men who had come among the scoffers, one was heard to say to the other, 'Well, Simeon is no fool, however.' 'Fool!', replied his companion, 'did you ever hear such a sermon before?'

In his later life, Great St Mary's was always crowded when Simeon preached. It is written that in November 1811 'the sight of the overflowing Church was almost electric'; in 1814 'there was scarcely room to move above or below'; in 1815 'the audiences were immense; attention candid and profound'; and in 1823, when he preached his sermon on the 'Excellency and Glory of the Gospel', many were unable to get inside the doors. But this movement in the direction of higher attendance, though ultimately profound, was not easily accomplished. The French Revolution in 1789 and the subsequent war provoked a 'Church and King' Tory reaction which regarded Dissenters as covert republicans, and Methodists and Evangelicals as little more than time-servers. Gunning recorded that in 1792 Sir Busick Harwood, who until that time had professed himself a Whig, remarked that, 'In general, every man ought to be considered honest until he has proved himself a rogue, but with Dissenters, the maxim should be reversed, and every Dissenter should be considered a rogue until he has proved himself to be an honest man.' A dissenting grocer named Gazam was hanged in effigy outside Emmanuel College with the approval of the master, and subsequently fled to America. It was at this time that Robert Hall, who was the minister of St Andrew's Street Baptist Church, was fiercely criticised by many undergraduates, and because in many ways he was popular, it was alleged that certain colleges shifted the times of dinner in hall so as to ensure that they clashed with the times that he was preaching.

In 1793, William Frend of Jesus College was prosecuted in the Vice-

Chancellor's Court and deprived of his fellowship for publishing a pamphlet in favour of peace and union between republicans and anti-republicans. Gunning himself was a supporter of religious liberty, and was branded as a Jacobin and an enemy of the government by the end of the decade. It is characteristic of this period that, in 1795, Gunning recorded that one Sunday morning, when attending the vice-chancellor to St Mary's, the vice-chancellor saw an undergraduate accompanying someone in military uniform in the opposite direction and. asked him why he was not going to St Mary's. The undergraduate gave no answer, so one of the constables was dispatched to get the man's name. He was summoned before the heads of houses, and Gunning was asked to give evidence as a witness. When asked whether he regarded the undergraduate's conduct as disrespectful and insolent to the vice-chancellor, Gunning said that he was simply there to say what had happened, not to pass judgement on the event.

In the first thirty years of the nineteenth century there was clearly a revival in university Christianity, and there was also an increase in the size of the university. Gunning said that the number of bachelors taking degrees about 1813 seldom exceeded eighty or ninety a year. By 1835, Romilly noted that 220 were admitted to the BA. It was reckoned that in 1830 the resident population of the university in term time was around 2,000: between 1,400 and 1,500 BAs and undergraduates, the rest senior members. (When it is remembered that the size of an undergraduate year group today is around 3,000, the way in which times have changed becomes clear.) In 1830 the population of Cambridge was about 21,000; the population of Great St Mary's parish in the 1790s and 1800s was about 760, by comparison with 1,100–1,200 in Holy Trinity parish and about 660 in St Edward's parish. Some increase in the number of people involved in university religion in the early nineteenth century was therefore to be expected.

Adam Sedgwick wrote in 1834 that 'someone entering the University Church at the hour of service may sometimes see six or seven hundred undergraduates in the performance of a voluntary worship and hanging with deep attention on the accents of the preacher'. The preachers who were popular were varied in churchmanship and theology, ranging from H. J. Rose, a High Churchman; Bishop Marsh of Peterborough, formerly Lady Margaret's Professor; Bishop Kaye of Lincoln, formerly Regius Professor; Maltby, the first Bishop of Durham appointed after Lord Grey became prime minister in 1830; and Charles Simeon. But the undergraduates were said to be only interested in what was called the modern school of preachers, and would go in crowds to the other churches if the more traditional style were encountered. This was described by R. M. Beverly in 1833 as follows:

> The general style of preaching, excepting always the sermons of the Evangelical Party, is dry, profitless, dull and anti-Christian. The Gospel is quite unknown, and indeed is rarely ever alluded to. They preach about virtue and justification by good works, a little against enthusiasm, a good deal about subordination and the duty of being a Tory . . . There is, however, nothing like eloquence, to recommend their bad doctrine. Their heathenism is too insipid to be palatable.

This is, presumably, the kind of thing referred to in Romilly's diary when, on 21 March 1832 – the general fast because of the cholera – he noted that 'Baines preached an indifferent & exaggerated sermon on the Cholera'; though perhaps his experience on 24 June was worse: 'an awful bad sermon from Huddleston, an incipient Dr (of) Div(init)^y who walks about in a Cassock &c – He said yesterday upon eating 4 times venison, "We preach against such things but sometimes the Flesh will prevail over the Spirit".' In 1834, Romilly commented on a sermon of Rose, at the time of controversy over whether Dissenters should be admitted to the university, that it was 'an intemperate and uncompromising High Church sermon. The language was very beautiful and eloquent, the delivery admirable, but I think a more inflammatory Party Sermon has hardly been preached since the days of Sacheverell' (i.e. in Queen Anne's reign). Romilly made other comments towards the end of the decade as well, talking about the times when the church was very full. On 10 November 1839 he arrived and had to elbow his way through:

> the place was awfully thronged: – the organ overpoweringly loud. – Melvill's text was Heb. XI.4 'he being dead yet speaketh' – It was a most eloquent eulogy on the ambition of being known after death, but there was nothing practical, without one may so call an address to the young man on its being praiseworthy to pursue vigorously the academical studies. – Last Sunday the throat clearing at the pauses was so marked & had so much the appear^{ce} of applause, that there was an attack in the Paper: – this Sunday there was less of it. – In the Evening I went to St Mary's again to hear Melvill preach for the Prop[agatio]^n [of the] Gosp: – I came 1/4 hour before the time & yet could get no seat: it was very hot. The organ was played as loudly as possible to the hymn 'loud anthems let us sing'. – The Text was

'The men of Nineveh shall rise &c'. He began with speaking of the extraordinary modesty of our Lord, & of the few occasions on wch He compared himself with others. He ended with saying that our Colonies would rise in judgm^t against us if we neglect their spiritual welfare.

Melvill, it should be noted, was in the list of popular preachers.

The vicars of Great St Mary's

One consequence of my emphasis on the university sermon is that the vicars have tended to be shadowy figures so far: indeed, I have not mentioned a single one. In the 214 years from 1742 to 1955 there were thirty-one incumbents; on average, therefore, each one served for seven years. But at least seven were vicar for a year or less and seven had ministries of eleven or more years. Moreover, between 1860 and 1908 there were only two, Henry Richards Luard and William Cunningham. What is the reason for this rather unusual pattern of incumbencies? The main reason is that Great St Mary's is a Trinity living, and until the mid-nineteenth century the custom was that if it fell vacant the clerical fellows could claim it in order of seniority. In the days before fellows were allowed to marry, that meant that the senior fellow could be very senior, and incumbencies could therefore be short. Between 1742 and 1798 there were fourteen incumbents, only one of whom, Henry Thezond, served over ten years. Thomas Spencer was vicar from 1798 to 1817, and was regarded as an eccentric. Gunning said of him that 'one day, after giving out the chapter appointed for the first lesson, he added, "A very good and a very long chapter; much too good and too long for you, I'll give each of you a verse," addressing half a dozen elderly females who formed his daily congregation: for at that time prayers were read daily at Great St Mary's'. (That practice of saying prayers daily dropped out in the early nineteenth century.)

William Carus (1802–91), Simeon's biographer and successor at Holy Trinity, was vicar from 1844 to 1851. One of his main achievements was to settle a long-standing grievance between the university and the parish. Between 1836 and 1840 the churchwardens, Thomas Hallack, a grocer, and William Bacon, a tobacconist, took the university to the Queen's Bench to clarify what seats should be appropriated for the university during university sermons. The judgement of 1840 was indecisive, but

Carus was able to guide the parties together. In 1843 William Whewell, Master of Trinity, who was also vice-chancellor, changed the time of the morning university sermon from 11.00 to 10.30. Previously the parish service had been at 10.00 and was rather rushed. Now it could be held at 11.30, which allowed time for a full service, and, indeed, a monthly communion. (The term 'full service' in the mid-nineteenth century denoted mattins, the litany and ante-communion.) It is true that some parishioners still complained that this made it difficult to make a hot Sunday dinner, but it is rarely possible to please everybody. The morning university sermon was obviously not very well attended: one of the Esquire Bedells said that the attendance was one head of house, two Professors (very irregularly), three MAs and six undergraduates. A vote in the Senate to abolish Sunday morning sermons except on the Sundays before the Commemoration of Benefactors and Commencement failed by twenty-three votes to seventeen in 1858 (although they were discontinued during the long vacation); but in 1860 it was passed by a large majority. The result was the development of morning sermons in college chapels. The afternoon sermons, whose preachers were chosen by the Select Preachers Syndicate, then became the main university sermons. They also were gradually reduced in number: the sermons in September went in 1866 and those in July and August in 1900. Those in the Christmas and Easter vacations ceased in 1896, and in 1921 the sermons on Christmas Day, Good Friday and Easter Day disappeared.

Henry Luard (1825–91) became vicar in 1860. He was also a Tutor of Trinity and University Registrary. In many ways he was a remarkable man: he completed the catalogue of university manuscripts which had been begun by Romilly, his predecessor; he edited eighteen volumes in the Rolls Series of medieval manuscripts; he was the first Trinity Fellow to marry and retain his fellowship. Yet his successor as Registrary, J. Willis Clark, wrote that 'though he was compelled intellectually to admit the advantage of many of the changes that had taken place in recent years, I doubt if he ever cordially accepted them . . . He was always casting lingering looks behind, and sighing for a past which he could not recall.' Clark regarded 'the restoration of the University Church to something like its ancient arrangement' as 'an the enduring monument of his parochial life'.

There always had been some who regretted the changes made to the church in the eighteenth century. In the 1840s, the Cambridge Camden Society had been founded to encourage church restoration on what it regarded as correct architectural principles – the restoration of the

Round Church in 1843 being an early example. In 1855, the committee of the Cambridge Architectural Society noted that the syndicate appointed to consider the state of Great St Mary's Church had presented their report to the Senate but had not been able to agree on a plan which they could confidently recommend: the difficulties in their way they had found great, but not insuperable. A committee was set up to raise money for the restoration, but by 1860 when Luard became vicar it had not made much progress.

Upon appointment, Luard published a pamphlet on the proposed restoration. He criticised the state of the church, both as a parish church and as the university church. First he pointed out that it was impossible to administer the sacraments: the font stood in a corner under a staircase leading to the doctors' gallery, and baptisms could only be administered in the presence of three or four persons instead of the whole congregation. Likewise with communion: if there were only a few communicants they could gather in the chancel; otherwise the clergyman had to read. the service in a loud voice in order to be heard from the communion table. Indeed until recently the first part of the communion service had almost always been read from the reading-desk (part of the pulpit towards the back of the church). Secondly, as a university church it was lacking. It ought to be as perfect a church as the country could show but instead it was a disaster. Archdeacon Hare in his Charge of 1840 had said that the churches could not be mere preaching houses:

> Unfortunately a Cambridge man may deem himself sanctioned in any licence he choose to indulge in by the strangely anomalous arrangement in S. Mary's; where the chancel is concealed from view by the seat in which the heads of houses and professors turn their backs on the Lord's Table; where the pulpit stands the central object on which every eye is to be fixed; and where everything betokens, what is in fact the case, that the whole congregation are assembled solely to hear the preacher.

'S. Mary's,' wrote Luard, 'is in some respects scarcely regarded as a church at all; and could a stronger fact be brought forward than the name which this gallery has acquired?' God's house could not be degraded into a mere preaching house: 'if the preaching of sermons were its only use, it would be better for us to have them in the senate-house, where we should have the building entirely to ourselves, and in no way be troubled about room.' But there were other university services, such as the litanies, where a better arrangement might improve attendance; and this might also be conducive to following the example of Oxford by having a university corporate communion at the beginning of each term or at least each academic year. Obviously the responsibility for the present state of affairs lay with the university, but Luard pointed out that if every college gave £100 the committee would have sufficient funds. But he also urged the parishioners to play their part, noting that if the churchwardens and parishioners had done their duty in 1757, the chancel would never have been blocked up.

However, Luard was successful. Although William Whewell, Master of Trinity, and George Pryme, one of the professors who most regularly attended university sermons, opposed the plans, the doctors' gallery was removed in 1863. The pit was also removed, and the old pews and gallery were swept away to be replaced by open seats, made of oak. *The Ecclesiologist* gave a qualified welcome, regretting that it was not possible to get rid of the aisle galleries at that stage and hoping that that would come some time in the future, whilst noting that the parishioners had a long-standing tendency to oppose anything that the university suggested. A new east window had been put in by Trinity after the fire in the shops at the back of the church on Peas Hill in the late 1840s had exposed the problems of the exterior; but it 'is by no means what it ought to be'. Furthermore the Committee had not yet received leave to remove the pedimented Grecian reredos; Essex's pulpit was retained and the organ still blocked the west window. The paper found it almost incredible that the University of Cambridge should have taken ten years to raise £3,300 for the restoration, and they were still more than £500 in debt.

A new (movable) pulpit, carved by Rattee and Kett, was eventually installed in 1872 at the expense of the university. The sole remaining parts of the three-decker pulpit are the black oak screens which separate the nave and chancel aisles on each side of the church. They were bought back for the church by Samuel Sanders in 1893. In 1865 the east end was remodelled. The panelling was removed and a new reredos, designed by Gilbert Scott, was given by Professor J. B. Lightfoot; a new communion table was given by the English Church Union; A. A. Vansittart, formerly a fellow of Trinity and a member of the Camden Society, gave the altar rails, the altar steps and the marble flooring of the sanctuary; and Luard paid for the tiling of the chancel at his own expense in 1871. Luard also gave the new glass for the east window in 1869, the theme of which is the birth of Christ. The chancel window on the south side was designed, like the east window, by Hardman to commemorate Charles Hardwick of St Catharine's College, and the north chancel window was also given by

Luard, in 1890, to commemorate his wife. The aisle windows – the roundels on each side – were given by Samuel Sanders in 1892, and the clerestory windows were begun in 1892 and completed in 1894. These follow the themes of the Te Deum: 'the glorous company of apostles, the goodly fellowship of prophets and the noble army of martyrs'. The most interesting, from a Cambridge point of view, are the six apostles, St Matthias, St Simon, St Jude, St Matthew, St Thomas and St James, in the two windows on the north side closest to the east end. The men depicted are Thomas Arnold, F. D. Maurice, A. P. Stanley, J. B. Lightfoot, Bishop Westcott and F. J. A. Hort. These two windows were given in memory of F. J. A. Hort, who died in 1892. Finally, the font was moved back into the main church from under the gallery staircase. So the restoration was complete.

Great St Mary's once more satisfied the ideals of the church reformers. This reflects a shift back towards the emphasis on the sacraments rather than preaching. In a way, it also epitomises the decline of the sermon. *The Ecclesiologist* had suggested that the galleries could be done away with because they were seldom full; on the other hand, *The Ecclesiologist* was prejudiced against galleries wherever they were found, and Great St Mary's was no longer the only place to hear sermons. College chapels were laying more emphasis upon them, and John Venn (son of the General Secretary of the Church Missionary Society and later President of Caius) noted Clayton at Holy Trinity and Harvey Goodwin (later Bishop of Carlisle) as preachers who were listened to in the 1840s. But Great St Mary's was full (and still is full) on great occasions: when J. B. Lightfoot preached his farewell sermon before leaving Cambridge for Durham in 1879, Bishop Welldon (later Dean of Durham) recalled that the University Church was packed to the doors. Furthermore, when the church was reopened in Lent 1864, this was marked by a special series of sermons. The preachers reflected Luard's churchmanship, and were a galaxy of High Church stars: Samuel Wilberforce, Bishop of Oxford; Henry Parry Liddon, student of Christ Church; T. L. Claughton, Vicar of Kidderminster; J. R. Woodford, Vicar of Kempsford; E. M. Goulburn, Canon of St Paul's; J. W. Bergon, Vicar of St Mary's, Oxford; T. T. Carter, Vicar of Clewer; Edward Pusey, Regius Professor of Hebrew at Oxford; William Hook, Dean of Chichester; W. J. Butler, Vicar of Wantage; and Harvey Goodwin, Dean of Ely. There is no space to dwell on these sermons, though they make interesting reading. What is most fascinating in view of some of the stereotypes of Evangelical hell-fire preaching is Pusey's sermon on 'David in his sin and his penitence'. 'Fear of Hell drives men to repentance,' said Pusey. 'Think if there is any way in which that awful truth of the eternity of woe could have been taught, in which God has not taught it.' The positive emphasis on the presence of God in W. J. Butler's sermon on 'God, the reward of the faithful' is different, as indeed is that of Liddon on 'Adam hiding himself from the presence of the Lord'.

J. W. Clark described Luard as an eloquent preacher, noting that his sermons in Trinity were 'plain, practical, persuasive; the compositions of one who was not above his congregation . . . but who spoke to the undergraduates as one who had passed through the same temptations as themselves'; and he applied the same principles at Great St Mary's, where 'his labours among the poor were unremitting, and . . . his generosity knew no limits'. Clark regarded him as a High Churchman of the school of Pusey and Liddon, rather than a Ritualist, a verdict echoed by Christopher Brooke. I am not very keen on the traditional labels, but I see him as a Cambridge High Churchman, with an unwavering belief in the catholicity of the Church of England. Thus his sermon on the death of F. D. Maurice in 1872 spoke of Maurice as a true and loyal son of the Church of England and his grasp of 'all Catholick truth'; 'his faith in the Triune Godhead, in the Divinity of our Lord Jesus Christ, in the efficacy of the grace of the Sacraments He left to be our helps in our struggles through life, in the presence of the Comforter in the soul of man, and the nearness which the Incarnation has brought about between God and man'. A few words from a Commemoration Sermon in St John's College on 6 May 1891 preached by the Reverend J. E. B. Mayor summed up Luard appropriately: 'In defiance of broken health . . . chastened in the school of suffering, constrained to dwell much abroad, he moved amongst foreign churchmen and authors, as amongst the poor of Great St Mary's, an ambassador of whom Cambridge need not be ashamed.'

Luard's successor, William Cunningham (1849–1919) was a very different kind of man. He was brought up in the Free Church of Scotland and was a student at Edinburgh University from 1865 to 1868 before he came to Caius in 1869 to read moral sciences. He hoped to make contact with F. D. Maurice, and moved to Trinity in 1872 after winning a scholarship along with his friend, F. W. Maitland. He was ordained in 1873 by Bishop Harold Browne, having already done practical work by teaching in the Jesus Lane Sunday School like so many Cambridge men before him. In 1874 he became one of the first university extension lecturers, and in 1880 chaplain at Trinity and assistant curate to Luard at Great St

Mary's – his duty was to preach one sermon on Sundays. Cunningham's academic reputation was as the first significant economic historian in the University of Cambridge. His book, *The Growth of English Industry and Commerce* was first published in 1882, and went through six editions (with revisions and amplification) in the next twenty-five years. In 1887 he was urged to apply for the living vacated by Luard because of ill health. The stipend at that stage was less than the £70 per annum that he had as Luard's curate; but Trinity allowed him to keep his Trinity chaplaincy and also gave him £50 per annum to pay for a curate at Great St Mary's. The first one was Alexander Nairne, Fellow of Jesus College and later Regius Professor of Divinity and Canon of Windsor.

Cunningham and Nairne tried to carry out all the instructions of the Book of Common Prayer, with daily services, holy communion on saints' days, and a choral holy communion on Sundays. In his first Lent, Cunningham tried a said mattins followed by choral communion and sermon on Sundays, but this was not a success because of the congregation's attachment to sung mattins. So Cunningham put the sermon back into mattins, whilst following it with a choral communion at noon. Attendance at the daily services was always small, but there was a regular nucleus. This new pattern of services reflects the way in which worship changed during the nineteenth century, and also illustrates that Luard was an old High Churchman.

Cunningham also invited several ladies to become district visitors to help distribute the communion alms. From his Scottish upbringing he brought the importance of preaching and catechising; he was reputed to know every child in the parish by name. At the suggestion of Mandell Creighton, Dixie Professor of Ecclesiastical History and later Bishop of London, Cunningham organised evening lectures on Sundays and Thursdays for undergraduates, though they actually attracted more parishioners than students. He started a guild to enable undergraduates to meet the preacher for coffee after the sermon, but so few came that he gave up. A plan to persuade the undergraduate religious societies to cooperate rather than compete on Sunday evenings also failed; but it did help E.G. Selwyn and Will Spens as undergraduates to set up the Church Society in 1906, which had Sunday evening sermons at 8.30. I think that was probably the origin of the tradition which was later revived by Mervyn Stockwood. Finally, Cunningham completed the restoration work in the church, particularly the windows.

Cunningham had been disappointed not to get the Chair of Political Economy in 1884, and after he became Vicar of Great St Mary's he resigned his university lectureship, and concentrated more on church work, apart from the duties of his fellowship at Trinity. In 1894 he became rural dean, and in 1907 he was appointed Archdeacon of Ely. Although he remained vicar until the union of the two parishes of Great St Mary's and St Michael's was complete, his duties thenceforward lay in the wider church. He had been discouraged by the decline in the congregation, but it was clear that his ministry had been valued. The Regius Professor of physics commented in 1909 that he had felt that Dr Cunningham was 'a teacher under whom he would like to sit'.

> Many of [the congregation] had heard a very great deal about theology; they had heard a great many controversies, they listened to a very great many arguments . . . but he thought they felt what they needed above all things, was to hear the exhortations of one who told them not so much what they were to think as how they were to live, and he thought it was that they had learned Sunday after Sunday from the pulpit of St Mary's Church.

A changing university in a changing town

The style of ministry established by the two remarkable vicars of the late nineteenth century was continued through the first half of the twentieth. Then from 1955 there have been six vicars, five of whom have become bishops and the other Dean of Westminster. In this last period the link between being vicar and being a Fellow of Trinity has been decisively broken. This reflects the outworking of a more profound religious change, which was developing during the time of Luard and Cunningham. Essentially the story is that of the decline of formal, compulsory religion and the growth of informal, voluntary, undergraduate-based religion. They almost passed one another during the nineteenth century as ships in the night. Religious tests at Cambridge University disappeared for undergraduates in 1856, and for fellows of colleges in 1871; though they survived for degrees in divinity until 1913. Cambridge was thus ceasing to be exclusively Anglican. As it did so, formal religion began to decline. The reduction in the number of university sermons was noted earlier, and the idea of introducing sermons into college chapels as a way of attracting undergraduates in the late 1850s illustrates the same shift away from expectations of formal observance.

At the same time undergraduate religion began to grow. The Evangelical influence of Simeon was the beginning of this, and it was reflected in recruitment for missionary work overseas, but even more in the foundation of the Jesus Lane Sunday School in 1827. King Street was the centre of an area in which the poor were concentrated in early nineteenth-century Cambridge; this gradually extended out towards Barnwell, whilst the development of Mill Road and beyond after the coming of the railway presented a further challenge. Castle Hill, by contrast, was an area of houses of ill-repute. William Cunningham's involvement in the Jesus Lane Sunday School is a reminder that such commitment was not an exclusively Evangelical activity. In the second half of the century undergraduate religion took off. David Livingstone's appeal for overseas missionaries in the Senate House in 1857, and the foundation of the daily prayer meeting in 1862 led to the formation of the Cambridge Inter-Collegiate Christian Union in 1877. The Moody Mission of 1882, and the Cambridge Seven who offered for the China Inland Mission in 1884 consolidated the Christian Union and opened up the undergraduate emphasis on missionary work overseas that led to the Student Volunteer Movement for Foreign Missions, or the Student Christian Movement, as it became in the 1890s. These were the activities of the religious societies, which Cunningham tried in vain to bring together in the late 1890s and 1900s. The issue which emerged then has remained: how can the university church take an initiative in undergraduate religion which will be less formal than the university sermon but also sit with the very different atmosphere of student-directed religious activities? It is not surprising that the initiatives that have been successful here have tended to be on the Middle to High Church side, such as the Church Society in 1906, because the Evangelical side was already well catered for elsewhere in the town. The dividing point here came in 1910 when the CICCU withdrew from the national SCM, which meant that a separate SCM branch had to be founded in Cambridge, though the division only became permanent after the First World War.

The First World War, too, saw the silent end of compulsory chapel, and the interwar years witnessed the flourishing of undergraduate religion, with the Free Church Societies as well as the SCM and CICCU reaching their largest numbers in this period. The aftermath of the Second World War, was rather different: there is almost a sense in which the 1945 religious climate did not really change until compulsory military service finished at the end of the 1950s. That is when the real tilt in twentieth-century Cambridge religion took place.

Cambridge itself was changing too. This chapter does not contain as much about the parish as it should; but the main feature of it in this period was its steadily declining population. Thus the amalgamation of the parish with St Michael's in 1907 reflected other pressures on the city centre. The developments in the eighteenth and nineteenth centuries had steadily removed the many shops and other dwellings originally surrounding the church. In this period, the leading figures of the town congregation were local shopkeepers, as was true of the leading Nonconformist chapels in the centre too. But the possibility for fellows of colleges to marry, and the declining attachment to specific parish boundaries, gradually created a new kind of congregation in the later nineteenth century. Some leading businessmen in the town remained, but to them were added senior members of the university and their wives (increasingly educated but not, as yet, employed). Indeed the changing role of women, especially after the establishment of Girton and Newnham, deserves attention. The development of Anglican 'congregationalism' (i.e. the crossing of parish boundaries to the church of one's choice), though officially always deplored if not denied, was essential for the survival of city centre churches in a town like Cambridge which, even in medieval times, had twelve parishes, more than twice as many churches as the five of my home town of Leicester, which was of similar size before the industrial growth of the mid-nineteenth century.

The story of Great St Mary's in the twentieth century is increasingly the story of that congregation, different from, but not unrelated to, the church in its role as the University Church and also the civic church. For most of the twentieth century, Great St Mary's was not, like Holy Trinity or the Round Church, marked by a distinctive party tradition, and in some ways perhaps it suffered from that. But that was the context out of which, in 1955, a new vicar, Mervyn Stockwood, attempted a completely different policy in relation to undergraduate religion.

Bibliographical note

The history of the university in this period is to be found in P. Searby, *A History of the University of Cambridge*, vol. III, 1750–1870 (Cambridge, 1997) and C. N. L. Brooke, *A History of the University of Cambridge*, vol. IV, *1870–1990*, (Cambridge, 1993). Earlier sources, referred to in the text, are W. Cooper, *Annals of Cambridge*, vol. IV (Cambridge, 1852), pp. 278–80, 626; C. Wordsworth, *Scholae Academicae: Some Account of Studies at the English Universities in the Eighteenth Century* (London, 1868), pp. 304, 330–4; and H. Gunning, *Reminiscences of the University, Town, and County of Cambridge from the Year 1780* (London, 1854), vol. I, pp. 26, 28, 262–3, 278–9, 334; vol. II, 9–10, 18–19, 286. The links between Cambridge and Lincoln Cathedral in the eighteenth century are described in D. Owen (ed.), *A History of Lincoln Minster* (Cambridge, 1994), pp. 219–20.

J. W. Clark, *Endowments of the University of Cambridge* (Cambridge, 1904), p. 91 gives the details of Worts' benefaction; and J. R. Tanner, *The Historical Register of the University of Cambridge* (Cambridge, 1917), p. 155 explains the origins of university sermons. The vicissitudes of university sermons in the nineteenth century are reflected in C. Smyth, *Simeon and Church Order* (Cambridge, 1940), pp. 108, 131, 132–3, 135, 144–5, and J. P. T. Bury (ed.), *Romilly's Cambridge Diary, 1832–42* (Cambridge, 1967), pp. x, 8, 17, 58, 181–2, and D. Winstanley, *Early Victorian Cambridge* (Cambridge, 1940), pp. 395–6. For the influence of Cambridge Evangelicals see H. C. G. Moule, *Charles Simeon: Biography of a Saint*, (London, 1892; new edn, ed. T. Dudley-Smith, London, 1965), pp. 31, 32, 64, 75–6, and J. Venn, *Early Collegiate Life* (Cambridge, 1913), pp. 268–9; the story of the CICCU and its split from SCM in 1910 may be found in O. R. Barclay, *Whatever Happened to the Jesus Lane Lot?* (Leicester, 1977), pp. 13–39, and D. M. Thompson, *Same Difference: Liberals and Conservatives in the Student Movement* (Birmingham, 1990), pp. 2–7.

A starting point for discussion of changes to the interior of the church is W. D. Bushell, *The Church of St Mary the Great, the University Church at Cambridge* (Cambridge, 1948), pp. 119, 125–6, 130, 133, 135–6, 137–8, 169, 192–3, 194–5, 198–9; however, more detail is found in three articles in *The Ecclesiologist*, 17 (1856), 149; 21 (1860), 160–2; and 24 (1863), 281–3. The sermons preached at the conclusion of the restoration are in H. R. Luard (ed.), *Sermons Preached During Lent 1864 in Great St Mary's Church, Cambridge* (Cambridge, 1864); the quotation from Pusey is on p. 183.

Luard is described in J. W. Clark, *Old Friends at Cambridge and Elsewhere* (London, 1900), pp. 328–43, and in [J. E. B. Mayor], Commemoration Sermon, J. W. Clark's Cambridge Collection, Cambridge University Library: see also H. R. Luard, *The Victory that Overcometh the World: a Sermon Preached at S. Edward's Church, Cambridge on the First Sunday after Easter 1872, Being the Sunday after the Death of the Rev. John Frederick Denison Maurice* (Cambridge, 1872) p. 14. For Cunningham's life, see A. Cunningham, *William Cunningham, Teacher and Priest* (London, 1950), pp. 83–9, 92.

PART TWO

Contemporary ministry

4 Between market place and Senate House: the parish of St Mary the Great with St Michael

JOHN BINNS

The parish and people of Great St Mary's

Note: the people who are quoted in this chapter are not identified individually in the text, but are identified collectively in the bibliographical note at the end.

To the right of the west door of Great St Mary's is a plaque marking the Datum Point. It was placed there in 1978 to mark the spot from which the distances were measured which were recorded on the first milestones to be set up in England since the departure of the Romans. Some of these milestones are still standing along the Trumpington Road. They have on them the crest of Trinity Hall since they were the work of the Vice-Master of that college, William Warren, in 1732. Warren selected this point at the entrance to Great St Mary's as the centre of the city. It was as good a place to choose as any, but the fact that he chose it is a pointer to what is the most significant fact about the church for its ministry. This is its location at the heart of the city of Cambridge.

To understand the complex and varied life of the church, we have to explore the different things that the church meant to the many people who used it, and understand their experiences and their faith.

Some of the events which are remembered took place because of the church's association with the university – such as the burning of the body of Martin Bucer in 1557 or the more recent visit of Mother Teresa in 1977. But members of the congregation will often remind you that as well as the 'university' there is a 'parish', and that the continuing daily regular routine of parish life is at the heart of the vitality of Great St Mary's. It was a parish church before it was a university church, and incumbents are appointed to the parish of St Mary the Great, Cambridge in the Diocese of Ely, or since 1908 to the united benefice of St Mary the Great with St Michael.

However, although this may be the title by which it is known, the geographical area of the parish is the least significant feature of parish life. The parish is the smallest and least populated in the diocese. It covers most of the market place, a small piece of land to the south-east of the market square including a part of Petty Cury, and another small piece of land to the north including Rose Crescent and a part of Green Street. A modern visitor stopping for a cup of tea and a cake at Auntie's Tea Room, the building closest to the door of the church is, as she enjoys her refreshment, in the pastoral charge of the parish priest of St Edward's. There are at present nineteen resident parishioners, the Roman Catholic chaplain to the university and the occupants of the flats above the shops on the east side of Rose Crescent, none of whom, to my knowledge, attends the church. Of such little importance is the ministry of the church to its geographical parish that there is not even any record held in the church of where the boundaries lie. The doubtful distinction of being the smallest parish in the diocese has implications for the ministry of the church. The clergy are relieved of the responsibility to minister to the institutions and people of a fixed area. The responsibilities which occupy so much of the time and energy of most parish priests – thinking of what to say at the weekly school assembly, supporting playgroups and local charities, and arranging the endless round of funerals for resident parishioners – hardly feature at all at Great St Mary's. This gives freedom for clergy to develop their own style of ministry but it also means that the uncomfortable question of what the church is for can never be avoided.

Earlier in the century, the centre of Cambridge was more densely populated and the parish was still, as it had been in earlier periods, home to a lively community. Great St Mary's could be recognised as a parish church and functioned much like town centre parishes around the country. Local people, both from the parish of St Mary the Great and from other parishes in the city centre, valued the church and are still vividly remembered.

Worshippers who have lived in Cambridge for fifty years or more remember a market town with its bustling centre and well-known characters. 'Guildhall Place was quite busy. Now it is a shopping centre but then it was a little row of houses all with front gardens – quite nice. King Street was in Holy Trinity Parish but the children came to us.' Many of the residents of the city centre between the wars played an active part in the life of the church and are still recalled with affection.

> There was one eccentric lady who had a lovely little shop in King's Parade, an art gallery. She was called Miss Crisp, and came to church dressed all in black. She said the Amen very loudly and after

everyone else. She had a very elderly mother who she used to bring in an old-fashioned wheelchair with a kind of windscreen all round it. She used to come into my father's shop and ask his advice about when she should take her mother out. My father was a chemist in King's Parade and he knew lots of people in the university and the town. In fact he was something of a figurehead and highly thought of. I remember him delivering medicines to people from the university living along Grange Road. He used to park his car in the Lion Yard car park – the old open air car park that is – and he would walk across the market place waving to all the people he knew.

Worshippers came from other parts of Cambridge too. Canon Essex, who became vicar in 1930, had once been curate of St Philip's Church in Mill Road, and people who had known him then began to come to evensong at Great St Mary's. 'We got people from his old parish coming to the evening service. It was quite a different group and he used to say that he had to preach a different sermon in the evening from the morning.' This was the start of a pattern of a 'town' evensong which remained a feature of life at Great St Mary's for many years.

The clergy of the twentieth century

This congregation of people who lived near the market place and those who came from further afield was served by a varied group of clergy. C. F. D. Moule was part-time curate from 1936 to 1940 and remembers some of the incumbents of the first half of the century.

> Anchitell (no less) Harry Fletcher Boughey, known as Old Boughey, had been vicar from 1908 to 1913, and I can remember seeing him – slightly built and lame. He was a fellow of Trinity, a fine scholar and a skilled bell-ringer. It was in his rooms at Trinity that I recall practising the hand-bells. Philip Napier Waggett, SSJE, was vicar from 1927 to 1930. He had won himself quite a reputation as a wit, though I doubt whether this drew a big congregation. Once in his time I dropped into a service and all I recall is his aside to the effect that 'what could be more dreary than the devout and honourable women' of Acts 13:50 (Authorised Version)? His congregation was, I suspect, just that. Edward Claude Essex (vicar 1930 to 1947), had a distinguished record – a double first in theology, winner of the university's Winchester Reading Prize, honorary Canon of Ely from 1943 to 1947. His fine gifts did not include an original mind or incisiveness. The congregations were small. But I made good friends, including

the verger and the organist, a Mr Fenn who came over from Bury St Edmunds. During World War Two my small and timid voice was sometimes heard to say from the pulpit that the Germans too were children of God and needed our prayers. There was a fiery ex-schoolmaster serving as a kind of honorary curate; and one day, just before I, as official curate and in the vicar's absence, was about to take the choir in for a service, his wrath boiled over. 'I can't walk in with anyone so disloyal,' he said. 'You go on and I'll follow when I've calmed down.' He did, still steaming a bit. Canon Essex was followed by George Elwes Allen Whitworth (1947 to 1955), no intellectual but a sturdy, honest, generous priest with a big commanding voice.

Canon Whitworth retired from his living in early 1955 and on Wednesday 1 June 1955, Arthur Mervyn Stockwood was licensed as Vicar of Great St Mary's, and a new era began. 'Mervyn changed everything' is the summary of his contribution from one member of the church. The Parish's Register of Services records the innovations of a single week at the beginning of October 1955, four months after Mervyn's arrival. In that seven-day period the contemporary ministry of Great St Mary's was set in place. On Monday the daily recitation of the offices of mattins and evensong, and the daily celebration of the eucharist began, and on the following Sunday was the first parish communion and the first 8.30 pm university service. That day there were 38 communicants at the parish communion, a number which rose to 84 a year later and then to 125 the following year. There were 415 at mattins, and 419 at the university service, although numbers were not always as great as these. This week set the pattern for the ministry of the church in the years which followed. It consisted of the building up of a eucharistic community drawn from all parts of Cambridge; the provision of a programme of preaching intended especially for students; and the maintenance of a continuing daily life of prayer and welcome offered to all who, for whatever reason, found their way inside the doors of the church. These three aspects were directed at different although overlapping groups of people.

Mervyn Stockwood had an extraordinary ministry. Forty years after his departure from the church, he is still spoken of with a mixture of awe and affection, and always simply as Mervyn. The character of his ministry is described elsewhere by Lord David Owen, and many could add to his account. Here is just one more set of comments, by Pamela Hill.

> I was an undergrad at Girton when Mervyn arrived. At that stage Great St Mary's was not the place where we undergrads went. My attachment started when a friend of mine, Paul Rose, was asked to

form a choir for the 8.30 pm service, and he invited me. For some reason we were mostly medics and vets, and we sang at St Andrew the Great in the morning and GSM in the evening. It was more than just a service, as we also spent time questioning and talking to the preacher, and this was important to us. I can't now quite remember how it all worked, since people stayed behind to ask the preacher questions, by the west door, but also went to tea at the vicarage at 39 Madingley Road sometimes. I was asked to help make the tea, and often so many people turned up that we did not have enough cups. Mervyn also started the Advent carol service and I'll never forget that service as long as I live. We sang the first hymn in the organ loft; the lights were put out; and then candles were gradually lit from the front. The atmosphere was magical. Later I was married to Norman (Hill). He was the Secretary of SCM and honorary curate at GSM. He did a lot a pastoral visiting, visited the members of the church, and took services. I also read the epistle one morning. Mervyn told me that I was the first woman in the history of the University Church to do this. Mervyn became a close friend and remained so for life.

Pamela's comments suggest that among the qualities of Mervyn's ministry were the exceptional quality of his pastoral care, and his ability, in spite of an unusual and isolated personality, to form lasting friendships which were based on a firm and even fierce loyalty on both sides. He claimed that he never took a day off during term-time, and knowing a little of the varied commitments at Great St Mary's and the excessive nature of Mervyn's personality, this claim does not surprise me. People came to Great St Mary's not only because of the rich diet of preaching, but because Mervyn spent lots of time with them. He described his daily routine to his successor, Joe Fison.

In the morning I deal with my correspondence and administrative work, (although) I try to dictate many of my letters on the previous evening. For the rest of the morning I either see people or prepare sermons or lectures. In the afternoon I visit. I would suggest that for the first few months you might like to work carefully through the electoral roll. This is what I did when I first came here and it was abundantly worthwhile. In the evening I either visit or else I go to meetings or discussion groups (or to dinners).

He then admitted one of his shortcomings. 'I am sure it would be an admirable thing if Mrs Fison were able to find time to interest herself in women's work. Not unnaturally they have felt somewhat neglected by me.' The Sunday congregation, increasingly focused on the parish communion, was built and sustained through this rigorous discipline of pastoral visiting.

Pastoral care

His successors were busy and distinguished churchmen who were active in church life at diocesan and national level. But it is clear from the recollections of members of the church that they also made the pastoral care of the congregation their first priority. Joe Fison had an intuitive ability to enter into people's experience and stand alongside them in times of suffering. Hugh Montefiore could walk past a regular member of the church in the street and not notice their existence, but had an unquenchable fascination with the lives of all those he met as well as an eccentric imperiousness which was able to communicate to people of all walks of life. 'I can recall many examples of Hugh's care. He helped my husband to reapply to be ordained priest, and continued to visit our family long after we had left GSM and were involved in parish work elsewhere in the diocese. He continued to support me during my husband's growing ill-health, and in fact continues to help today.' Stanley Booth-Clibborn maintained a punishing and demanding schedule of visiting, and could be irrational and demanding, but had a delightful down-to-earth quality. 'Stanley called a spade a spade, and he gave us curates a real freedom to do our job. He was also extraordinarily humble and slightly uneasy in Cambridge life. He felt that he wasn't a brilliant preacher, and at one point did not include himself on the list of term-time preachers.' Michael Mayne had a remarkable memory for pastoral detail, and invariably administered communion to the large and diverse congregation using their Christian names. 'He was strongly committed to a remodelling of the parish structures and many of the groups date from his time. He was a humane colleague.' David Conner brought pastoral and teaching gifts of a high order, and gained a reputation for spiritual direction and counselling for a wide range of people. A later chapter discusses the varied talents of the vicars of Great St Mary's. However different they may have been, their commitment to a pastoral ministry as the basis of all parish life was common to them all.

The curates of Great St Mary's were vital to this extraordinarily committed pastoral ministry with its endless time and energy given to spending time with the people who came to church. They too, like the vicars of the church, were a group of men and women of great ability and dedication. Curates, after leaving the church have gone on to become provosts of cathedrals; chaplains of hospitals, schools and colleges; diocesan directors of ordinands and of mission; fund-raisers for national charities; a lecturer in homiletics and a suffragan bishop – a broad range of occupations suggesting that ministry at Great St Mary's had a capacity to nurture a variety of gifts. They played a significant part in the great plan of pastoral care, and especially the detailed strategy of parish visiting. The congregation became accustomed to the arrival of the curate at their front door, which they could be sure would happen once a year and probably considerably more often. 'The curates had a lot to do with building up the feeling of belonging. They used to travel miles on their cycles, until, that is, they were eventually provided with motor scooters. There was a system of dividing up the city into areas for them to look after.' 'We clergy divided the parish into sectors. I had a degree in geography so I was given the job of redrafting the map of the areas. We used to put pins in the map – one for each member, and we had to get round all the pins in a year. Each staff meeting you had to report on the visits of the previous week.' Occasionally short cuts were taken to complete the required total. 'We used to be amazed at how many visits X did, until we discovered that he used to cheat, and included a five-minute chat with someone he met in the market place as one of his visits.'

One method of ensuring that nobody was missed out of this inexorable visitation system was the Birthday Book. Michael Mayne revived this custom, and took care to ensure that the names of all the congregation were included. They were prayed for on the Sunday before, and then there would be a visit and a card on the day itself. 'These were the days of the mopeds, and we would often call at 9.30 pm after the evening meeting, wish the person many happy returns, and hand over a crumpled and damp card which had been in our anorak pocket since 9.30 in the morning.' The congregation was well aware that the basis of the life of the church were the hours spent in visiting the homes of the city. 'This may sound sentimental but we really did feel we were part of one big church family.'

The scattered congregation needed more than a group of clergy on mopeds – however energetically they scoured the streets of Cambridge. There was an awareness that there were many different sorts of people with varying needs. Children's church took place in St Michael's, and the youth club in a room above the Maypole pub in Portugal Place. There was also a strong ministry to young unmarried professional people. A discussion group was started for young adults called 'oi ichthoi', but this produced a stern note of correction from one member of the congregation who taught in the Divinity Faculty, pointing out that the plural of ichthus (or fish) was irregular and therefore not 'ichthoi'. The founder of the group never discovered the correct form of the plural of this noun and decided to change the name to 'fishes'. The group gained something of a reputation as a marriage bureau, with one of its organisers, James Atwell, being among those who met their future spouses at its meetings. Study groups and parish conferences were also important in holding the congregation together, and Stanley Booth-Clibborn took especial care to invite people round to the vicarage for discussions and meetings. It was however Michael Mayne who was especially sensitive to the need for a network of groups to help the congregation grow together. Within a few months of his arrival, seven prayer groups had been formed to provide a focus both for developing friendships and for the spiritual growth of the congregation. A year later a more ambitious scheme was launched when the city was divided into thirty-two neighbourhoods, and a 'link person' invited to provide basic pastoral care and communication for each area. These groups were supposed to meet every couple of months – and often did. The scheme enabled Christmas cards to be distributed to the congregation, newcomers welcomed and a network of personal relationships to be nurtured. The neighbourhood links have remained as a basic part of the church's pastoral strategy since then. Through them members of the congregation shared in the task of sustaining the cohesion of the congregation.

'Never forget that it all depends on your regular congregation, and especially those who come to the parish communion.' So Hugh Montefiore admonished Stanley Booth-Clibborn, who was to succeed him, and a former curate, Colin Slee, commented, 'I am a great believer in knocking on doors. GSM put it into my bloodstream and it certainly works.'

Although Great St Mary's may not have a parish it certainly has a congregation. Many people are attracted to worship at it. The church is just one of over twenty Anglican parish churches, to which must be added the much greater number of churches of other denominations, and the chapels of the colleges, many of which attract substantial regular congregations from the city. What is it about Great St Mary's which draws people to worship at it? How does it contribute to the richness and variety of ecclesiastical life in a city which was and is, from a present-day point of view, heavily over-churched?

Worship and politics

A survey in the church conducted in 1989 stated that the aim of the church was to 'provide a constantly available pastoral presence in the centre of Cambridge, especially available to those who are not at ease with pastoral help close to their residence or place of work'. Its position in the centre of the town overlooking the market place had the result that it was a familiar and much-loved building for the inhabitants of Cambridge. Because it was clearly visible to all shoppers and others who found their way to the market place or King's Parade and because it was always open to all visitors, it was a familiar and comforting place. A building is non-challenging. You do not have to make any statement of faith or to have any desire to pray to go inside. It can play whatever function you want it to, and it can accept whatever form of faith you bring to it. So a building which is there and open to all can easily become a natural home for people of any kind or degree of religious faith. People felt that it was their property and in practice Great St Mary's has functioned as an alternative parish church for the people of Cambridge. Many of its congregation are those who never discovered where their own parish church was situated, or, if they did, found that they did not like the services, or felt stifled by the demands of the community life of a local church.

The churchmanship has fluctuated with successive incumbents, but Mervyn's pattern of eucharistic worship has remained the basis of its life. The parish communion, which is now celebrated at 9.30 am, remains the centre of the life of the church. There are eucharistic vestments, a processional cross and candles though no incense, a robed choir, a nave altar; and the Alternative Service Book is used (although this will no doubt change when another service book is authorised for use in the Church of England). In addition there is sung mattins and evensong. It is seen as important that this weekly pattern of worship does not vary, so that all worshippers, whether regular communicants or occasional visitors, can know what to expect.

Cambridge has a deeply rooted and vibrant Evangelical tradition, which reaches back over many centuries. Not only is this shown by the strength of the Evangelical churches in the city centre, which include Holy Trinity, where Charles Simeon was vicar from 1783 to 1836, and the Round Church, now worshipping in St Andrew the Great, but also by the influence of Evangelical patronage trusts. For example the six parishes along the Newmarket Road and Mill Road cover the area to the south and east of the city centre. All have, as their patron, the Evangelical

Church Trust (or an incumbent appointed by the Church Trust). This sharply defined division of the city by style of churchmanship has an inevitable effect on people's choice of church. So some of the congregation of Great St Mary's came to the church seeking an alternative to the Evangelical worship offered in their own parish churches. 'I decided to look for another church when I discovered that my vicar had never heard of Julian of Norwich.' 'We became uncomfortable with the increasingly "Evangelical" form of worship at our own church so we tried GSM in the early 1960s, where we have worshipped ever since.' This worshipper goes on to say what he finds attractive about Great St Mary's. It provides 'a traditional mid-style of worship with high quality music and a strong preaching tradition. No gimmicks! People know what to expect.'

Great St Mary's could be described as a church for the people of Cambridge. It does not, as some other churches in the centre of the city, attract people from a wide area, and thus should not be described as serving an eclectic congregation. It has retained a local base, resulting from its central position at the heart of the city and the conscientious pastoral ministry which has, over the years, built up strong loyalties among a broad range of Cambridge people.

But there has always been more than an unadventurous brand of middle of the road worship. The church also gained a reputation for being ready to experiment and innovate. This was in part a consequence of the preaching ministry to the university, which encouraged the church to absorb new and unconventional elements of the Christian life, and also a result of the influence of successive incumbents who introduced the church to their distinctive commitments and enthusiasms. Thus a radical streak developed.

The church gained a reputation for its work with young people. Robin Howard began a youth club, mentioned earlier, in a room above the Maypole pub in Portugal Place. Then there were the famous jazz and then beat services. At one beat service organised by Ian Ogilvie in 1964 a band from the Leys School, the Chaperones, played a selection of popular songs before the service started. The church was packed, and a number of outraged letters were sent to the *Cambridge News*. The Reverend J. Joyce of Waterbeach complained that this beat music was the basis of 'frenzied dances, the devotional worship of the corrupt religions of heathenism' (*Cambridge News*, 8 November 1964).

Controversy became a familiar feature of life at Great St Mary's. In 1967, a lecture by Hugh Montefiore to the Modern Churchman's Union contained the speculation of a possible homosexual orientation in Jesus. Later that same year, on 20 September, a service took place to coincide with the Cambridge Conference of the World Congress of Faiths. There were readings from the Scriptures of different religious traditions, a Jewish blessing and Muslim prayer. In his sermon Hugh Montefiore reminded the congregation of God's love expressed through all religious traditions. At the same time a service of protest was held outside the church, conducted by the Reverend Christopher Wansey, of Roydon in Essex; and a letter appeared in the *Cambridge Evening News*, signed by eight Cambridge incumbents, protesting at the event. The Bishop of Ely said that he had not been aware that it was going to be a full multi-faith service. He did however authorise a service of 'open communion' during the Week of Prayer for Christian Unity in 1966 at which 300 people of many different churches accepted the invitation to share in the eucharist together. Attempts to gain authorisation for a Roman Catholic mass to be celebrated in the church had to wait until 1984.

Stanley Booth-Clibborn's experience of ministry in Kenya brought a strong sense of commitment to the church in Africa. On the occasion of the fifth centenary of the building of the church, the congregation decided to raise money not only for essential building work in Great St Mary's but also for a water project at Milo in Uganda. At the height of this activity a poster appeared in the town advertising the Grim St Mary's May Ball. Music was by the Black and Blacker Minstrels, an encounter group in the Clay Cross Chapel was to discuss 'Christ and Turbo-Engineering' and at dawn there was to be a Festal Picket of Peterhouse (bring the Kiddies), all to be washed down with Free Sparkling Cocoa. Tickets cost fifteen roubles for a double ticket with a reduction for tribes. Stanley was delighted with this tribute to his ministry.

The strong relationship of Great St Mary's with the inhabitants of Cambridge was built out of a painstaking and at times sacrificial pastoral care of its congregation, combined with a liturgical tradition which combined the apparently contradictory qualities of predictability and innovation. These three distinguishing features were attractive to a wide variety of people, and indeed it could be argued that the church had developed an instinctive grasp of the main features of English Christianity – a commitment to the welfare of individual persons, an attachment to tradition and regularity and a practical desire to adapt their religion to whatever is happening in modern society.

University church

Ministry to the university is slotted into the life of the parish. Mervyn's strategy, which he set up in that week in October 1955, was to alternate 'parish' and 'university' services. So, after an 8 am holy communion, there was a 9.45 am parish communion for people from the town. 'So far as I know no undergradutes come to us regularly on a Sunday for communion,' he commented. Then mattins at 11 am was for the university. It was shortened, and there were sermon courses. Since most college chapels did not celebrate sung mattins this proved popular with undergraduates. Evensong was for the town and undergraduates were not encouraged to attend. Then, of course, came the great university service at 8.30 pm. Timing was tight, especially between parish communion and mattins, and this encouraged the formation of the famous queues to get into church, which were, especially for the celebrated moments such as mattins on the Remembrance Sunday of Suez year, long, and grew in the folk memory of the church to fabulous proportions, reputedly stretching to Hobson's Conduit and beyond.

Alongside the regular services which were planned with undergraduates in mind were the official university occasions. These included university sermons. In 1968 the time of these was moved from the early afternoon to the morning, taking the place of mattins. This change led to great heart-searching from Hugh Montefiore, the vicar at the time. He was worried that the character of mattins as a student service would be lost. It turned out to have a happier result in integrating the university sermon more fully into the worshipping life of the church, being included as a focus of either the Sunday evening or morning programme of preachers. The list of university preachers is distinguished and many of the episcopal bench, most professors of theology and several authors and broadcasters have preached the university sermon. Attendances vary, but the sermon is, at present, an important and established part of the ministry of the church.

Behind all this lies the presupposition that the university church provides a ministry complementary to that of the college chapels. The services of mattins and the university service were deliberately timed so that they did not clash with the regular chapel services of holy communion and evensong. It was made clear that undergraduates were expected to have gone to their own chapel first. The Great St Mary's blend of short services, popular style and famous preachers was intended to have a missionary thrust which would commend the faith to enquirers who could then be referred to the chaplains. The university service, said Mervyn,

> is not evensong, and I have made it quite clear to the undergradu-
> ates who come to us who are practising Anglicans that they should
> go to evensong first. One of the really encouraging features of this
> service is the number of keen Christians who come with friends who
> believe very little. And I think that is one of the main functions of
> our 8.30 service – a service to which people on the circumference
> can come to learn more about the faith and its application to life. I
> am told that the CICCU had the worst attended services last term
> for many years. I am not concerned with scoring points. I mention
> it for one reason – I believe that while the CICCU will always attract
> a certain type of person, yet in the past it has got hold of others
> simply because nothing else was provided. Those are the people I
> most want to help, the man on the circumference – and when I have
> met him, to pass him on to you [the college chaplains].

The church was especially involved with colleges which did not have their own chapels. Those founded before the Oxford and Cambridge Act of 1877 had a legal obligation to provide Anglican worship and instruc-tion, but later foundations, and women's colleges which were not techni-cally colleges of the university until after the admission of women in 1948, were not bound by these requirements. As a result Great St Mary's came to be more directly involved in chaplaincy provision. Undergraduates from Newnham and New Hall often came to the parish communion, those at Girton presumably preferring the church in Girton village.

A more formal arrangement was made by which Great St Mary's pro-vided a chaplain for Girton College. Colin Slee was the second chaplain of Girton College, from 1973 to 1976.

> Muriel Bradbrook, the Mistress, went to see Stanley who said he
> had already advertised for a curate but was prepared to make the job
> half at GSM and half at Girton. So I applied for a job as a curate but
> found that I ended up doing this split job. I found myself doing far
> too much, but this was my own fault as I tried to do two full-time
> jobs. I did an 8.30 am communion at Girton, then had breakfast with
> students, leapt on my motorbike and arrived at GSM just in time to
> join in the procession at the start of the 9.45, taking my motorbike
> helmet off as I started up the aisle, then it was the 11.15 mattins, then
> lunch before some Girtonians arrived for tea. There was evensong
> at Girton at 6 then the preacher came back to supper with about
> twelve of the students, then I shot back to GSM for the 8.30.

Not all chaplains operated at this strenuous pace, but the combination of a curacy at Great St Mary's with chaplaincy at the college with the third largest number of students in the university was always a stressful assignment.

The post of chaplain to Girton College was, in 1996, combined with an experimental ministry to the departments of the university, rather than with a curate's ministry. The growth in the importance of research had led to increasing numbers of research students, assistants and fellows who were employed directly by the university departments and so were not members of colleges. This group falls outside the community network provided by the colleges, and therefore the development of chaplaincy provision for them is especially urgent. But it also presents particular difficulties due to the scattered and disparate nature of this group. Jeremy Clark-King was the first to be appointed to this shared post, the future of which will depend on whether it proves possible to set up a new style of chaplaincy in the university, based more on practices developed in industrial mission or ministry in non-collegiate universities rather than college chaplaincy. He is based at Great St Mary's and this development is a further example of ways that the church has sought to contribute to ministry within the university as a whole.

This varied relationship with the university is facilitated by the patrons of the parish, Trinity College. While the practice of appointing fellows of the college came to an end with Mervyn Stockwood, the college maintains a close interest in the life of the church. The combined post of Chaplain at Girton and Curate of Great St Mary's was brokered by the college, as was the evolution of the task to include chaplaincy to university departments. Usually the involvement of a patron of a parish is limited to the appointment of the incumbent. For Great St Mary's – since the crown always appoints a successor on the occasion of a priest becoming a diocesan bishop – this task has not always been required. But the geographical proximity of the college and the church has led to a much closer and continuing relationship, which has been especially important in developing this ministry to the university – a complex and changing organisation.

There has been little sign of tension and conflict between town and gown in Great St Mary's. Occasionally unpleasantness arose to sour this otherwise harmonious situation. The archives contain a set of letters showing how Mervyn arranged for a music student to become deputy organist and the holder of the post, Mr Haycock, considerately, although under some pressure, resigned to make space for this new arrangement. Colleagues in the music faculty were incensed and a declaration condemning the church appeared on the music faculty notice board. An angry correspondence ensued between the PCC and the music faculty as a result of which retractions were made.

The greater enemy to the ministry of church to university, however, was not hostility but indifference. While people remember the occasions when the chuch was packed for the visit of Mother Teresa, they forget that, for example, a couple of terms earlier a certain Reverend Desmond Tutu, then on the staff of the World Council of Churches, preached to a congregation of fifty-eight. Small attendances were frequent, and the maintenance of the programmes of visiting preachers at mattins and the university service was a source of great stress. Michael Mayne considered that this part of his work could occupy half of his time in busy periods. The demise of the university service in 1993 was an inevitable if regrettable decision.

Visitors

In the life of Great St Mary's there is a third group of people who come to it, in addition to its congregation and the members of the university. These are the many visitors who do not attend services but who value the existence of the church. These come with an infinite variety of concerns, needs and interests. Among them are the groups of foreign students who come in the summer holidays to Cambridge as a centre of English culture, the people who like to call in as a break from a busy morning shopping and who stop to light a votive candle and sit quietly for a while, and those who are homeless or lonely and who need company or practical help.

Awareness of the multiple needs of visitors has led to the growing importance of the building itself as a centre of ministry. The secretary's office is the focal point. Julia Jepps was parish secretary from 1979 to 1991, and described her impressions on being introduced to the little room tucked into the west end of the church.

> The office was bursting at the seams with cupboards (visible and invisible), various obviously well-used office equipment, and every available space occupied with papers and files. There was no window, and to my horror, my pet aversion, strip lighting. I was not reassured when the verger mentioned that an urn containing the ashes of some poor soul would be arriving from Eaden Lilley's and would I please receive it. At the first weekly staff meeting I was introduced to the other members of the staff – two curates and a

director of music. They introduced me to Fitzbillies' chelsea buns which we consumed on Thursdays (the vicar's day off). Many well-known figures from all walks of life came to speak in Great St Mary's, and I would often arrive in the office on Monday mornings to discover an odd assortment of clothing and overnight bags belonging to weekend visitors – and on more than one occasion a bishop combing his hair. At the opposite end, other footsteps found their way to the office door, some seeking help and a sympathetic ear, or a cup of coffee and a bit of warmth; visitors wanting to climb the tower who had come to the wrong door. Many were quite astonished to discover this bustling office in the University Church. I had always dreamed that the office would one day be transformed from a stuffy, overfull, untidy, dusty, room for the use of all, into a clean light place, streamlined and germ-free. But then I suppose it would have lost its hospitable welcoming air, which is after all what it's all about.

In 1986 the interior of the west end was remodelled. New offices were created so that there are now five rooms, and a small kitchen and toilets, providing a more substantial base for the life of the church. Their existence has contributed to a change in the style of the pastoral ministry of the church, which is now much more clearly based on the building itself. A typical day begins when the church doors open at around 7.30 am, for the early daily eucharist at 8. Once it is over the first visitors come. These are the people who are out early, and regularly call in for a cup of tea, not necessarily homeless but often isolated and vulnerable. The office opens after mattins at 9 and the church staff, clergy, secretary, verger and steward (or bursar) begin work. An early job is to open the tower and bookstall. From then on until the doors close after evensong at 6 pm there will be a galaxy – or a kaleidoscope perhaps puts it better – of visitors, tourists from a wide range of countries, choirs to sing lunchtime concerts, local people to light a candle or leave a note on the intercessions board, a cameraman to take some shots of Cambridge from the tower. Great St Mary's is large enough to provide staff to welcome visitors every day of the year, but small enough for it to be the same four or five people who can therefore get to know the regulars.

St Michael's Church

The picture of the life of the Parish of St Mary the Great requires two further elements to make it complete.

It contains not one church building but two. The Parish of St Mary the Great was joined to that of St Michael in Trinity Street in 1908. St Michael's is over 150 years older than the present Great St Mary's Church, having been built in 1324. It is an unusual church since it was built as a parish church and college chapel combined. An earlier experiment had taken place in Merton College, Oxford in 1290, but there the parish church section was never completed. St Michael's has a large chancel and small nave – a pattern copied by later college chapels. It was built for Michaelhouse College, and was also used by Gonville Hall – with the two colleges occupying alternative sides of the chancel. Its use as a chapel was brief, since its two colleges were to become constituent parts of Trinity College and Gonville and Caius College, and it then was used solely as a parish church. Although it is a building of great historical significance and architectural interest, it now has little pastoral or liturgical function, and, from the time that its parish was combined with that of St Mary the Great, there has been continual debate as to how it should be used.

Its main use during the first half of the twentieth century was for children's activities, which took place in the church on Sunday. But other institutions were interested in the church. The building is surrounded by Gonville and Caius College, and on several occasions there were discussions as to its possible conversion to become the college library. The failure of these negotiations benefited the college eventually, since in 1996 the former Squire Law Library became the college library, a far larger and better appointed building for this purpose. Another possible user was the Roman Catholic Chaplaincy, then based at Fisher House, in the parish. John Fisher had, when a fellow of Michaelhouse, worshipped at St Michael's and so there was a historical link between the chaplaincy and St Michael's. The difficulty with both possible schemes was the need of Great St Mary's for extra space for meetings, social events, children's work and other activities. Although both college and chaplaincy could offer some alternative space, they would not have been so easy of access or so convenient. And so these promising plans did not come to fruition.

Hugh Montefiore decided on a positive response to this problem. 'Mervyn Stockwood had more or less promised it to Monsignor Gilbey for the RC chaplaincy – and then he left. Joe Fison had more or less promised it to Caius College for their library – and then he left. I decided we needed a parish hall and launched an appeal.' The work cost £12,000, of which the parish contributed £5,000 and the appeal £7,000. The nave was divided from the choir by a brick screen and became a hall. A small kitchen and larger toilets were built in the north aisle, and a couple of meeting rooms were created on a higher level. It proved to be a useful resource. Dog shows, antique sales and craft fairs brought in an income. A language school was a regular user and there were numerous plays. One winter it was a night shelter for the homeless. 'Few buildings in Cambridge can have witnessed more cups of coffee and second hand bric-à-brac sold for love of God and care of neighbour near and far than St Michael's.'

However, this solution did not meet with everybody's approval. John Betjeman said he thought it was the most expensive way of ruining a beautiful building that he had encountered. Many agreed with him that a bare brick screen across a thirteenth-century church, and a plywood false ceiling and cast iron lighting gantry obscuring the roof of the oldest college chapel in Cambridge, lacked architectural sensitivity. Worse, new health and hygiene regulations made the kitchen unusable for catering of even the most modest dimensions, and there was no access for the disabled. As a result the 1966 alterations have become outdated, and the use of St Michael's is once again under discussion. It may be difficult to work out the best use for St Michael's, but it is clearly vital for the future of the parish that this resource becomes fully effective. The facilities in Great St Mary's are limited to a large space for worship and several small rooms for offices. A modern parish community life needs more than that, and St Michael's is the only place where social functions, group discussions, and of course eating and drinking can take place.

As well as its official connection with the Church of St Michael, Great St Mary's has worked alongside many other civic and charitable organisations. Some of this work reaches back many centuries. An example of the sharing in the life of the city is the long history of the Jackenett Charity. In 1469 Thomas Jackenett, burgess, gave a row of four alms-houses, later increased to eight. They were built in the churchyard itself, and were occupied until 1788 when, with the assistance of Trinity College, eight new houses were built in Walls Lane, now King Street. These have been a home to some sad and impoverished townspeople. Gladys Cannon remembers her early days as a trustee.

> There was an old lady who was always getting drunk and the police were running her in. Mervyn said we would give her a chance and so he gave her an almshouse. But it did not go smoothly. The other residents came to the church office saying she was coming home drunk and making a noise at night. Mervyn wanted me to go round, and when I did I found she just had a room with a table, a chair and

a bed – and nothing on the floor. She was struggling to get a bit of lino down, and I tried to help her. Another time I went round with Joe Fison and we were so horrified. She was washing herself with a bowl of water and her legs were black. They had not been washed for years. We had to get the health people round. I stood at the door while they got to work. One said 'you should come and look at this, there is a whole family of bugs on the bed'. It took three visits for them to fumigate that place. Later she went blind and went to the Red Cross Home. They finally got her clean there!

In 1971 the Jackenett Charity was amalgamated with other charities, the Merrill Charity of Great St Mary's, the Wray Charity of Holy Trinity Church and the Elie Charity administered by Caius College. The properties of the three charities were sold, and a piece of land purchased in Chesterton, to the north of the city. In November 1972, New Court, consisting of thirty purpose-built flats was opened, and and in 1980 a second block of flats was built. This was named Cannon Court, commemorating the remarkable life of service to the church of Gladys Cannon.

It is fitting to finish by remembering Gladys Cannon. She was born in 1901 and was baptised in Great St Mary's in the same year. She was a Sunday school teacher, a PCC member continuously from 1941 to 1970, sacristan from 1954 to 1994 and made the first eucharistic vestments to be worn in Great St Mary's since the Reformation, and an almshouse trustee from 1956. She occupied this position until 1998, interviewing applicants for vacancies in the almshouses. She seldom leaves her home now, and her familiar seat in the front row of the nave is usually unoccupied, but she retains a keen interest in the church to which she has given so much of her energy and devotion. She has been a member of the church through the incumbencies of fourteen vicars and a far larger number of curates, whom she has supported, encouraged, and prayed for. The naming of a block of almshouses after this most tireless of members of the congregation is a reminder that the distinguished ministry of Great St Mary's within the city of Cambridge during the last seven hundred years, and especially since 1955, rests on the Christian witness of its many members.

Bibliographical note

The sources used are mainly members and former members of the congregation: Gladys Cannon, Pamela Hill, Julia Jepps, Walter Mitchell, C. F. D.

Moule, Betty Orange, Margaret Pearson, the Very Reverend Colin Slee, the Reverend Canon Geoffrey Walker, Michael Wallis. Documents are from the parish archives and include a talk given to the deans and chaplains of the university and a letter to Canon (as he was then) Joe Fison both by Mervyn Stockwood; and a letter from Stanley Booth-Clibborn.

1. Great St Mary's from the Market Place *c.* 1870.

above

2. Great St Mary's from the west, eighteenth-century drawing.

right

3. Edward Blore's design for a spire *c.*1820. A spire was intended when the tower was built in the sixteenth century.

4. Lavenham, Suffolk, nave arcade. An arcade very similar to Great St Mary's, but without galleries.

5. Great St Mary's, nave arcade.

6. Lavenham, late medieval screens. Great St Mary's had similar screens.

7. Font, 1632.

8. Pulpit, 1618, given to Orton
Waterville church after 1736.

9. Bell-ringing
chamber, sixteenth-
century panelling.

ECCLESIA B. MARIÆ VIRGINIS CANTAB.

10. Great St Mary's from the south, David Loggan engraving, 1690.

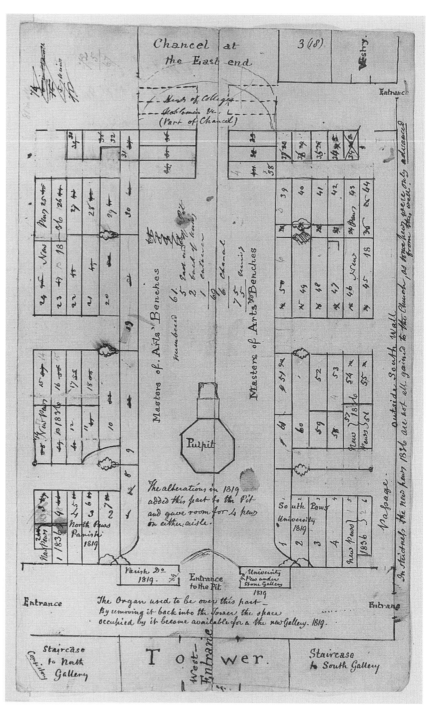

11. Ground-plan of the nave *c.* 1820, showing central pulpit and seating.

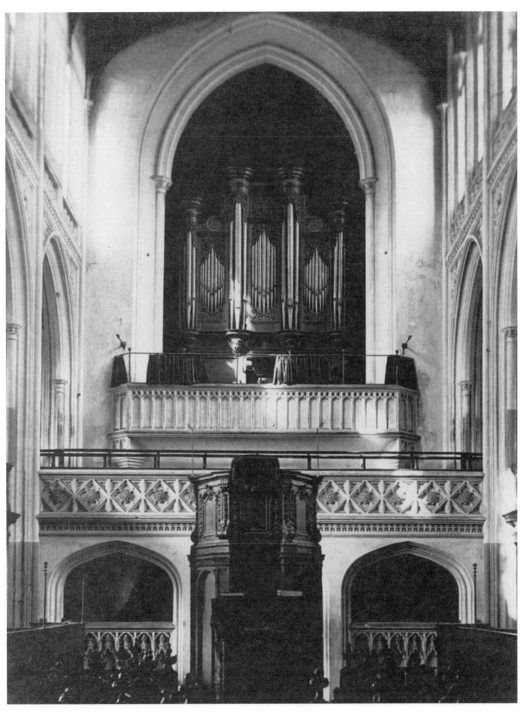

12. Nave looking west *c.*1860. Eighteenth-century pulpit and Edward Blore's west gallery.

13. Nave looking east *c.*1860. The Doctor's Gallery fills the chancel arch.

14. Nave looking east after 1870. The Doctors' Gallery removed, the chancel refurnished and the nave reseated.

15. East end after 1960, and Michael Mayne, Vicar 1979–87.

16. Plaster model of the *Majestas*, by Alan Durst, 1959. It replaced the Victorian reredos at the east end.

17. *The Risen Christ*, a bronzed fibreglass sculpture by Gabriella Bollobas, 1982, in St Andrew's Chapel.

18. Martin Bucer (1491–1551), reformer. He was buried in Great St Mary's but his body was exhumed and burnt at the stake in Queen Mary's reign.

19. Henry Richards Luard, Vicar 1860–87.

20. William Cunningham, Vicar 1887–1908.

21. William Steers, thirty-seven years clerk of Great St Mary's.

22. Mervyn Stockwood, Vicar 1955–9, greeting students after a university service.

23. The reopening of St Michael's, September 1996. *(left to right)* Edward Roberts, Bishop of Ely; the Vice-Chancellor; J. B. Collins; Marcus Bradford, Mayor; Joe Fison, Vicar 1959–63; Hugh Montefiore, Vicar 1963–70; George Pace, architect.

above 24. University procession.   *below* 25. Civic procession.

26. Queue for a service.

27. Cows which apparently strayed from Coe Fen, discovered in the churchyard, May 1971.

above
28. Kenneth Kaunda, President of Zambia, at Great St Mary's.

right
29. Duke Ellington, musician, playing in Great St Mary's.

30. Mother Teresa, June 1977.

31. Bishop Michael Ramsey and Billy Graham, evangelist.

32. Parish choir, 1977. Stanley Booth-Clibborn, Vicar, and Graham Sudbury, Director of Music.

34. John Binns,
Vicar 1994–   ,
with Bishop Mano
Ramalshah,
secretary of USPG

33. David Conner, Vicar 1987–94.

5 Cambridge religion 1950–1970

HUGH MONTEFIORE

There was certainly a great boom in the practice of the Christian religion in the fifties, and to a lesser extent in the sixties, and what took place
was really a very remarkable phenomenon. Pre-war, there was no weekly
undergraduate service at the university church; during the fifties and
sixties many congregations of over a thousand people are recorded in the
register book of Great St Mary's. One Cambridge dean of that time who
was an undergraduate before the war tells me that in Trinity College, the
largest of Cambridge colleges, there were only twenty to twenty-five
communicants in the college chapel pre-war. Post-war, the chapel – and
it is one of the largest in Cambridge – was almost always full. Another
correspondent, who was dean of one of the smaller colleges, tells me that
when he came in 1959 he could expect ninety-six communicants on a
Sunday morning. A former chaplain of another college, again one of the
smaller colleges, tells me, and I quote his words: 'I used to go through the
college list towards the end of the academic year, and I found that, several
years running, about half the undergraduates were doing something
about public worship – i.e., more than once a term.' In addition, students
flocked to city churches with their particular churchmanships on
Sundays at 11 am. These numbers, we will find, began to run down
halfway through the sixties, until they reached their present levels; and I
was told on good authority the other day that in one Cambridge college,
which must be nameless, only three communicants could now be
expected on a Sunday morning.

Clearly something rather remarkable happened, and it is right to seek
some kind of cause, even though a complete explanation may be impossible. It is difficult to be certain, for it all happened over a quarter of a
century ago, and accurate statistics are not available, and so I have to rely
on my own impressions and on those of deans or chaplains of that period
who have kindly replied to my enquiries. Let me start by speaking out of
my own experience. I came to Cambridge in 1948 as a theological student
at Westcott House, and I remember that religion already seemed to be

93

booming in the university by then. Charles Raven was at the time not only Regius Professor of Divinity but also vice-chancellor of the university. I recall him preaching at a packed undergraduate service, organised by the SCM, in Great St Mary's one Sunday evening; the SCM was still at that time a power in the university. I recollect Raven saying with great passion and with an agonised look on his face, 'I need to be broken', and it was certainly very impressive to a student to hear the chief representative of Cambridge University speaking with such Christian conviction. Doubtless this was not without effect. Raven, however, was quite atypical. He later told me that he had to abandon conducting missions because he found that he tended to hypnotise congregations. Booming Christianity in Cambridge was not due to him. To what or to whom then was it due? I think it had a great deal to do with the war. Indeed, it actually started during the war. One of my correspondents tells me that in 1942 the Divinity Faculty arranged for Dr C. S. Whale to give a series of lectures on Christian doctrine (which was later published). To the great surprise of the Divinity Faculty the response was so huge that the lectures had to be held in the examination schools, the largest lecture hall in the university. My correspondent describes it as the first harbinger of spring before the coming blooms of summer.

Later, by 1949, Oxford and Cambridge were both full of returning warriors like myself. I do not think that people today realise that service in the armed forces during the last Great War was the best recruiting ground that the Church of England has ever had. As a result the number of candidates for the ordained ministry swelled, and the number of clergy, in contrast to their present decline, actually increased; so much so that a new theological college was mooted, and a new wing was built to Queens College, Birmingham. A former chaplain, however, who left Cambridge to serve in what was then known as CACTM (now the ABM, which has responsibility for training for the church's ministry) tells me that in the mid-sixties too many charming but weak ordinands were accepted for training at theological colleges. He writes: 'The selection conference from which I returned most unhappy was the only one in my experience when we recommended the whole lot – because there was not a single strong candidate to set the standard.' Perhaps we are seeing some of the results of these weaknesses in the ordained ministry today.

But that is to anticipate a decade. Many returning ex-servicemen, when commissioned in the armed forces, were bereft of their customary props of family and school. As officers they often found themselves in positions of considerable responsibility where they faced extreme situations in which their own and their men's lives were at stake; and in such circumstances many found God. Of course religious ex-servicemen were not unique to Cambridge. I had started in 1946 to read the Oxford honours school of theology. The late evening service at the university church of St Mary's, under the leadership of Canon Dick Milford, was usually crammed. Although I am told that not all Oxford college chapels were full on a Sunday evening, mine was, despite the fact that the chaplain was a shy, remote and academic man whom no one would have approached for pastoral advice. One of the questions we shall have to ask is why religion in Cambridge continued to boom for nearly two decades, while in Oxford it declined much sooner. It is necessary to think back to the situation at the end of the last Great War. The Labour Party had been swept into power not because the country was ungrateful to Winston Churchill for his part in winning the war, but because of a widespread conviction that a new start was needed to win the peace. In contrast to our present 'culture of contempt', idealism was abroad. R. A. Butler had already introduced a great new Education Act. In 1941 a committee was formed under the chairmanship of William Beveridge which produced a plan against what he called the 'Three Giants', which included poverty, and which led to a social insurance fund. Beveridge also advocated a National Health Service which Aneurin Bevan triumphantly introduced after the war. There was a determination in the country that those who had given up so much to win the war – and that meant ordinary people – should share in the fruits of peace. But people felt you couldn't build a new Britain simply on the basis of a political welfare state. Something more profound was needed on which to ground it in a country which was then still basically Christian. Christian England must do better than devilish Nazidom. As one distinguished correspondent has put it: 'The platitude that we were still reasserting traditional values, which Hitler and Co. had put under direct threat, must be a backcloth.' And basic to those traditional values was their grounding in God revealed in Christ. The church was in good heart, and its morale was high. Believe it or not, there was even talk of the conversion of Britain. In contrast to the needless defeatism so common today, Christians were fired with optimism and good hopes for the future. As we shall see, this idealism and high morale which was generally widespread throughout the country had its spin-off among the undergraduates of Cambridge.

After a short spell in a northern curacy, I returned to Cambridge in 1951 to join the staff of Westcott House. During the next two or three years I was often asked to preach in college chapels, and acted at one point as unofficial chaplain to Girton College. Despite the attractions for women of worshipping in a men's college, Girton College chapel was pretty full, as were the college chapels as a whole. There was, however, no central service in the university for undergraduates here at Great St Mary's, although other city churches had their good measure of them. In 1954 I became Dean of Gonville and Caius College, and I found that I had inherited from my predecessor Eric Heaton a full chapel on Sunday evening and a large number of communicants.

It is sometimes said that the Cambridge boom in religion was due to the influence of Mervyn Stockwood here at Great St Mary's. Now it is true that Mervyn had a vast influence on religion in the university as a whole. From 1955, in three and a half short years, in a truly remarkable way he transformed this church. He made the Christian religion a talking point in the university. I remember preaching in Great St Mary's on a Trinity Sunday on recruitment to the sacred ministry – as we then had to do – before Mervyn came, and finding that the majority of my congregation sat behind me in the choir stalls, as was the case at the Assize Sermon here. However, we must not despise small numbers: one undergraduate present on that occasion heard the call, later became a curate here, and is now a bishop. But Mervyn filled the church – including the galleries – Sunday after Sunday. As I have remarked, the church registers regularly recorded a congregation of over a thousand, both at mattins and at the university service at 8.30 pm. His personal magnetism, his Christian commitment and his combination of humour with trenchant Christian teaching, worked wonders. Cambridge religion blossomed greatly under Mervyn, but the boom did not start with Mervyn. I remember John Burnaby, the Dean of Trinity College which holds the patronage of this living, asking me whether I thought college chapels were strong enough to withstand a great central university place of worship, such as would be likely if Mervyn were invited to the benefice. Of course they were. After Mervyn arrived in 1955 I did not notice any diminution of attendance in my college chapel, which is after all only over the road. Perhaps I may put the point in this way. If Mervyn had lived fifty years later and had recently been appointed Vicar of the university church, I doubt very much whether his impact today would in any way resemble what actually happened here in the fifties.

Why was Cambridge religion still booming? In the first place, there was, as I have explained, a general feeling of high morale and optimism in the country as a whole, and the church also was optimistic, and this had an effect on the ordinary undergraduate of the day. Moreover there was a far greater knowledge about the Christian religion among students than there is today. Everyone knew the outlines of the Christian faith, in contrast to today, when many students arrive with their minds and hearts a *tabula rasa* so far as Christianity is concerned.

Secondly, National Service was then operative, and the majority of those coming into residence had done National Service; and this to some extent had the same effect as wartime service had done. The effects of World War Two were continued from the returning warriors to the National Servicemen; and the idealism only gradually declined. Moods don't alter overnight. However, one former dean tells me that when National Service ended, while numbers at holy communion continued in treble figures, attendance at college Sunday evening chapel dropped like a bomb from full house to some twenty-five or thirty, unless there was an outstanding preacher. Ex-National Servicemen, instead of arriving here as adolescents, came up as adults. Politics was not a matter of concern to most: religion took its place. National Service had an important effect on Evangelicals. Whereas formerly the Intercollegiate Union had been a bigoted sectarian minority, they were now to a large extent (but not wholly) a more mature body under a sensible and dedicated leadership. This situation hardly helped the Student Christian Movement, which still maintained a chaplaincy in Cambridge, but it sowed the seeds of good Evangelical leadership in the future, the results of which we are now seeing in the present. Cambridge at that time was blessedly free from a narrow ecclesiasticism. Apart from King's and St John's, music and singing did not dominate chapel worship, as it tends to do when worship becomes only one of many options and the interest of a small minority, instead of an accepted expression of corporate life and an essential constituent for those concerned with the great problems of life. Apart from a few 'professional Christians' among the student population, undergraduates as a whole, prompted by their college chaplains, wanted to do their bit for those less fortunate than themselves. They wanted actually to do something. Many organisations flourished: Aid to South Africa, Refugee Adoption Groups, assistance to students who came from Eastern Europe, JAGUAR – that is, Joint Action Group for Understanding the Races – and of course the very popular Friday bread and cheese lunches for War on Want. The United Nations Association (CUUNA) was the strongest university society!

In the third place, there was in those days still a strong corporate sense. Tradition was important and college traditions were upheld by undergraduates. Present-day individualism had not yet caught the nation in its grip. The college chapel was part of this corporate tradition: and it actually bestowed a sense of corporate identity, in the same way as wearing gowns and eating in hall did. The chapel was not just the habitat of a clique: when a third of the college was present at worship, it could properly be called, to the amazement of the more atheist or agnostic dons, a real expression of the corporate life of the college. I remember the time of breakfast being accommodated to fit in with the college equivalent of the parish communion. Even if fellows sat in different pews from undergraduates at evening prayer on a Sunday, they all worshipped together. I found, in the college of which I was a member, that a large percentage of the fellowship body practised their religion.

A fourth reason has been suggested to me by more than one former dean for the persistence of the practice of religion in Cambridge; and that is, quite simply, class. One of them mentioned to me that many of his regular communicants then had been to a public school, from which they had derived this habit. Another noticed a fall in chapel attendance when his college took in more grammar school boys. I do not however think that this was a general reason. I recollect one of the colleges where almost all undergraduates were ex-public school men; and while its chapel was full of dons, I did not notice queues of ex-public schoolboys in the congregation. In the college where I served there were comparatively few public school boys – the college was alleged, falsely I hope, to have had at that time a positive prejudice against them. But I recollect many young men from northern grammar schools were among its keenest Christians.

I do not think that we can account for the Cambridge religious boom by the continuance of university or college missions. I do not doubt that they did good. The university mission taken by Michael Ramsey in 1953, in his deeply religious yet witty style, undoubtedly greatly affected some people. But it was too highly organised. Everybody concerned with it was so exhausted by the end of the week that chapel attendances actually dropped; and such a mission has never been repeated in Cambridge over the last forty years, although Oxford still continued with its triennial university mission.

It is particularly difficult to generalise about religion as a whole, and in any case it is only possible to quantify its outward expression; but my impression was that it was flourishing all round. So far I have only mentioned Great St Mary's and the college chapels. It is interesting to note what undergraduates were prepared to do out of term. The Franciscans would round up some sixty young men for a parish mission; there were missions organised by the Cambridge Pastorate and by the Cambridge

Inter-Collegiate Christian Union (CICCU), not to mention the Hopping and Fruiting Missions; and there were college groups, too, visiting parishes. And during term the Free Church chapels and their fellowships were also thriving. 'Meth Soc' seemed to draw on large numbers, and, as we would expect, there was strong fellowship among the Methodists, both in town and gown. The same could be said of the Baptists and Congregationalists and the Presbyterians. There was a real ecumenical spirit. Although in parish churches members of other churches could not yet be invited to share in Holy Communion, an exception was made for college chapels in view of their strong corporate life, and many Free Churchmen were strong supporters of their college Christian fellowship.

There was also the Cambridge Pastorate, which did great work based on Holy Trinity. Bill Skelton, a World War Two war ace, an ex-RAF pilot and then chaplain of Clare, was one of its figureheads. And there were the brown brothers. In particular Brother Michael Fisher had an enormous influence on undergraduates. I remember when the poor man was trying to write essays while he was studying for the ministry at Westcott House, it was almost impossible to stem the tide of undergraduate callers. Anglo-Catholics tended to gather at what is surely the most beautiful church in Cambridge, Little St Mary's. Meanwhile Father Gilbey was carrying out with great distinction his role as Roman Catholic chaplain to the university, until he felt he must resign over the issue of the admission of women to the Newman Society. A strong traditionalist, he was a man of deep spirituality, wide sympathies and old-fashioned courtesies. He used to breakfast every Sunday with Mervyn Stockwood, where he was reported to have said: 'Mervyn, I have no objection to your being an Anglican, but I do object to you reading the *News of the World* over breakfast.'

And of course there was the CICCU. It was very strong in the fifties and sixties, and it had no real central competitor until Mervyn Stockwood came to the University Church and began the Sunday evening service for students. CICCU had its well-attended bible readings in the Union on Saturday nights, and also its Sunday evening service then held at Holy Trinity. Its members on Sunday mornings attended services in city churches (not particularly the Round Church in those days). It had (and still has) a triennial mission, with college missioners appointed, and Mervyn Stockwood allowed this to take place in Great St Mary's. It passed off happily, though there was some reluctance on the part of the more extreme brethren when he insisted on himself leading prayers in the vestry before the mission service began. Of course some young men in the CICCU were then, as doubtless today, suspicious of anything to do with established religion. I remember an undergraduate saying to me, 'Dean, it would help if you were a Christian' – but that same undergraduate is now a very tolerant diocesan bishop. I have already commented on the good sense of the CICCU in those days, and I have always thought that, like the old Oxford Group, it was an excellent thing, provided you passed through and came out the other side. In any student pastorate it is necessary not to look at the present, but what a student will be like ten years hence, and I have to say that, of those who had fundamentalist views, the lapse rate among their members was very large after they had gone down.

In those days there was fairly tight control of the CICCU from IVF (The Inter-Varsity Fellowship); but in college cooperation depended upon personal relations between its members and the dean and chaplain. They could be very loyal members of the college chapel. There was a wide spread of evangelicalism in Cambridge, and a wide measure of cooperation. Eric James tells me that when Billy Graham took a CICCU mission, he was very happy to lunch with him and Harry Williams, neither of whom could remotely be regarded as coming from his stable. In those days the CICCU certainly did not dominate the religious scene, although when I once visited the Jewish Society, I was told that their view of Christianity did largely consist of fire and brimstone, because it was members of the CICCU who had tried unsuccessfully to convert them to the Christian faith. So far I have hardly mentioned the deans and chaplains. In the post-war period there were some brilliant pastors and thinkers and communicators among them. One former dean commented to me that the post-war chaplains in several colleges were ten times better in 1949 and 1959 than they were in 1939. Another don said to me that 'among the deans there were more ten-talent men than there are now'. There was such a galaxy that it is difficult to know whom to omit. Among the chaplains at Trinity were Simon Phipps (later Bishop of Lincoln), Hugh Dickinson (later Dean of Salisbury) and Eric James (later the initiator of 'Faith in the City'). Peter Nott (later Bishop of Norwich) was Chaplain of St John's, Murray Irvine (later Provost of Southwell) at Sidney Sussex, Martin Coombs at Emmanuel, Simon Barrington-Ward (later Bishop of Coventry) at Magdalene, and John Drury (later Dean of Christ Church) at Downing. Tony Tremlett (later Bishop of Dover) at Trinity Hall and Noel Duckworth at Churchill, both older men, had great influence on the undergraduates in their colleges.

Among the deans were many 'aces'. Henry Chadwick, a polymath who later became Dean of Christ Church, Regius Professor of Theology at

Oxford and Master of Peterhouse, was Dean of Queens' in the fifties, while his brother Owen, later Master of Selwyn and Regius Professor of History (and awarded the Order of Merit) was Dean of Trinity Hall. Alec Vidler was the idiosyncratic and learned Dean of King's. John Robinson, Dean of Clare and later Bishop of Woolwich, and Harry Williams, Dean of Trinity, each achieved bestseller status with *Honest to God* and *The True Wilderness*. Roland Walls, the eccentric Dean of Corpus Christi, was much loved. Ian Ramsey at Christ's (later Bishop of Durham), George Woods (later Professor in London), and Peter Baelz at Jesus (later Professor) were all outstanding theologians. At Trinity Hall, Lancelot Fleming (later Bishop of Norwich) was succeeded by Bob Runcie, who was to become Archbishop of Canterbury.

Of course the influence of these deans and chaplains was large, as was that of Charlie Moule, the humble and approachable Lady Margaret Professor of Divinity, and Donald Mackinnon, the Norris Hulse Professor, profound but extremely eccentric. These all helped to maintain the boom in religion but they did not themselves create it. What happened was that the chaplains made friends with undergraduates, the deans produced the theological stuffing and Great St Mary's produced student preaching of high quality and enabled them to listen to well-known people of distinction.

In Oxford the chaplain of a college is customarily a teaching fellow in the college, who can have little time and energy left over for personal contact with the whole undergraduate body. In Cambridge the religious provision was (and still is) more generous. The chaplain was usually not a fellow, did not teach theology (that was left to the dean) and was a young man with a limited term of appointment. He had time to make friends with all undergraduates – say, one pastor for three or four hundred students. A hard line was not drawn between the church and the community. Because chaplains were not members of governing bodies they did not belong to the college establishment, so they could be approached as friends with whom caution was not needed. They could cover almost the whole range of student activities, from cycling behind the college boat on the river, joining college societies, to drinking and partying with undergraduates. The college chaplain might well have been the first clergyman to whom a freshman ever spoke. Does this account for the fact that religion continued to boom in Cambridge when it did not in Oxford? Dr Vivian Green, former Rector of Lincoln College, wrote a book called *Religion at Oxford and Cambridge*. It spanned eight centuries, and he wrote this about pastoral care in the mid-twentieth century:

It is possible that the subtle quality of Cambridge religious life, as mellow as the old rose brick of the colleges themselves, may have been in part the effect of a system which placed the responsibility for the pastoral welfare of the undergraduates in many colleges in the hands of a Dean, who was usually a tutorial fellow ranking high in the college hierarchy, and of a Chaplain who acted as his assistant.

I do not think, however, that the Cambridge collegiate structure can be held to be the principal reason for the continuance of the Cambridge religious boom into the late sixties. Good chaplains do not on their own stir these strange movements of feeling and opinion; and, in any case, since the same chaplaincy establishments in Cambridge still hold, why did not the boom continue indefinitely? Undoubtedly the chaplains did a splendid job, and helped to maintain religious commitment; but they could not have been its principal cause. I think that Green is probably right in seeing one reason for the differences between religious life in Oxford and Cambridge in the 'intrinsic domesticity about the Cambridge scene which forbade the fiercer intellectual debating at Oxford; anticlericalism had been less deeply entrenched there than in nineteenth century Oxford'.

Cambridge theology in the fifties was really rather dull! There were still some old-fashioned liberals about, but John Robinson, then Dean of Clare, was gaining considerable acclaim by what he called 'biblical theology', and he was the most popular lecturer in the faculty. I remember going along with Howard Root, then Dean of Emmanuel, to see Alec Vidler at King's. We found all this a bit stuffy. We asked Vidler if he would chair a group which was prepared to take a more radical look at theology; and this was the beginning of the Cambridge symposium published in 1962 called *Soundings*. It made quite a stir when it was published, although – apart from Harry Williams' contribution – it was modestly orthodox. It may be of interest to cite the beginning of Vidler's Introduction:

The authors of this volume of essays cannot persuade themselves that the time is ripe for major works of theological construction or reconstruction. It is a time for ploughing, not reaping; or to use the metaphor we have chosen for our title, it is a time for making soundings, not charts or maps. If this be so, we do not have to apologise for what we hope will be possible for a future generation. We can best serve the cause of truth and of the Church by candidly confessing where our perplexities lie, and not by making claims which, so far as we can see, theologians are not at the present in a position to justify.

In the same year, 1962, the Faculty Board of Divinity put on a popular series of open lectures, published later under the title *God, Sex and War*. As Professor Mackinnon wrote in the Preface: 'The first series of lecture subjects were chosen which were known to be of burning interest to undergraduates.' They were delivered during the term of Tripos examinations; nevertheless they drew immense crowds which, like the open lectures of twenty years before, had to be held in the examination schools as the only large enough lecture hall. They were followed the next year by a series which was published later under the title *Objections to Christian Belief*. These were not intended to give answers to such objections, but in the words of Dr Vidler in his Preface 'to plumb the objections without complacently assuming that answers were readily available. Above all in a university Christians must seek to understand the fundamental doubts to which their faith is exposed at this age of the world.' These lectures also drew large audiences, and people were encouraged to listen to Christians honest enough to articulate doubts.

I resigned my university lectureship and the deanery at Caius to become Vicar of the University Church of Great St Mary's in 1963. Although a visitation of the parish revealed only twenty-seven residents, the church was the best attended in the city, and we reckoned that house-to-house visiting covered sixty square miles! (The curates had to be provided with motor scooters.) This meant that we deliberately undertook no pastoral work among undergraduates, and actively discouraged them from attending any service on Sunday other than the 8.30 pm student service. At other times the college chapel should be their place of worship.

I found that I had entered into a splendid inheritance from gown as well as town bequeathed me by Joe Fison, Mervyn's successor, who left to become Bishop of Salisbury. There were bulging congregations and there was undergraduate enthusiasm. But I came to realise that such numbers could only be maintained if preachers of first-class eminence could be obtained: archbishops, cardinals, people like Pastor Niemoller. I also discovered that students would listen with particular attention to distinguished lay men and women who were prepared to speak openly of Christianity. I also invited leading politicians like Enoch Powell and Ted Heath to speak. These sermons from Great St Mary's were posted to subscribers and published in book form. I was determined that under-graduates should realise that Christianity affects the whole of life, so we had poetry readings by W. H. Auden and C. Day-Lewis, and Duke Ellington brought from America his Concert of Sacred Music. We tried to involve students in the religious issues of the day by means of teach-ins. In those years when the Divinity Faculty did not have open lectures, I arranged popular courses covering the Christian faith, one of which was published under the title *Truth To Tell*. I think it is possible to categor-ise most of the Cambridge theology of that time as 'critical theology'. This term applies also to *Honest To God*, *God, Sex and War*, and other Cambridge writings. They were in their different ways attempts to restate Christian orthodox thinking in more contemporary terms. They succeeded because they were mainstream, and at the same time they stimulated or satisfied enquiring minds.

But time was beginning to run out. College chapels were already beginning to feel the draught in the 1960s. By 1967 I realised that Cambridge student religion was indeed beginning to wane, and large congregations could no longer be guaranteed. University revolution was in the air; and although it only mildly affected Cambridge, attention was moving to student rights and student politics. The increasing secularisa-tion of society, which earlier had passed Cambridge by, now made itself felt.

I do not think that we can neglect the wider movements of thought. Individualism was gaining ground. Post-war idealism had faded. Religion was giving way to politics. Students concentrated on work to get good degrees and foster their careers. Theological liberalism hardened into radicalism, and in Don Cupitt's case, into belief in a non-real God. Instead of a confident Gospel there was substituted either a sectarian or a tentative voice. Perhaps there was even what has been called 'funda-mental academic fatigue'. So the pendulum swings far from one side to the other; and doubtless will swing back again. We cannot explain these great movements of the Spirit. They are a mystery. 'I don't think I shall ever know the reason for that great resurgence of Christian belief and practice in the fifties', writes one correspondent. Another says: 'It pushes one in the realm of mystery.' A lecturer can only point to some psycho-logical and sociological factors and describe the scene as he knew it. Why did it happen? I think it would be best to end with a verse from St John's Gospel (3:8): 'The wind bloweth where it listeth, and thou hearest the sound thereof, but canst not tell whence it cometh or whither it goeth: so is everyone that is born of the Spirit.'

Bibliographical note

For further background, see V. H. H. Green, *Religion at Oxford and Cambridge* (London, 1964). Other works referred to are *Soundings*, ed. A. Vidler (Cambridge, 1962); D. M. MacKinnon and others, *God, Sex and War* (London, 1963); H. Montefiore, *Truth to Tell* (London, 1966).

6 Mervyn Stockwood, a personal recollection

DAVID OWEN

Arriving in Cambridge

I want to try to capture the atmosphere of Cambridge in the autumn of 1956. I was an eighteen-year-old medical student. I had just come from my first experience of earning my own living helping to build a sewage plant in Plymouth. During that summer the Suez controversy erupted. I will never forget it because it taught me a new view of life. I had hitherto instinctively taken an *Observer* newspaper, anti-government, anti-Anthony Eden view on Suez. One day the best-selling *Mirror* newspaper (this was in the days before the *Sun*) printed a slashing attack on Anthony Eden, and during our lunchtime break the Irish labouring force, who formed the majority of the workforce, were absolutely incensed about what they saw as an attack on Britain, and they vowed that they would never buy this newspaper again. What Anthony Eden was doing, they said, was absolutely right, and the Egyptians (wogs or gippies, and I've no doubt a few other pejorative terms) were absolutely in the wrong. It was the first time that my eyes were opened to the fact that there is in this country a very strong strand of working-class patriotism – and that includes the Irish. This group are not by any means always identified with the Labour Party; and their politics are not always the outcome of rational thought but follow deep emotions. Henceforth I never assumed that I could anticipate the political positions of anyone in any walk of life.

So, it was a somewhat changed young man who arrived in Cambridge to find the university in a total ferment. It is very hard to recapture those moments, but there was a deep-seated anxiety about the international situation, particularly what was happening in Hungary, and which was unfolding day by day. We felt we had to act. Some of my contemporaries actually dropped their studies and drove to Budapest.

I remember going to a rally on Parker's Piece, where there was virtually no green grass to be seen at all, so packed was it with people. One of the rally's most striking features was that, apart from the normal political speeches, there was a deeply political speech by a rather strange and striking clergyman called Mervyn Stockwood. Then in Great St Mary's Church at 11 o'clock on Sunday 4 November 1956, I heard Mervyn Stockwood preach on the Suez crisis. It was an unforgettable moment. The church was packed to overflowing – the galleries absolutely full all around, and there was a crowd outside who were unable to get in. Mervyn led us through the moral quagmire that faced us all. His words were to me electric, because, among many other things, they had none of the moral equivocation which I tended to associate with the Church of England.Here is an extract to give a flavour of the sermon which Mervyn preached.

> Now let us examine the issue as fairly as we can. Let us take the government case. Anybody who listened to Prime Minister Eden last night [he had given a television broadcast] must, I should have thought, have realised that they were listening to a man who honestly believed he was acting in the best interests of his country. A man does not easily court unpopularity, risk political suicide, divide the nation as it has not been divided for years, estrange our allies and hurt our friends, unless he is absolutely convinced in his conscience that he must do what he is doing, and that ultimately the world will believe that he is right.

That taught me, perhaps, the first lesson about Mervyn, which was his capacity first of all to take on the argument from the other person's point of view. (I later discovered that he had been taught this skill by Aneurin Bevan who believed that you could never really develop an argument of your own until you had first addressed your adversary's argument and that your own argument would be greatly enhanced in the ears of your listeners if you had done full justice to the strength of an argument which you were opposed to.) Mervyn made it clear that no nation and no party could be proud of its record in the Middle East. He said: 'It is a squalid tale of deception, broken promises and double crossing, and, if we as a nation or as a party say we have no sin, we deceive ourselves, and the truth is not in us.'

Then he went on to say:

> What of the other side? The basic charge of the critics is that the British, by taking the law into their own hands, by acting as their own judge, by disregarding their covenanted word, have committed a crime against the whole edifice of international law. The fact that we have shocked our allies, dismayed our friends, united the Arabs against us, brought comfort to the Communists, is not what matters most. What does matter is that Britain, thought to be leading the

world towards a new international conception of law and order upon which the future of civilisation depends, stands convicted by sixty-four nations, and we find ourselves in the dock alongside Soviet Russia.

And this was the tragedy – that, as he spoke on 4 November, we all feared that the actions that had been undertaken in Suez, with Britain and France putting themselves on the wrong side of international law, were going to be used by the Russians as a justification for stamping out the revolution in Hungary. And two days later Soviet tanks rolled into Budapest. For my generation, things were never the same again, particularly for those of us on the left who might have flirted with Communism. The nakedness, the sheer oppressive nature of Soviet Communism was revealed for all to see and I, for one, never forgot it. Furthermore, it was reinforced for me in Czechoslovakia when the Soviet military stamped on the flowering of the 1968 Prague Spring.

Mervyn reminded us that people like himself had grown up during the First World War and suffered acute bereavement – as practically everybody had – and had then lived through Abyssinia, Mussolini and Hitler, fought from 1939 to 1945, and then experienced Hiroshima. They had seriously believed that, with the founding of the United Nations in 1945, something new had been born, something which, although like a child was still weak and immature, would nevertheless grow up to give hope to a poor, sad, war-weary world. He went on to say:

> And our sin last week, and as a Christian I advisedly use the word sin, is that we did our best to kill the child. Although as a nation we may be successful in our political venture, yet our guilt remains. For God is not mocked. What to me is the most tragic thing of all, is that today, when Russia has offended the conscience of the world, instead of being able to condemn her with clean hands, we are in the dock alongside her.

He ended that remarkable sermon by reminding us of a man who had often preached in Great St Mary's Church 400 years ago, Thomas Cranmer, Archbishop of Canterbury. He told us that we should use the words that are known to English-speaking people throughout the world, and that we should say together the general confession, and to say it, not just for ourselves, not just for our country, but for the tragic disorder that rebellious man has brought to this world.

It was controversial of course. The city council was so outraged that the university church had not supported what they felt to be the proper

Tory party line that they declined to attend the traditional Remembrance Day service a few weeks later. It was however a boycott for which Mervyn was profoundly grateful. When the word went round that the Remembrance Day service was being boycotted by the mayor, the church was packed with undergraduates on that occasion as well, with queues around the market place.

But although there were Conservatives both in Cambridge and around the country who were incensed and furious about the sentiment of that sermon, I think there were very few Conservatives who were actually in the church that day who were incensed. For they had listened to their vicar honestly try to put the issues, and to come to firm and clear conclusions based on Christian principles. I personally found that to be the crucial element in Mervyn's character.

Mervyn's table talk

No record of Mervyn's ministry at Great St Mary's can avoid recounting his anecdotes and recollections. He enjoyed telling how he had been asked to consider going to the university church at Oxford about three years before he came to Cambridge. However, the then Bishop of Oxford (Kenneth Kirk) was very traditional and High Church and firmly rejected the choice of Mervyn, remembering previous disruptive vicars of that church. Then three years later, he was asked to go to his own university church. Previously, Great St Mary's had had a don from Trinity College as its vicar. Until the end of the last century all dons had to be clergymen so it was not difficult to find someone for Great St Mary's from amongst the Trinity dons. They did many jobs in the town and being vicar of Great St Mary's was one of them, because Great St Mary's was never quite a parish church in the way we understand it. It was however becoming harder to find Trinity men – preferably nearing retirement and of sufficient means to maintain themselves on the modest stipend provided. Considering the difficulties the college was remarkably successful in finding able men.

Let Mervyn himself take up the story.

> When my predecessor, Canon Essex, retired in 1954, they tried again to find a suitable incumbent. First they tried Canon Raven, Master of Christ's College, a very distinguished theologian and Regius Professor of Divinity. He was a great preacher, and he had married for the second time to an American millionairess. Now,

unfortunately, she had died on their honeymoon, so he seemed ideal. But Raven, who was a great prophet and an outstanding man in so many ways, declined. Then a couple of other candidates also turned the job down. Raven then firmly said that it was time things changed. There should be a vicarage (which the church had never had before) and a proper salary for the incumbent (which in those days was about £700 a year). And so it finally came to me.

He would continue, with clear enjoyment when he used the word 'ordinary':

I set out to run the church as an ordinary sort of church for the first time in its history. When I arrived there was an eight o'clock communion service, attended by about ten or twelve people. Then mattins at eleven, attended by another handful and evensong at half-past six attended by people from the town. The university really had nothing to do with the church. The church only became the university church every Sunday afternoon and then the vicar simply had no rights in it except at the altar. The bishop used to ask me to go to sit in his chair at the altar from time to time to remind the university that they had no authority over the sanctuary. The university sermons were learned sermons on very technical theological subjects, drawing a congregation of something like thirty to forty people, except for those days when a very distinguished person like the Archbishop of Canterbury or some very controversial person like Bishop Barnes of Birmingham preached, when people would flock in. Nobody could make out whether I was High Church or Low Church but they did know that I was not 'long' church. I could not stand any service that went on for more than one hour.

Mattins was celebrated strictly in accordance with the Book of Common Prayer, but again things were kept short. Short lessons and a short psalm, and the preacher was told that he would always be in the pulpit by twenty-five minutes past eleven. After the sermon there were never more than three prayers. Slowly the thing built up and before long there were occasions when the congregation numbered 1,500. There would be one queue down King's Parade to Corpus Christi College and another around the Market Place. He tried to make evensong, which was mainly for the town, as lively as possible. Then there was a service at 8.30 for both the university and the town. He started a daily mass and a daily mattins and evensong which he claimed had never happened before in the history of the church. Each weekday began with mattins and communion, and a half-hour meditation every day during term. And there was always evensong.

He claimed that during the term he never took a day off and was always present at every service. That was for many reasons. For one thing, he thought that it was very important to be accessible to the undergraduates. And, secondly, he knew that there would be criticism that the church was just a place for left-wing politics or for atheism or for all the other things of which people liked to accuse it. Sometimes he was criticised for being too left-wing and not praying for the Queen enough. He said,

> Look here, before I came here the Queen was prayed for at mattins and evensong about three times a week, and now we have three services a day and sometimes more, so the Queen is prayed for about thirty times a week. Can you tell me any time since the building of this church that there have been more services provided or where the undergraduates have a greater part to play?

Of course a bachelor could do all sorts of things which one could not expect a married man to do. He remembered,

> Almost every night I was out, going round the colleges. Of course, in those days you had lock-up and, many times, like St Paul, I had to be let down over the wall – although not actually in a basket! I can't tell you how many times that happened. I reckon it was very rare for me ever to finish my day's work until after midnight, sometimes two or three in the morning. Sometimes I would even be in the college all night. I was only thirty nine, something of that sort, at the time.

He had an unusual and surprising, but also visionary, range of interests and commitments. He had always been interested in psychical research and he used to get well-known mediums to come to Cambridge to talk on psychic phenomena. He found Cambridge a sympathetic environment for this interest, and at least one professor shared his enthusiasm. There are reports of a visit to a certain Mrs. Twigg, a medium in London, with notes taken as part of an experiment.

He was also a great believer in the priesthood of the laity. He brought them in as much as possible. The readings – both epistle and gospel, which in those days was regarded as the vicar's job – were always read by the laity.

Mervyn's personality

Now what about Mervyn the man? He gave an address to a group of theological students on Ash Wednesday that same year, 1956, and I want to recall his words. I do not believe Mervyn was a great thinker. I do not think that he himself considered himself a great thinker; nor was he a great wizard when it came to the written word, but he had the capacity to use the spoken word in a very remarkable way. He said this to those students of theology:

> Religion has been described as what a man does with his loneliness. It is, of course, an inadequate definition, but it is partly true. Have you ever thought of how little you know of other people? Even your closest friend or fiancée? How little you know of yourself, of those strange moments of awareness, doubt, or queer exaltation, of agonising despair? And the Christian life is a paradox. On the one hand we must be gay and light, be passionate, understanding, giving ourselves in friendship to anybody and everybody, and in so doing we may attract a host of friends. On the other hand, in spite of the friends and the laughter, we know that in large tracts of our life we are quite alone. And it is there, especially, that we stand before God and pray that He may abide in us and we in Him. You will appreciate that we are now dealing with things that are difficult to put into words, but as this realisation of the loneliness develops, it should lead us beyond despair to a yearning desire for union with God, and for that identification with the eternal which makes us most truly individual.

Nobody knows the inner thinking of any man, but I believe that these words summed up a great deal of what Mervyn was: on the one hand a strangely gregarious showman, apparently super-confident; and yet, on the other hand there was a man who spent hours on his knees, who was strangely humble, who agonised over his religion. A man who wanted in a way to live a more simple life than that of the bon viveur which he slipped naturally into, and who really thought he would only have been capable of existing on a frugal diet in a monastery. We all knew, of course, that he would only have been able to live in a monastery where wine was a fairly basic ingredient in the diet!

In 1958 Mervyn gave eight addresses during Lent in Great St Mary's which were published by SPCK as *The Faith Today*. In the fourth of these addresses entitled 'The Cross', Mervyn invoked the words and the thoughts of someone who was, really, his hero, Archbishop William Temple. Mervyn told us that Archbishop Temple had begun an address to a university audience on the meaning of the Cross with two quotations. The first was 'Let there be light, and there was light', and the second quotation was 'And Jesus was parted from them about a stone's cast and he kneeled down and prayed saying "Father if thou be willing, remove this cup from me. Nevertheless, not my will but thine be done." And being in an agony he prayed more earnestly, and his sweat was, as it were, great drops of blood falling down upon the ground.' And then Mervyn went on to say this:

> In those two quotations there is depicted the difference for God between creating a universe with all its millions of stars, and the making of a selfish soul into a loving one. To create was easy. But to convert a heart, like our hearts, from the self-centredness which is natural to them into the love which is God's own nature which they must reach if they are to be in fellowship with Him, costs the agony and the bloody sweat, and the death upon the Cross.

And he asked his audience to remember that contrast – creating the universe, and converting a single human heart – as we tried to come to grips with the scandal of Christ's death, because it would help us to see the situation in true focus.

So there was a deeply spiritual side to Mervyn's religion and, quite frankly, without it he would never have packed Great St Mary's. Nor would the appeal that he had for undergraduates then ever have been so potent. Whatever the students, however young they may be, or can or cannot do, without doubt they can spot a fraud and if they had believed that Mervyn, with all his flamboyance, with all his admitted failings, was a fraud, they would never have been there. They believed, and I believed then and I believe today, that subsequent events showed he was an exceptional man, definitely worth listening to.

But another fascinating aspect of Mervyn's time was that he did not often ask people to come to listen to him. It sometimes seemed to me that we very rarely heard from him. Rather, what he managed to do was to assemble a quite remarkable galaxy of talent to speak to us, particularly politicians. I heard Aneurin Bevan speak on two occasions: the first time when I was aged eleven, when I went to a meeting in Devonport Guildhall, an occasion which made a tremendous impression on me. The second occasion I heard Aneurin Bevan speak was in Great St Mary's. Bevan had a fairly pronounced stutter. I do not remember much of what he said but I remember how he said it. At one time he described a golden salver and said it 'ssh-sh-ssh-sh-shimmered', and I tell you that, as he spoke, the gold shimmered before my eyes. I saw then how you could use a speech impediment to dramatise words and to use them in a way that enhanced their meaning and lent cadence to an utterance. It was an amazing speech. A great many other people of all political persuasions became Mervyn's friends and acquaintances. It is worth trying to recall some of the influences in his life. One of the strongest was Sir Stafford Cripps, the Labour Chancellor of the Exchequer. Another was the Conservative Member of Parliament for Bristol, Walter Monckton, and Minister of the Crown. It was an extraordinary feature of Mervyn's life that he had many close friends who were quite prominent Conservatives, but were as devoted to him as were members of the Labour Party. Mervyn himself was a Conservative as a young man, something one tends to forget. Then he was greatly influenced by his experiences in a very poor part of Bristol before he came here to Great St Mary's. The thing that had counted most in influencing him to become a committed member of the Labour Party was his feeling that the church had lost touch with ordinary people. He described this feeling in the introduction to a book called *The Cross and the Sickle*, published in 1977, in which he wrote about Soviet Communism, and to which he asked me, as Foreign Secretary, to contribute a Foreword.

He described Stafford Cripps as one who

> coupled socialist conviction and Christian devotion. He was a brilliant lawyer who joined the Labour Party when he felt that the religious organisation to which he belonged would make no real impact. As the so-called National Government lurched from folly to disaster, Cripps moved further to the left and became the red bogey man of the press. Distrusted by the moderates in his party, he adopted an independent position and was expelled. [Mervyn was also expelled from the Labour Party at this stage when he became a supporter of Stafford Cripps.] Distrusted by the moderates, however, his following was considerable, not least among those who were convinced that massive social reforms were long overdue. As I was now among their number I became an eager disciple. Few churchmen shared my conviction. Bristol Cathedral refused to allow Stafford Cripps to preach to the youth organisations of the city, and his own clergyman in Gloucestershire banned him from reading the Scriptures at morning service for fear that the gentry would be offended. It was experiences of this sort that made me reconsider much of what I had been taught in church and theological college.
>
> Matters came to a head when I was denounced in the press for opposing Chamberlain's deal with Hitler at Munich, and when some months later I was reported to MI5, it dawned on me that religion, especially as practised by the Established Church, was being used to supply the spiritual varnish for the *status quo*. It talked about brotherhood and justice, but it was usually on the side of those forces in society which were determined that changes should be restricted to modest amelioration. Moreover the congregation of

the churches, and still more of the legislative assemblies were desti-
tute of representatives of the working classes. The Church of
England was, as it still is, largely a middle-class institution. A
national church it certainly was not.

He wrote this when he was Bishop of Southwark.

The person who spent a considerable time persuading Mervyn to
leave us in Cambridge and go to be Bishop of Southwark was Harold
Macmillan, then Conservative Prime Minister. Again, one meets the
paradox in Mervyn's life. He was passionate about his politics, but he was
actually in many respects a moderate in his political views, with little
understanding of extremism. Religious revival was going on in
Cambridge in the late 1950s and this was not just happening in Great St
Mary's. Mervyn agonised probably too much about whether or not he
should go to Southwark. He rather enjoyed this period when people were
wondering 'will he, won't he?' The whole idea of saying no to being
Bishop of Southwark rather appealed to him. I have always thought it
was the prospect of going into the House of Lords that finally clinched
his decision, though, of course, he did not automatically enter the House
of Lords by becoming Bishop of Southwark. When he gave his farewell
sermon there was hardly a dry eye in the audience. I want to quote something of what he said in this sermon.

> Throughout I've been anxious for you to realise that the church is
> the divinely created community concerned with moulding the stuff
> of society, and with incarnation itself in the rough and tumble of
> human experience. And I have been anxious that you should bring
> your intellectual resources to bear upon your faith, to follow where
> reason leads, and to relate what is said here to what is said in the
> lecture room and the laboratory. For the Christian faith, like the
> Christian church, is not a departmentalised issue. If properly
> understood both give coherence and meaning to every issue.

At Great St Mary's issues were being discussed that we were indeed
discussing in the Medical School laboratories and the other departments
of the university – eugenics, abortion, homosexual law reform – as well
as religious questions such as the truth of the Virgin Birth. After services
had ended, at the back of the church (which Mervyn called Mars Hill)
the preacher was subjected to very considerable questioning, and vigor-
ous discussion took place. I remember Archbishop Ramsey preaching a
sermon in Great St Mary's, no doubt after having had two or three other
services that Sunday. After two hours of discussion, with the Archbishop

having to answer questions throughout, Mervyn said, 'Look, this cannot go on any longer, I'm going to take the Archbishop home; I'm going to take him back to bed.' Archbishop Ramsey seemed to me the most 'Christian' Archbishop who has held that office since Temple, and the effect of hearing him has never left me.

The final thing that Mervyn said to us, in his farewell sermon preached on 8 March 1959, at the 8.30 pm service, was this:

> And if you and I are to register in the twentieth-century world, it means that behind the normal exterior, behind the laughter and the argument, behind the brilliant brain, the carefully trained mind, must be the experience of the mountain ledge, the loneliness, the wind brushing the face, the marks of the Passion, and that moment of supreme revelation, when the Spirit speaks, bone of my bone and flesh of my flesh, and so we find our consummation and our peace.

Earlier in that sermon he had spoken of man being at bottom a lonely creature; 'no matter how close one's ties might be with other people, much of one's life was spent alone'. I suspect that this most gregarious of men spent far more of his life alone than any of us were ever conscious of. Yet he brought something unique to a generation of undergraduates in this church and to all those parishioners who knew him during the period that he worked and preached here. His incumbency was in the highest traditions of Great St Mary's and of what this church has accomplished for Cambridge. I personally owe Mervyn an immense debt, and if I have discharged it with this tribute even in one little particle, then I am a happy man.

7 Vicars of Great St Mary's 1959–1994

JASON BRAY

Joe Fison 1959–1963

Mervyn Stockwood's last service at Great St Mary's was on Easter Day 1959. Undoubtedly he had made a remarkable contribution to the life of Great St Mary's. He was exceptionally energetic and had a clear vision of what he wanted. He introduced many features into Great St Mary's which we in the Anglican church have come to regard as standard for a parish church, such as parish communion on Sunday mornings, or preachers from other denominations, but which were then surprising innovations. His courage to do these things in the face of sometimes very stiff opposition was one of the important factors of his ministry.

According to canon law, when the incumbent of a parish is appointed to be a diocesan bishop, as happened in the case of Stockwood, it is the crown, and not the patrons of the parish – in the case of GSM, Trinity College – which appoints a successor. Such was the case with the appointment of the next Vicar of Great St Mary's – Joe Fison.

One of the things that has surprised me in working on this chapter has been the fact that almost everyone I have spoken to has told me that Joe Fison was not in GSM for very long. What they do not seem to realise is that he was there for around the same amount of time as Mervyn Stockwood. Possibly 'he wasn't there very long' is an unconscious acknowledgement that his impact on the life of the church was not as great as that of his immediate predecessor or indeed of his successor. Or possibly it is a reflection more on the character of Fison which appears to have affected people like a strong gust of wind: powerful in its intensity while it is present, but, while it lingers in the memory, is soon gone.

Although they were both very remarkable in many ways Joseph Edward Fison was a very different person from Mervyn Stockwood, and it *was* to some extent a surprise to him and possibly to the parish that he was appointed at all. For a start, he was in fact older than Stockwood, having been born in 1906 in Hereford where his father was a teacher at

119

the Cathedral school. Despite having been born in the West Country, both his parents came of East Anglian stock, and it was in East Anglia that Fison spent much of his youth after the early death of his father in 1919. Both his parents came from staunchly religious backgrounds: his father was an Evangelical Anglican, and his mother a Congregationalist. This strongly Protestant background coloured much of his early life, and during his time at Oxford Fison became a founder-member of the re-established Evangelical group OICCU (the Oxford Inter-Collegiate Christian Union). Having read classics, he went on to read theology while in residence, although not technically training, at Wycliffe Hall. Fison felt that his vocation was not to the priesthood, but to be a missionary, and accordingly he tested his vocation by travelling to Africa in the company of Alfred Buxton (a founder-member of CICCU, the Cambridge forerunner of OICCU). While still in Africa, Fison was suddenly asked to become a member of staff at Wycliffe, and having accepted the offer, was duly ordained. A few years later he served on the staff of St Aldate's Church, Oxford, a thriving Evangelical church where the contact he had with both the townsfolk and students would serve him in good stead during his time at Cambridge.

During the war he served as a forces chaplain first in Cairo, and then in Jerusalem, where he developed a friendship with Martin Buber, the great Jewish philosopher. His experiences there provided him with an intimate knowledge of the Holy Land which rekindled his love for the Old Testament and the Jewish people, which had first developed after a briefer stay with the Anglican Bishop of Jerusalem. Also during his time at Jerusalem he married his wife Irene, who gave birth to their first child there.

After the war Fison was a residentiary canon of Rochester, and then sub-dean and parish priest of Truro (the bishop was at that time also Dean of the Cathedral). Both these appointments gave him the opportunity to write monographs on various subjects including a beginners' guide to his beloved Old Testament and a book on the Holy Spirit. In addition to this, Fison was a popular speaker at missions, study and quiet days, and other events, as well as a noted leader of pilgrimages to the Holy Land. Then in 1958 Fison was asked to be Chancellor of Lincoln Cathedral, a post which he accepted. In the meantime the crown offered him the post at GSM, and, after much heart-searching, he accepted, having been released from his promise to go to Lincoln.

Fison was a contrast with Stockwood in many respects. Whereas

Stockwood was a very efficient and organised man, capable of the large administrative burden of running the church which GSM had become in his incumbency, Fison was a man with little administrative skill. It is interesting to compare the time when both of them were diocesan bishops: Stockwood rose to the challenge magnificently, whereas Fison, who was sent to Salisbury, was less of a success on the administrative and routine work fronts, even if he was better loved by his diocese. This basic difference in character is shown in the sermons which Stockwood and Fison preached. Stockwood's sermons were clear, well organised and transferred well to the printed page. Fison, with his strong voice and robust pulpit manner, was sometimes likened to an Old Testament prophet, speaking with no written notes, and going where the spirit led him, the congregation being enthralled because they never knew what he was going to say next, or indeed how he was going to say it. All this is despite the fact that Fison was by far the more scholarly of the two.

A further contrast lay in the fact that while Stockwood was from a High Church background, but had become more liberal, Fison came from a strongly Evangelical background. Over the years, however, he came to value symbolic forms of worship more and more, and during his time as bishop would readily attack both those who 'tape God to the altar' as well as those who 'think they have taped Him to the lectern'. This said, he was apparently never entirely comfortable with the eucharistic vestments which Stockwood had introduced at GSM.

If Stockwood put GSM on the map in his guise as a controversial social reformer, as well as a great preacher, Fison added to the image the power of the evangelist, as concerned with the agnostics in Cambridge as with the people on the edges of the church, Stockwood's concern. However, like Stockwood, Fison also showed great concern over the issues of the day, preaching on one occasion on Britain's entry to the EEC. He kept the same basic format as Stockwood, but was successful in different services: in his time the congregation at the parish communion which Stockwood had instituted grew considerably. Fison, nevertheless, continued Stockwood's policy that as far as its ministry to undergraduates was concerned, GSM was there to supplement the work of the college chaplaincies, and not to replace them.

Stockwood had been very much a social animal, but Fison's great successes were with individuals. F. W. Dillistone, writing of his time at St Aldate's, Oxford – words would be equally applicable to his time at GSM – says,

It was in personal relationships . . . that he proved irresistible. He was so genuinely interested in people and entered so readily into their feelings in life's crises – births, marriages, deaths, that he was soon as well known as a pastor as he was a preacher. He had an extraordinary knack of breaking down barriers of shyness and reserve in every kind of social environment. Without a trace of superiority, either of class or of learning, he drew people out and almost at once they felt completely at ease in his presence. Yet he was not aggressive. It was all spontaneous and natural: no pretence or hypocrisy.

A personal recollection of Joe Fison may serve to illustrate what the average member of the congregation of GSM felt about him. Peter Arthur writes of an encounter during the first year of Fison's ministry:

I suffered a major slipped-disc and was lying at home waiting to go into Addenbrookes Hospital. Joe came to see me. He stood by my bed and looked down at me. 'Peter,' he said quietly, 'You're in pain.' Nothing more; there was no miracle, the pain did not go away, but a great outpouring of love swept over me and I was at peace. He came to give me communion in the old Tipperary Ward at Addenbrookes and, later, at home with my wife, Jean. I treasure the memory of those moments.

Another of the major contrasts with his predecessor, as we have noted already, was Fison's lack of general organisational ability. Again Peter Arthur's recollections shed some light on this subject:

I was on Joe's PCC and was GSM's first Director of Stewardship . . . PCC meetings were a riot and rarely finished before eleven o'clock at night. But, however chaotic were the meetings, they were always fun; there was laughter and a wonderful sense of camaraderie. It did not seem to matter that we never finished the agenda, nor that we were never quite certain what we had decided!

Things were no different in Fison's next appointment: his successor as Bishop of Salisbury, George Reindorp, once remarked of Fison, 'I followed a saint but a saint who kept no files.'

There is, however, a more practical side to Fison's ministry. During his time at GSM he initiated a building programme which would radically alter the shape of the west end of the church. This involved the creation of a series of vestries where the clergy could see visitors in private, and also the installation of toilets since the church had previously been forced to use those in Market Hill. Fison also looked at the situation at St Michael's, a redundant church some yards away from GSM on Trinity

Street. He hoped to turn this into a centre for church activity. The problem of what to do with St Michael's has been a perennial problem at GSM, and although Fison looked into the problem and initiated work there, his solution was by no means the final one.

An important point of contrast with Stockwood was Fison's ability to speak to both sides of the Cambridge community, both the city and the university, and to get them to share some sense of common witness. His ministry was to both town and gown at the same time, whereas Stockwood to some degree always felt himself to have been the vicar of the university church. The more balanced nature of Fison's ministry is perhaps more than any other the reason for the fact that whereas Stockwood, the Anglo-Catholic, had begun the parish communion, it was under Fison, the erstwhile Evangelical, that it really started to flourish – a fact that may have upset Stockwood. When Fison's move to Salisbury was announced one of the parishoners wrote of him: 'Those of us in the town congregation felt how marvellously he drew together the town and gown threads and built up a wonderful sense of fellowship.'

The university, however, plays a large part in the life of GSM, and it was a change in the make-up of the undergraduate constituency which was to cause Fison some difficulties in the latter half of his ministry, and which made the decision to leave GSM easier than it might have been. In the first two years of his incumbency the vast majority of the undergraduates had undergone a period of National Service, and were thus older when they came up to Cambridge. From 1960 onwards the majority came straight to Cambridge from school, and he felt in some sense nervous of them, and they failed to respond to him in the same way as the older undergraduates of earlier years. In fact it may be argued that the reason that GSM enjoyed such a great – and in some ways rather traditionalist – revival in the late 1950s was because of the very fact that students were older – they were arriving in Cambridge when they were the same age as the later students when they graduated. Those who had done their National Service were more disciplined and more mature and were able to remember the austerity of the war years, and had probably had more time to think about what religion meant to them than later students. It is also the case that there was a general, if mild, resurgence of interest in religion in the 1950s, and that, even if the GSM of Stockwood and Fison formed the vanguard of this movement, it was part of a much wider phenomenon. When Fison was appointed to Salisbury, GSM would need a different sort of vicar, a man more attuned to the present and able to rise to the challenges which the 1960s would bring. In this those responsible for the selection of a successor to Fison were highly fortunate in their choice of Hugh Montefiore, surely the man for such a moment as this.

Hugh Montefiore 1963–1970

Hugh Montefiore was born into a Jewish family in 1920, but had become a Christian at school. After Oxford, he trained for the priesthood at Westcott House. A somewhat turbulent curacy followed in Jesmond, a suburb of Newcastle, and then Montefiore returned to Westcott as Chaplain and Tutor in 1951, becoming Vice Principal in 1953. In 1954, after a row with the principal, he left without a job to go to, and was fortunate enough to be offered the post of Dean of Gonville and Caius, and he stayed there, a matter of a few yards from Great St Mary's, until he was appointed its vicar in 1963. He, therefore, witnessed the revival under Stockwood and then Fison from close quarters, becoming a personal friend of both.

Montefiore was a 'Cambridge man' through and through. He knew the town and the structures of the university as well as anyone else, but, when he was appointed to Great St Mary's, he was determined that he would be a parish priest, and not an academic. Accordingly, he resigned his fellowship at Caius and his university lectureship in the New Testament. He is reported as saying, 'I'm all set to give everything I've got to the parish of Great St Mary's.' Montefiore's schedule was punishing, for, in addition to running the busy life of the church with its endless round of services, he insisted on visiting as many people as he could, and, in addition, continued to write and lecture at a ferocious rate.

Montefiore describes the situation when he arrived at Great St Mary's in these terms:

> When I first went . . . I found an almost non-stop Sunday, with a fair inheritance from Joe Fison. What surprised me was the very variety of people at the different services, and the comparatively little mix. There was a small 8 am of about twenty communicants. Parish communion at 10 was around 100-plus, some families, rather middle class, few dons, no undergraduates. There was a largish up-market mattins of about 200 . . . The university sermon at 2.30 pm had a minimum quorum of dons. At evensong there could be a large attendance, between 100–200 I think, mostly humble people from down Mill Road. At the 8.30 pm university service students still came in large numbers, and there were never less (when I first came) than

200, and up to 1,400. The church obviously had the affections of both town and gown, as could be seen by the vast numbers that attended Advent carols (gown) and Christmas carols (town).

It was a source of regret to Montefiore that there was little contact between what were in effect two separate congregations, as he himself said, 'The only real combined town and gown occasion . . . was my Institution with the reception in the university combination room.'

A further disappointment was the fact that the university sermon, which for so long had been at 2.30 every Sunday afternoon, was rearranged: from spring 1966 it replaced mattins on certain occasions in full term. Montefiore, who consulted both Stockwood and Fison about the matter, knew that this was the only way to preserve the link between the church and the university. However, the price to be paid was the relatively large regular attendance at mattins, since the university sermon was off-putting to many of the regular congregation.

Fison's hopes that St Michael's would become a focus for the life of the parish had been abandoned, and when Montefiore became vicar, the church was in the final stages of negotiating the leasing of St Michael's to Caius to be used as the college library. Caius were keen on having St Michael's as their library because, while it is on Trinity Street, it is also surrounded on all sides by the college. Since Montefiore had been Dean of Caius, the college expected, not unreasonably, that the matter would be settled relatively quickly. The matter was in fact settled quickly, but not as Caius had hoped, for Montefiore broke off negotiations, deciding that it should be converted into a parish hall. In June 1964 he set up an appeal to raise the necessary money. The architect Montefiore appointed to oversee the task was George Pace. By 28 September 1966, the project was complete, and the new parish hall was officially opened by Joe Fison, then Bishop of Salisbury.

The 1960s, of course, saw enormous upheaval in the life of society at large as well as in that of the Church of England. During this decade, the central concerns of the immediate post-war years were sidelined, and a mood of questioning swept away much accepted wisdom. Not the least reason for this mood in the field of religion in the country at large was the publication of Bishop John Robinson's notorious *Honest to God*, which rapidly became, after the Bible, the best-selling religious book of those turbulent years. In Cambridge, however, theological radicalism had arrived somewhat earlier. The process started with the 1961 'Open letter on intercommunion' which a large number of academics, led by Geoffrey

Lampe (then Ely Professor of Divinity), wrote to the Church of England, encouraging it to allow members of all denominations to receive communion in Anglican churches. Slightly later there came a series of lectures organised by the Faculty of Divinity on the subject of 'Objections to Christian Belief'. These were held in the Arts School, and attracted literally thousands of hearers on a weekday evening during term.

Thus in the years before Montefiore's transfer to Great St Mary's theological radicalism was very much to the fore in Cambridge. For his own part, Montefiore was concerned that the ideas current at the time needed to be expounded and responded to correctly and effectively, and was in two minds how he should go about this: whether these aims were best served by an academic theologian, or by a parish priest with a strong preaching role. He chose the latter. Part of the allure of the church for Montefiore was the fact that it had become so well known that the vicar was almost *ex officio* a public figure.

In addition to his own role as preacher and spokesman of new theological trends, Montefiore also invited some of the leading preachers and thinkers of the day to preach, including Martin Niemoeller (who preached on Remembrance Sunday in 1964), Bishop John Robinson, Billy Graham, Enoch Powell, Malcolm Muggeridge, Harry Williams, Kenneth Kaunda – the President of Zambia, and Archbishop Michael Ramsey. Attendances at services to hear these preachers were high, but Montefiore found it difficult to sustain the high numbers for all services, attributing this to the changing theological and social climate of the times.

In his autobiography Montefiore writes of his efforts to have Roman Catholic preachers invited as part of ecumenical initiatives of the 1960s.

> I was determined to have some Roman Catholic preachers, which at that time was forbidden according to the rules of that Church. I thought if anyone could get round this, it would be a Jesuit; and I was right. I invited Father Thomas Corbishley to come and give an address which would not be part of a service. The Bishop of Northampton, in whose Roman Catholic diocese Cambridge lay, was at the time in Rome for the Vatican Council. Corbishley saw him briefly, and said, 'By the way, I've been asked to give an address at Great St Mary's: it's not part of a service' and permission was given. We had the ordinary university service, and after the last hymn I said, 'This service is now ended: we shall sit for a short violin solo as a voluntary.' At the end of this Corbishley preached.

Montefiore was also very much involved in local discussions when it seemed possible that the Methodists would reunite with the Church of

England. The newsletters from his time are full of references to joint services with Wesley Church, King Street, and a series of debates on divisive issues was held. It was a source of great distress to Montefiore that the talks between the two churches came to nothing.

It was during the early 1960s that the liturgical movement was finally revealed as one of the major driving forces in the modern church, and its influence once again was felt at Great St Mary's. In February 1962, the church first used the Series 2 Communion Service for the parish communion on an experimental basis, Montefiore says 'almost as soon as [it] became legal'. By summer 1968, it was being used for the parish communion every week. Another liturgical innovation was the nave altar, which was given as a leaving present by one of the curates, Guy Mindelssohn, in 1965. A further aspect of liturgical change in Great St Mary's was the licensing of lay people to assist with the chalice in October 1967. This was a change which was at first resisted, but, once the lay assistants had been decently clothed with cassocks, it was accepted.

The church also enjoyed a flourishing in pastoral activity during Montefiore's time as vicar. This was often difficult with the town congregation, for in a lot of cases they remained anonymous. With the students he adopted a wholly different policy: 'I wanted to have an "anonymous ministry" to undergraduates, so that they could come and go without being "got at"; but I opened lists for daily readers and servers so as to encourage loyalty among those who did not need to remain anonymous.' Montefiore's sensitivity to students was no doubt as a result of his experiences as Dean of Caius. Much of the burden of the pastoral work in general was borne by the vicar himself, although his team of curates was expected to work just as hard.

Without doubt the most notorious event of Hugh Montefiore's incumbency was the furore over his statement in a public lecture that it was possible that Christ may have had homosexual inclinations. An unrepentant Montefiore describes the events in his autobiography in his own inimitable fashion:

> I still think that the lecture was rather a good one. My argument was that, if Jesus was to reveal God, then there would have to be certain aspects of his character which did this. I analysed those characteristics which he had in common with mankind, those which he shared with the Jews of his day, and those which were peculiar to himself. Among the last named, I especially noted his self-identification with those who were despised in the world's eyes. I pointed out that he was believed not to have been procreated by his

legal father, that he was born away from home like a displaced person, that during his ministry there were times when he did not have anywhere to lay his head, that he suffered the most ignominious death known to the Roman world, and that he died between two revolutionaries. It was as though God, in becoming man, was determined to identify himself with the most despised and unfortunate of his human creation.

I then speculated that it could be that he was also homosexual in orientation. If so, this would fit in with these other points I had made about his identification with the outcast, for the Jews hated homosexuality. I went on to suggest that there could be pointers in this direction. He had not married, and Jewish males were supposed to have produced a male heir by the time that they were twenty, unless they were Rabbis, which Jesus was certainly not; and at the Last Supper St John uses a somewhat strange phrase about him leaning on the breast of the beloved disciple. All this took up barely a page in a twenty page lecture; but the press were there, it was during the silly season, and it was blown up into a colossal scandal.

I realised something had gone badly wrong when I was woken up in the middle of the night with a message that the *Daily Express* wanted badly to speak to me. I drove back to Cambridge, and as I got in the front door of our flat, I heard the telephone ringing. I took the receiver off the hook, and heard a voice say: 'Have you any comment on the Archbishop's statement about you?' Well, of course, I did not know anything about a statement, but the Archbishop, urged on by his lay assistant, had been persuaded to issue a statement, saying of course that I was utterly wrong. That was only the beginning of troubles. All the papers took it up. I was subjected to a barrage of reproof. Over two thousand letters arrived, some of them 'more in sorrow than in anger', but most of them written in a state of fury. Of course these people had no idea of the context in which I was speaking, but had only read a few sentences taken out of a long lecture, and published in the press. Pride of place must go to a Belfast telegram: 'Bible Protestants of Ulster abhor your smear on Christ and charge you with diabolical blasphemy – Ian Paisley.'

I sent a copy of my lecture to the Archbishop and to my Bishop, Ted Roberts. The Archbishop wrote in a very kindly way, ending 'I am sorry you have been involved in a turmoil which I hope will die down.' The Bishop, when he heard the context in which I had spoken, was simply splendid. He said, 'Hugh, I want you to preach on this next Sunday evening, and I will come and sit under you just in front of the pulpit.' So I did. There was a large congregation, and

I explained just what I had said and why I had said it. Of course it was inevitable that there were some members of the congregation who were somewhat distressed. The churchwardens, however, stood by me very strongly, and there seemed to be nothing to do but to ride out the storm. I was, however, grieved that I had caused such pain to so many people, and also that it had given people an opportunity to speak ill of the Christian faith.

A year or so later, in summer 1969, as a result of his schedule Montefiore suffered a collapse. He spent nearly three months off-duty, recovering. He had been under more and more pressure, and now felt that he had given all that he could give to the church. It was now time for him to move, but it would take a brave man to give him an appointment now. The man who was prepared to take the risk was Bishop Mervyn Stockwood, who invited him to be Suffragan Bishop of Kingston late in 1969. Montefiore left Great St Mary's in spring 1970.

Montefiore's incumbency had in some ways been a difficult time for the church. The vicar himself could be exceptionally abrasive, and offended a good number of the congregation, both by his personal style, and by his controversial views. It was a time of theological questioning for the church and also of (mild) liturgical experimentation, both wholly in keeping with the times. During Montefiore's time the onward momentum of Stockwood's revival was kept up, but after Montefiore Great St Mary's, to some extent, needed a period of recuperation. Unfortunately this was not to be the case since its energies were to be expended further under Stanley Booth-Clibborn.

Stanley Booth-Clibborn 1970–1979

If Hugh Montefiore's time at Great St Mary's had been a period of theological discussion and exploration which reflected the intellectual climate of the 1960s, Stanley Booth-Clibborn's incumbency may be characterised as a time of heightened social awareness on a world-wide scale.

Stanley Eric Francis Booth-Clibborn was born in 1924. He studied at Oriel College, Oxford, and then trained for the priesthood at Westcott House. After serving as a curate in Sheffield he spent the period from 1956 to 1967 in Kenya, returning to Britain to become vicar of one of the city centre churches in Lincoln. His time in Africa had a profound influence on his subsequent ministry, adding to his awareness of social and political issues.

Booth-Clibborn apparently regarded the appointment to Great St Mary's with a good deal of trepidation, and gives the following account of his first full Sunday:

> It was Sunday evening, the first Sunday in the university full term. The new vicar was sitting at his desk in his study in the tower, making a few last minute adjustments to the sermon due to be preached shortly at the 8.30 service. Suddenly I noticed that my hand holding the pen was shaking. Good gracious, I thought with shock. Has it come to this already? I've only been in the place a few weeks and I'm going to pieces already. Then the reason for the shaking dawned on me. The whole tower was shaking with the swinging of the bells. I could blame it on the bell ringers after all.

Like many of the vicars of Great St Mary's he found the routine very demanding, especially the round of services on Sunday. At the time these were the same as those Mervyn Stockwood had initiated, the 8.00 said Holy Communion, the parish communion at 9.45, and then mattins at 11.15. In the afternoon the vicar would entertain undergraduates at Sunday tea, where there would be an opportunity to meet the guest preacher. There then followed evensong and finally the 8.30 student service, which was always followed by a debate.

Of these services increasingly the most important was the regular parish communion, which had gone from strength to strength in the years since it had been initiated by Stockwood, and its regular congregation was in many senses becoming the backbone of all activities in the church. Booth-Clibborn recounts:

> My predecessor . . . said to me, 'You know, Stanley, what everyone knows about GSM is the glamour side of it, when you get the famous preachers and with any luck, a good turn-out of town and gown to hear them at the evening service. But never forget that it all depends on your regular congregation, and especially those who come to the parish communion.' And how right he was. It was the congregation which really made the ministry of the church during my years there, and it was wonderful to serve Christ together with them, drawn as they were from almost every side of the life of Cambridge.

It appears, then, that by the time of Booth-Clibborn's arrival the gap between the university and city congregation was finally being closed. The Great St Mary's term card still carried the words 'The University Church is intended to be a supplement to, and not a substitute for College

Chapels', but now it went on, 'All students in Cambridge are welcome to its activities.'

Great St Mary's was, nevertheless, not unaffected by external social trends, and Booth-Clibborn's incumbency coincided with a time of increasing apathy towards religion in general. This was particularly noticeable in the undergraduates who came up to Cambridge at this time. Booth-Clibborn himself noted that he was fighting a losing battle on his own, remarking of his regular congregation:

> I often wished that more of them had supported our ministry to the university through that evening service, started by Mervyn Stockwood in the years when, as Colin Morris once put it, 'large numbers of short-haired undergraduates turned out to praise God in Cranmer's English'. Those days had gone, and it was a hard task and a strain for successive vicars both to tempt the right men and women from all walks of life to occupy our pulpit, and to encourage people to hear them, especially among students.
>
> But there were many wonderful occasions at those evenings with even the galleries crowded with people who had come to hear distinguished preachers of every denomination. I was particularly grateful to successive Archbishops of Canterbury who found time for us in the midst of all the pressures, and even stayed behind to face a barrage of questions. Sometimes the turn-out was small, though as I was reminded by Lord Longford as I whispered an apology as we processed in together, 'many a politician would be grateful for an audience like this'.

One of the occasions when Great St Mary's was full to capacity (and beyond) was on 10 June 1977, when Mother Teresa of Calcutta delivered an address to some 1,300 people who packed the church and the church-yard, where there was a live relay set up. She was introduced by Malcolm Muggeridge. A collection was taken in aid of her Sisters of Charity which totalled more than three thousand pounds, and included some items of jewellery.

From the parish's point of view, however, probably the most important series of events were those with which Great St Mary's celebrated the fifth centenary of the commencement of work on the present building in 1978, during which the church was floodlit by the city council. The celebrations lasted for a year, during which an appeal was set up. The appeal raised in excess of ten thousand pounds and the money was divided between the church and a scheme in Milo in Tanzania. Milo originally grew up around a mission station set up as a result of an appeal by David

Livingstone to the university in the Senate House. The aim of the Great St Mary's appeal was to help them to provide hydro-electric power for the local hospital, school and mill. The money that was retained by the parish went to provide the church's first proper choir vestry, a church office and an office which, it was hoped, would be used for ecumenical purposes.

The celebrations themselves started in January with a sermon delivered by Lord Ramsey, former Archbishop of Canterbury. This was followed by a series of sermons by Peter Baelz, then Professor of Pastoral and Practical Theology at Oxford, and later Dean of Durham. Throughout the year former curates were invited back to preach; these included Professor C. F. D. Moule who had served at Great St Mary's before the advent of Mervyn Stockwood. Bishop Mervyn Stockwood (now a fairly regular visitor) returned on 23 April to dedicate some new hassocks and to preach on 'What this church stands for' at 11.15, to be followed by Edward Heath, former Prime Minister, at the university service at 8.30. Two weeks later the then Archbishop of Canterbury, the Most Reverend Donald Coggan, also preached at the 8.30 student service.

During the year, a series of exhibitions was held in the church both on issues of immediate concern to the church like the exhibition on Milo, or the display of old documents pertaining to the church, but also on wider issues such as the exhibition of pictures taken with an electron microscope, or one on the frontiers of space provided by the University Astronomy Department. In the latter part of the year the very active Wider Concerns Committee organised an exhibition called 'Overseas' which highlighted the many contacts which Great St Mary's had with overseas projects.

On Tuesday 16 May 1978 a service of thanksgiving was held at 7.30 to mark the actual quincentenary. The Bishop of Ely, Peter Walker, preached to a congregation which included the mayor, the vice-chancellor, the deputy lieutenant of Cambridgeshire, as well as many other civic and ecclesiastical dignitaries. Five episodes from the history of Great St Mary's were chosen: the Reformation story of the burning of Martin Bucer's corpse; the story of an accident on the tower in which John Warren the churchwarden, was killed; memories of the use of the church by town and gown in the eighteenth century; an account of the ministry of Charles Simeon the great preacher; and some words from Mother Teresa of Calcutta's address from the previous year. These were read by representatives of the Roman Catholic church, one of the serving churchwardens, representatives of the city council and of the university (Bishop John Robinson, then Dean of Trinity College), a Methodist minister as representative of the city centre churches, and a Kenyan priest who was studying in Cambridge at the time.

As well as the special occasions for which Great St Mary's had become well known, the more ordinary life of the church prospered in Booth-Clibborn's incumbency. We have already mentioned the increase in the importance of the parish communion in terms of numbers. At this time another new rite (Series 3) was slowly introduced to Great St Mary's, being first used in January 1972, and regularly from March 1973. A new setting was written for it by Alan Tranah, the Director of Music, who had also written music for Series 2 when that had been introduced by Hugh Montefiore. The 1662 Communion Service (actually in its 1928 revised form) was still being used on occasional Sundays, and on the fourth Sunday of every month there was also communion at 6.30 pm. At the same time as the introduction of Series 3, the Parish Communion was brought forward to 9.30 from its previous time of 9.45. This was to allow the clergy more time between the two services to meet people over coffee, which had now become a regular feature of Sunday morning, and from June 1975 mattins, which had been at 11.00, was moved to 11.15 to allow even more time. Bishop Hugh Montefiore suggests – possibly, one suspects, tongue in cheek – that allowing more time between the two services was a mistake, because previously people had thought that Great St Mary's was better attended than it was because there would always be a queue outside the church waiting for the eucharist to finish before mattins started. In November 1977 the sharing of the peace was introduced at the parish communion.

The main emphasis of Stanley Booth-Clibborn's ministry, as we have suggested, was very much on world-wide social issues stemming in part from his experiences of poverty in Africa. In this he was supported wholeheartedly by his congregation. Many fund-raising activities were organised in addition to those connected with the fifth centenary celebrations. In his first year of office, for example, the vicar ensured that a bell was tolled to mark the beginning of Christian Aid Week as a reminder of hunger and malnutrition in the world, and a few months later a 'starve-in' was held outside the church to highlight the same issues. One of the more regular activities was the fact that church members were encouraged to send charity cards at Christmas, and in later years these were actually produced by the church. Each Christmas a gift table was placed at the back of the church in aid of the needy of Cambridge. In

1974 Christian Aid Week was commemorated by a shack made of tins which was placed on King's Parade and was made by young members of the congregation.

From 1975 onwards, members of the congregation were encouraged to donate 1 per cent of their net incomes to the church, and much of this money went to the World Development Movement, and the rest was shared between such charities as CMS, USPG, Christian Aid, Oxfam, Save the Children, as well as smaller projects sometimes suggested by members of the congregation e.g. the Sanyu Babies' Home in Uganda. One of the more ingenious ways of raising money for charity was a stall which was set up to sell sunflower seeds to passers-by as part of Christian Aid week in 1976. The seeds were then planted in the north-west corner of the churchyard.

The church also raised money for a remodelling of the west end and for the redecorating of St Andrew's Chapel, which was completed in October 1975. The west end project was on a much larger scale. Work started in the summer of 1978 on plans prepared by Gordon Steele to build a new choir vestry, office and study. Much of the money for this came from the Quincentenary Appeal. The result was that excellent facilities were available on church premises, and saved the vicars from the incessant toing and froing to the vicarage on Madingley Road.

Booth-Clibborn's incumbency also saw a proliferation of different organisations in the church serving different age or interest groups. This was a process that went back at least as far as Hugh Montefiore's time with the 'Back Benchers' group that he had initiated for young people. There had been, of course, a branch of the Mothers' Union which Miss Gladys Cannon had run in Mervyn Stockwood's time, but which folded in Joe Fison's time. The Mothers' Union was eventually replaced by the Focus Group for women of any age or status which aimed to foster 'friendship, understanding, growth in Christian faith, and concern for the needs of the community', as the Great St Mary's 'Church Organisations and Information' card put it. The Focus Group was supplemented by the more formal Women's Afternoon Fellowship, which met in church where there would be a short service, an address and a discussion followed by tea.

For younger people there were several groups. The Children's Church met in St Michael's during the parish communion, at which they would appear at the offertory. For eleven- to fifteen-year-olds there was the Thursday Thinkers, which met fortnightly from September 1972, and aimed at 'preparing for Christian life in its widest sense, by developing a sensitivity for one another within the group, and also an awareness of the world around and its needs'. For fourteen- to eighteen-year-olds there was The Group, which met weekly. There was also another organisation called The Fishes, which, while being technically open for anyone to join, was made up mainly of people in their twenties – and in fact originally called the Over Twenty Group. They met in members' homes and their programme included among other things discussions and social activities, as well as more practical things like decorating the curate's house on Eachard Road in preparation for the arrival of David Richardson and his family. The majority of these groups were coordinated by a very active and committed team of lay people.

In addition to the special groups, social events were organised for all members of the congregation such as the annual harvest supper. There was also a series of Great St Mary's evenings, which met periodically in the vicarage, and took the form of discussions or Bible studies.

When in 1979 after a relatively long incumbency, Booth-Clibborn was appointed Bishop of Manchester, his replacement was announced as Michael Mayne, then Head of Religious Broadcasting at the BBC.

Booth-Clibborn's incumbency came at a difficult time for the life of the church in general. It was a time of declining numbers and growing apathy, but, despite this, or possibly even because of this, Great St Mary's became very active in social concerns. However, it is possible that some of this was at the expense of a deeper spirituality. Many of the liturgical innovations which had been introduced by both Stockwood and Montefiore were dropped – the fact that Michael Mayne reintroduced lay ministers for the eucharistic elements is evidence of this. It is also somewhat surprising that such an active church did not have regular Bible study groups, or prayer groups, neither did the parish organise retreats. Furthermore, virtually all the church organisations were concerned with social issues, both internal and external, and rarely was there any mention of any 'religious' activity other than the regular services. When he arrived, Michael Mayne at once became aware of this lack, and sought to rectify it.

Michael Mayne 1979–1986

Stanley Booth-Clibborn left GSM in January 1979 and was consecrated bishop in York Minster on 2 February, and enthroned in Manchester on 15 February. Since he had become a diocesan bishop, the crown was entitled to appoint the next vicar, and chose Michael Mayne, then Head of Religious Programmes on BBC Radio, who was instituted and inducted on 1 June.

Michael Clement Otway Mayne was born in 1929 and had studied in Cambridge at Corpus Christi College, graduating in the same year as Mervyn Stockwood's arrival as Vicar of Great St Mary's. In a letter published in his first university term card, Mayne says of his memories of Great St Mary's when he was an undergraduate: 'I only remember going in twice: once to hear a wise and stirring mission address by Bishop Michael Ramsey, and once to hear a Sunday afternoon university sermon of quite unbelievable tedium.'

After Cambridge, Mayne went on to train for the ministry at Cuddesdon. After a curacy in Harpenden, he became the domestic chaplain to Mervyn Stockwood, then Bishop of Southwark. From Stockwood, Mayne learnt many things, and in some senses their style of ministry was similar: for example Michael Mayne reintroduced the Birthday Book for members of the congregation, and birthdays were then read out as part of the intercessions in the parish communion. The original Birthday Book which Stockwood had started had long since fallen into abeyance.

In contrast to that of his immediate predecessor, Michael Mayne's incumbency was one in which the church became more spiritual and more focused on its life as a community in faith. He writes:

> My initial reactions and immediate concerns on arrival had been that the parish was extremely active, vocal in the field of social and political concern, and rather over-busy. My aim was to make it more prayerful; to build up the fellowship within the Church family; to order the worship with great care; and to present an interesting and challenging series of events on the Sunday nights of term.

The term card for Mayne's first term was a sign of things to come. At the Sunday evening services, the preachers included the Reverend Harry Morton, the General Secretary of the British Council of Churches; Rabbi Hugo Gryn; Gerald Priestland, the BBC Religious Affairs Correspondent; Leonard Cheshire, founder of the Cheshire Homes; Metropolitan Anthony Bloom (the first of three visits he made during Mayne's years); and the Director of Christian Action, Canon Eric James. By this time the university sermon was preached at 8.30 and in Michael Mayne's first term this took the form of the founders' and benefactors' sermon, and was delivered by the distinguished Cambridge church his-

torian, David Thompson. During term time there was no evensong, but
outside term it was held at its old time of 6.30.

For the Sunday evening university service Mayne always tried to
invite preachers who were in the public eye, of whom undergraduates
would have heard, as he says,

> It was almost always someone who was a familiar name to under-
> graduates, and that was quite hard because people go out of fashion
> quite quickly. And it was always politicians or churchmen, artists,
> journalists, all kinds of people who had some sort of religious vision
> in the broadest sense, not always Christians. . . . And planning the
> thing, and getting people to agree to come a term ahead, for the term
> card, and planning it so that it was a balanced kind of thing, that was
> the hardest part of the whole job.

Mayne gives a vivid insight into his hectic life as vicar of Great St
Mary's:

> They [the preachers] would always come to supper first, and I would
> brief them. Then at 8.30 there was a brief act of worship, and then
> it was theirs for thirty to forty minutes for an address, followed by a
> question session until ten o'clock. And some of those question ses-
> sions were very lively indeed. And at 10, we always ended, but there
> were always people who wanted to talk to them, and by the time
> you'd got home, and they'd unwound, and had a drink, and were
> staying the night, it meant a terribly long night.

The problem which added to the strain on the vicar, as Mayne himself
admits, was that the 8.30 student service had simply ceased to appeal to
the average undergraduate.

> During my time it was dying, it began dying in the 1970s under
> Stanley Booth-Clibborn. If you got the right person then you could
> still fill the church, not the galleries, but downstairs – just occasion-
> ally the galleries as well. I remember the great debate between Billy
> Graham and Michael Ramsey, the place was packed. People like
> Hans Kung would fill it, but otherwise, you would get between 70
> and 80 up to about 200, that would be the average. On the whole,
> GSM people didn't come to it, didn't really support it. Occasionally
> I would put three line whips out, and they would, but one could
> understand – it's not the thing one wants to do on a Sunday night.
> I think Cambridge had changed, and students had changed so much
> in what they wanted from when Mervyn came.

Over the years, however, those who did go to the various services were treated to some very fine preaching from, amongst others, Archbishop Robert Runcie (who preached on no fewer than five occasions), Cardinal Basil Hume, the ever popular Michael Ramsey, Hans Kung, Lord Soper, Rabbi Lionel Blue, Lord Coggan, distinguished politicians such as Edward Heath, Shirley Williams, Dr David (now Lord) Owen, Roy Hattersley, and Enoch Powell; literary figures like R. S. Thomas and Christopher Fry. There was a series of dialogues between different public figures such as that between the vicar and Cliff Richard, Bishop John Robinson and Don Cupitt discussing belief, and Dame Cicely Saunders and Brian Redhead discussing death and dying, and also the famous dialogue between Bishop Michael Ramsey and Billy Graham on the Mission of the Church in January 1981. There were also visits from actors and entertainers such as Sir Alec Guiness, Donald Swann, Timothy West and Prunella Scales, and Judi Dench and Michael Williams. The value of the Sunday 8.30 services was possibly summed up by a Cambridge GP, Dr Christopher Cornford, who told the vicar, 'I am very thankful for GSM, for I have been there this year for discussions on nuclear war and on the Third World and the Brandt Report; and because these human concerns are being considered. Many Cambridge people who aren't Christians and don't worship there feel in a strange way that GSM is their church and they belong there.'

As part of his concern to enhance the spiritual life of the parish, Mayne increased the number of daily celebrations of the eucharist, having them at different times of the day so that people would be able to go when it suited them. Another innovation which led in the same direction was the setting up of eight independent prayer groups in different parts of Cambridge. Once these were organised, they ran without any further involvement on the part of the vicar. At the same time a neighbourhood links scheme was launched in an attempt to bring the congregation which is spread throughout Cambridge into closer community. Mayne's incumbency also saw the introduction of the regular Bible study after a short series taken by the Reverend Nicholas Sagovsky, then one of the curates.

One of Mayne's proudest achievements was the production of the splendid *Great St Mary's Service Book*, which was designed to enhance and enrich people's understanding of, and involvement in, the liturgy. It contained the *Alternative Service Book 1980*, Rite A, with a devotional and liturgical commentary on the facing pages. Together with this, it contained suggestions for morning and evening prayers and prayers for use before and after the eucharist. Before the new rite was used for the first time, a series of three teaching groups was held to introduce members of the congregation to it. At around the same time as the introduction of Rite A a number of church members received permission from the Bishop of Huntingdon to administer the chalice. This innovation was first made under Hugh Montefiore, but appears to have fallen into abeyance in the intervening years. A rota of lay people was also formed to bring the bread and wine to the altar at the offertory, and to be involved in the intercessions.

As well as a series of Annual Parish Quiet Days which were held initially in the vicarage, but later at Little Gidding, and an annual parish retreat, Michael Mayne also organised four more formal teaching weeks. Two of these were on prayer and spirituality, one on belief in God and one, aimed mainly at the university, called 'Encounters', which was led by the Archbishop of Canterbury. The first of these courses was called 'The How and Why of Prayer', and was billed as a 'novice's course in prayer and spirituality'. It was led by Bishop George Simms, Dr Una Kroll, Dr Rowan Williams, now Bishop of Monmouth, and Father Bob Ombres. It was held over four days, and included a guided meditation at lunchtime, a prayer workshop in the early evening and more formal sessions later on in the evening.

During Mayne's time the St Andrew's Chapel became increasingly the focus of the spiritual life of the church; and so plans were drawn up to have it redecorated and improved to fulfil this purpose. A figure of the Risen Christ was sculpted by the Hungarian Gabriella Bollobas; a carpet was laid; and a new altar frontal which had been woven by the Benedictine nuns of Turvey Abbey was dedicated. There was also a new tapestry in memory of Geoffrey Wood made by Alec Pearson, which was to hang over the priest's stall; an aumbry light by David Peace; and candlesticks by Gordon Steele. As well as these additions, new and more portable furnishings were made by Tony Woolstenholmes. The chapel was refurbished using money given mainly in memory of Dr Erwin Loewenfeld, Church Treasurer from 1944 to 1973. The chapel was rededicated by the Bishop of Huntingdon on Sunday 25 March 1984, kept that year as the patronal festival.

Perhaps one of the more surprising insights which Michael Mayne provided was his reflections on what the congregation, especially those academics who attended regularly, felt they needed from the church, and needed from its vicar.

When I arrived, I was horrified to find on my first Sunday in the congregation, Geoffrey Lampe, Charlie Moule, Henry Chadwick, Mark Santer, Norman Pittenger, and so on, and I thought, I can't cope with this, all these academic theologians. And I came to realise that what people wanted of that church was the experience of coming to a normal parish church set up where things were done with care, but which was not demanding. They gave of themselves during the week, they were working on an intellectual plane during the week, and they wanted to come to a place on a Sunday where they could actually be relaxed. And they didn't want to be met on a level where one couldn't be. They simply wanted what one could get out of a good normal parish situation. And I think it's very important that GSM didn't have pretensions above its station, even when some of its congregation was quite high-powered.

In the July of 1985 Michael Mayne came down with a serious illness. The initial diagnosis was that it was viral pneumonia, but it later proved to be ME. This put him almost entirely out of action from then until his departure to be Dean of Westminster in June 1986.

Great St Mary's was lucky since Mike Hobart, a churchwarden, was prepared to take over the effective running of the church. His reminiscences provide a valuable insight into the latter stages of Mayne's incumbency:

Michael Mayne was something of a benign autocrat. Round-table discussions between churchwardens and clergy, or with other church officers were never held. The churchwardens met with Michael fairly occasionally, and with a restricted agenda largely set by him. Michael did not delegate. The onset of Michael's illness was, therefore, not only a great personal tragedy and loss of spiritual leadership, but an immense challenge in terms of keeping the show on the road. An *ad hoc* steering group consisting of the assistant clergy and churchwardens formed. There was a most difficult moment when we decided that we needed to take over the decision making and temporarily supplant Michael. This *coup d'état* was a very painful decision and Peter Arthur had to do the difficult bit. In some ways, the challenge was easier than it would have been if Michael had been suddenly removed from the scene, since we had the opportunity of taking advice from him. On the other hand, we had to work more circumspectly than was the case after Michael left, and, indeed, the experience put us in excellent shape for the interregnun which was to come.

Michael Mayne had been totally exhausted by the job of running Great St Mary's. His contribution to the parish had been enormous, but it had been at the cost of his health. The stresses upon him were greater than they had been on any other vicar since he found it exceptionally difficult to fill the church on a regular basis, and, instead of accepting that the days of glory were finally over, he attempted to keep the revival going. It is interesting that he considers the job of Dean of Westminster a good deal less stressful than that of Vicar of Great St Mary's.

David Conner 1987–1994

It was David Conner who was eventually chosen by Trinity to be the next Vicar of Great St Mary's. Conner was in some ways perhaps an unusual choice since he had no previous connection with Cambridge. His academic training had been in Oxford, where he had also been trained for the priesthood at St Stephen's House. The entirety of his ministry had been spent as a chaplain in various schools, although he had acted as a team vicar as part of his duties in one of the schools. Before arriving at Great St Mary's, he had been chaplain at Winchester College. His attention was alerted to the vacancy at a time when he felt that it was time to move on from chaplaincy work, and so he applied for the job.

Conner admits that, although he had of course heard of the church, and of course of Mervyn Stockwood, he had formed little idea of what being the Vicar of Great St Mary's would involve until he arrived on the scene in January 1987. He immediately started to feel the pressure that had caused Michael Mayne so much trouble. The problems were twofold: by the time Conner arrived in the parish there was already an expectation that vicars of Great St Mary's would go on to greater things, and people inevitably said to him from the very moment of his arrival, 'You're not going to be here long.' As a means of coping with this pressure Conner told himself that he would only stay in Great St Mary's for seven years, and that at the end of that time he would start looking for a new job. The second cause of pressure was even greater. All churches to some degree or other hark back to a time they see as a golden age, and if this is true of all churches Conner felt that it was tenfold true of Great St Mary's, because the golden age had in fact been real, not imaginary, and, furthermore, it was within relatively recent memory. The new vicar therefore felt that people were looking to him to start the revival afresh, to do what Michael Mayne had found impossible, to restore Great St Mary's to the ecclesiastical powerhouse it had once been.

By the time Conner came to be instituted as Vicar of Great St Mary's it was increasingly evident that circumstances had changed, and a resurgence of the Great St Mary's revival was virtually impossible given the pervading attitude of the times. Churchgoing in general had, or appeared to have had, reached an all-time low, whereas in the late 1950s when Stockwood was at Great St Mary's, churchgoing was enjoying a great resurgence. There was also a seemingly universal apathy towards any sort of idealistic organisation, and church attendance was further affected by this trend. Furthermore, in contrast with Stockwood's time, the undergraduates who had once formed the backbone of the revival had to work a good deal harder, especially since the harsh economic realities of the late eighties and early nineties meant that not even Cambridge graduates were certain of finding jobs on leaving the university. The undergraduates who came up at this time were also younger than the students who had been forced to do National Service in the 1950s, and were in general a more sober lot than their predecessors. All these external factors meant that the likelihood of a repeat of Stockwood's success was nearly impossible – indeed even Stockwood himself would almost certainly have found the going tough.

A further, perhaps more deep-seated cultural change which made the external circumstances of Conner's time different from those of Stockwood's was the move that Conner noticed away from the spoken word as a medium for expressing and conveying the depths of religious experience, and he suggests that music has by and large taken its place in this regard. When he attended one of the first deans' and chaplains' meetings, he recalls that they said that there were only three speakers in the world who could guarantee a full house: one was Mother Teresa, one was the Pope and one Desmond Tutu. And indeed the only time during Conner's incumbency when Great St Mary's was full to capacity was when Desmond Tutu was invited to give a public lecture. On that occasion, and that occasion only, the vicar was forced to close the doors and turn people away. However, more generally the only times when the church was full was for the Christmas carol service which Great St Mary's held for the town and for other such musical occasions. Indeed Conner recalls that it was never difficult to attract large numbers of people to any sort of musical event. Particularly memorable for him was the visit of the great cellist Paul Tortelier, who came to Great St Mary's to give a masterclass not long before his death, and in whose playing

Conner found the depths of religious experience expressed in audible form.

Because of this shift from words to music, Great St Mary's invested time, money and effort into all sorts of musical endeavour. The parish organ was refitted and restored, and a paid Director of Music was appointed. It was also at this time that the church choirs came into their own, so that between them, at any one time, there were often more than sixty young people in either the parish choir or the girls' choir.

This is, of course, not to say that the preaching ministry of the church was in any way neglected. University sermons continued to be given, and for the first few years the 8.30 student services also continued, although their importance decreased as time went on. However, Conner felt that it was the ministry to the regular 9.30 parish communion that was becoming more and more important, and indeed to a very great extent during his time *that* congregation became in effect *the* congregation. This was particularly the case because by the time Conner came to exercise his ministry in Cambridge, undergraduates were being actively encouraged to attend the 9.30 parish communion, whereas previously, they had been discouraged from attendance, and encouraged to go to their college chapels. Nevertheless, the vast majority of members of the congregation were not undergraduates, but people from the town, or senior members of the university. However, despite the fact that the 9.30 congregation was meeting for a celebration of the eucharist, Conner still perceived that the major reason they were there was to be fed in some way by a sermon, not necessarily a long treatise-type sermon, but a solid piece of teaching, lasting between ten and twenty minutes. Despite his Anglo-Catholic training at St Stephen's House, Conner did not attempt to alter in any significant way the already rather Catholic liturgy that he had inherited from Michael Mayne, although he did place a great emphasis on the importance of the already established pattern of daily celebrations of the eucharist, and on the saying of the daily offices. The prayer groups and the neighbourhood links which Mayne had introduced flourished during this time, and in this way the main town congregation continued to grow and to nurture itself.

Ministry to the university community still continued to play a very significant part in the life of the church, but Conner was very careful to ensure that Great St Mary's did not enter into competition with either the college chapels or with the other city centre churches, and Great St Mary's did not attempt at this time to be all things to all undergraduates. There was in fact a general feeling at the time that all religious institutions had fallen on hard times, and that unwelcome rivalry would cause more problems than it would solve. Collaboration became more than ever the order of the day. So for example if one of the other city centre churches wanted to put something on for students at 8.30 on Sunday evenings, Conner's policy was that there should be nothing at Great St Mary's to allow any who wanted to go to the other church to do so. Throughout his time, relations between the clergy of the city centre were good, and they would meet to pray together at least once a week. Conner felt that the best way to minister to undergraduates and other students was to organise small discussion and Bible study groups for them, and this continued throughout his ministry, to the extent that, a few months before he left, he was one of the prime movers in organising an Affirming Catholicism group, mainly made up of people from Westcott House, but open to all.

However, Conner ensured that the ministry of Great St Mary's in his time was not solely focused on the university or the 9.30 congregation. He tried to develop a role for the church as a parish church for the whole of the town centre, thus recalling the church's ancient name, St Mary's in the Market Place. As part of this ministry he ensured that the church was always open during the day so that people could come in at any time and find a quiet space in the middle of a busy day. He attempted to make sure there was always a member of the staff – preferably a priest – at hand to give advice to occasional visitors. So over the years a steady stream of townsfolk came to the church for advice or help of some kind. This also facilitated his broadening of the church's ministry to other visitors – tourists and the like. They were encouraged to come in, and possibly to say a prayer, and the concept of pilgrimage was developed to embrace them. At the evening office prayers were always said for these pilgrims, and any prayer requests they may have made were offered.

A further group of people on whom the ministry of the church was focused was the increasingly large numbers of homeless and disadvantaged people living in and around the centre of Cambridge. This was not always a popular ministry with all members of the congregation at all times, but the vicar was determined that Great St Mary's should support such organisations as Wintercomfort and the Emmaus Foundation, who help such people.

Perhaps the most important symbol of the refocusing of ministry at Great St Mary's during the incumbency of David Conner was the final abandoning of the 8.30 student service on Sunday. There had been a slow and steady decline, and by the time of Michael Mayne it had become almost impossible to sustain. Under Conner it reached the stage where the vicar was more often than not embarrassed by the small turn-out. It also became evident that the people who did turn out on a Sunday evening were much more likely to be from the town congregation than from the undergraduate body. Times had changed, and David Conner was forced to take the decision that the 8.30 services had outlived their function, and simply did not attract sufficient numbers of students any more. For him the decision was a hard one, but he may have felt in a better position to take it, since, unlike Mayne, he had no personal loyalty to Mervyn Stockwood. In some ways Conner feels that it was an admission of defeat, but the church still had its increasingly healthy ministry to undergraduates who were, perhaps more than ever before, increasingly integrated into the mainstream life of the church. This change in tack in the ministry of the church, and the recognition that, particularly with regard to undergraduates, it was impossible to recapture the past, made a significant difference to the amount of pressure under which the vicar found himself: whereas being vicar of Great St Mary's had nearly killed Mayne, Conner appeared to come out of it relatively unscathed, describing the experience as 'invigorating'.

Conner was no doubt helped in this by the formidable team of volunteers and officers that a church as lively as Great St Mary's is capable of producing, and he and the other clergy attempted to work together with them, perhaps in contrast to the benign autocracy of Mayne. Conner pays particular tribute to Giles Ecclestone who was the Great St Mary's curate during the interregnum, and for the first part of Conner's incumbency, and who made Conner's arrival much easier having made arrangements for the events of the first half-year or so. During Conner's time one of the curates was also Chaplain of Girton, a post which enhanced Great St Mary's relations with the university.

In conclusion, one could say that Conner was a very gifted, pastorally sensitive incumbent, who ministered at a time when Great St Mary's was being forced to face the fact that the world and the university to which it ministered had changed significantly. The years of radicalism and experimentation were over. More than anyone else Conner – perhaps because he had no preconceived ideas about the church – was able to foster an atmosphere where the congregation did not feel that the name of the church had to be on everyone's lips all the time. Pastoral care for the 9.30 congregation and a changed, more personalised ministry to individual members of the university became the order of the day, although the more formal ancient links with the university were maintained. The great revival was finally and emphatically over. Now it was time for the church to relax, and face the changed situations of the late 1980s and 1990s . It was time to take stock, to let the past be the past and to allow Great St Mary's to become the normal city centre church it had perhaps never been before.

David Conner left in January 1994 to be Suffragan Bishop of Lynn in the Norwich Diocese He was replaced by John Binns, then at Holy Trinity, Tooting, in the Diocese of Southwark, a graduate of St John's College, Cambridge, who had trained at the College of the Resurrection, Mirfield, and had recently completed a doctorate on Patristics from the University of London, a new incumbent to face a new set of circumstances.

Bibliographical note

I have drawn extensively on letters, transcripts of interviews and other documents in the Great St Mary's archives. In addition there are several biographies – and one autobiography – about the figures discussed here. Joe Fison's life is covered in F. W. Dillistone, *Afire for God, the Life of Joe Fison* (Oxford, 1983), see for the passages quoted pp. 27, 132, 33, 140, 89. Hugh Montefiore's is the subject of both J. S. Peart-Binns, *Bishop Hugh Montefiore* (London, 1990), and I have quoted from pp. 163, 110; and Hugh Montefiore, *Oh God, What Next?* (London, 1995), see pp. 130, 144–5. Some of the sermons preached during Hugh Montefiore's incumbency were published as *Sermons from Great St Mary's* (London, 1968). For some of the background to the religious life of post-war England, see Adrian Hastings, *A History of English Christianity 1920–1990* (London, 1990), especially pp. 141–2, 536.

PART THREE
The building

8 The fabric and furnishings

LYNNE BROUGHTON

Great St Mary's is a grand building in the Tudor Perpendicular style, dominating the market place of Cambridge and complementing its more famous sibling across the road, King's College Chapel. On entering, however, many visitors feel a sense of surprise. Darkened by the galleries, filled with brown woodwork and with its intricately carved roof equally dark, the interior may not immediately attract. But the furnishings have considerable historic interest and can best be understood in the context of the theological and liturgical developments which have occurred in the centuries since it was first built.

Original state

The church is built of high-quality creamy-coloured limestone, with a much altered chancel essentially of the early fourteenth century. Nave and tower were rebuilt in the late fifteenth to early sixteenth century to a design almost certainly by John Wastell, who was working on King's College Chapel at the time and who also designed the contemporary church at Saffron Walden. The latter can give a good idea of what Great St Mary's would have looked like without the galleries; spacious, elegant and filled with light. The wardens' accounts for 1522 twice mention stone brought from Weldon, a quarry the other side of Peterborough. It was brought by water and unloaded at Jesus Green. By this date the main body of the church was finished and being richly furnished; the entry refers to stone required for the tower or vestry, both still under construction. But it is likely that the same stone had been used for the earlier work. The highly carved stone of the interior is clunch, a local stone, used also in the Lady chapel at Ely. A kind of chalk, it is unsuitable for exterior use because of its poor weathering qualities but soft enough for intricate carving.

The nave is said to have been finished in 1519, but it may have been in use well before that date. The great inconveniences of such major rebuilding programmes were generally ameliorated by methods which allowed use of the church, or part thereof, for as long as possible. Aisles and arcades were frequently built just outside the outer walls or arcades of the previous church, which could thus remain in use until the time came to cut through the walls and remove the old arcades. This may explain why the present nave is wider than the tower, which has been extended on its east side to provide abutment for the arcades. The tower may have been built on the foundations of a predecessor. Once the new arcades and lower walls had been built the partially completed church could be temporarily roofed. This made the new work inhabitable while providing a stable platform for those working on the clerestory walls and roof.

The nave roof is of flat pitch, its tie-beams supported on curved braces with traceried spandrels. The large roof bosses contain some figure carvings. These include two demi-angels holding a shield with the crowned monogram MR for Maria Regina – Mary (the Virgin), Queen (of Heaven); St Michael fighting the dragon; a Pelican-in-its-Piety; a priest kneeling before a crucifix; and two demi-angels holding a star or molet which could be the arms of the Earl of Oxford. Other bosses are carved with foliage; one has the Crown of Thorns in foliage. Shafts rise from the piers to corbels supporting the wall posts of the roof, dividing the clerestory windows into pairs. In the original arrangement the alternate corbels of the nave roof were also supported by shafts and seem to have had above them on the wall posts niches containing figures such as survive in Lavenham church. By the eighteenth century these were in a mutilated state; the niches, being of wood, may have rotted too badly to be retained. In 1783 shafts and niches were removed. The figures most likely represented saints, but no evidence of their identity has survived.

In its original, newly completed, state the interior would have been resplendent with colour on pews, screens and roof, as well as in the windows. The rood screen, so-called because of the great rood or crucifix which was suspended above it, stretched right across the aisles as well as the chancel arch, and was reached by the spiral staircase still surviving at the south-east end of the south aisle, which now gives access to the south gallery. It was an unusual arrangement for a church with separate chancel, although common in churches, such as many in Devon and Somerset, where the nave with its aisles and the chancel also with aisles are all of a height with no architectural separation. The screen at Great St Mary's may have been similar in effect to that surviving in Attleborough, which also stretches the full width of the church.

The contract for the rood screen of Great St Mary's survives, and raises some puzzles. The screen was supposed to be patterned on those already in place in Thriplow and Gazeley churches, parts of which have survived. It seems strange that a large, important church in the university town should be looking to village churches for inspiration. What is more, the screens in these churches are of different dates and styles, that at Thriplow of the early fourteenth century, and hence very old-fashioned by the time that Great St Mary's screen was commissioned. The answer may be that the joiners, John Nun and Roger Bell, happened to be acquainted with those screens, perhaps from making the one or mending the other. The similarity required by St Mary's churchwardens is likely to be not of style but of materials and standard of workmanship. It would be much easier for those not expert in the technicalities of a craft to inspect a screen which was already in place and take it as their agreed measure of sufficient quality.

Other screens there would also have been, closing off sections of the aisles for use as guild and chantry chapels. Eight to ten guilds are recorded at one time or another; the major guild being that of St Mary (which combined with that of Corpus Christi to found the college of that dedication). These guilds would have needed chapels for their services and space, usually provided within the chapel, to store their books and vestments. A surviving, much restored, piscina at the east end of the south aisle indicates the presence of an altar there. Another would have balanced it in the north aisle, and altars were probably also placed against the rood screen on either side of its central doorway. Lavenham church retains north and south parclose screens of the early sixteenth century. These divided chantry chapels from the aisles and can provide some idea of what the arrangement may have looked like.

The westward extensions of the aisles, now enclosed and used as offices, probably also formed chapels, screened across their east ends, where the present walls are situated. What is now the vestry was a Lady chapel; the north chancel chapel was dedicated to St Andrew; a Domesday chapel is recorded as being in the south aisle. There were also chapels to St Lawrence and to the Trinity. Since there was a Trinity image on or above the rood screen a nave altar may have been dedicated to the Trinity. Masses said or sung at the high altar would have been only partially visible to a congregation standing or kneeling in the nave. But the masses taking place at other times in the chapels would have been more visible and audible.

In the chancel it seems that the Sacrament was reserved, as in many other churches, in a covered pyx suspended above the high altar. This is probably what is indicated by two entries in the churchwardens' accounts for 1504: 'Item a pix of laton with a Clothe of Chaungeable Sarcenet in ecclesia. Item a Clothe of olde silke for the said pix in ecclesia.' 'Changeable sarcenet' seems to have been a two-coloured shot silk. The brass container would have been covered by a hanging cloth, weighted at the corners with large beads as is the rare example surviving from Hessett church, now in the British Museum.

The north wall of the chancel contains an arch framing a recess. It was probably built as a monument to some local person, with the intention that it should also be used as an Easter Sepulchre. Monuments placed in similar positions have survived in better condition in some other churches. Many of these contain imagery of the resurrection of Christ. In the later Middle Ages all churches would have had some form of Easter Sepulchre, although many of these were not permanent parts of the building but collapsible wooden structures, erected for the Holy Week ceremonies. During the liturgy of those days the story of the death and resurrection of Christ was dramatically re-enacted. On Good Friday, after the reading of the Gospel story of Jesus' death on the cross, the consecrated bread from the hanging pyx was taken in procession through the church and then deposited in the Sepulchre to symbolise his burial. A watch was kept until the midnight vigil of Holy Saturday. The churchwardens' records retain references to this. For instance in 1539 John Capper was paid a small sum for watching the Sepulchre.

The most complex of the surviving Easter Sepulchres is that in the church of Hawton in Nottinghamshire which is carved with scenes of the resurrection and ascension of Christ. Great St Mary's probably never had carved imagery, though there may have been painting, such as the resurrected Christ on the arch of the Clopton monument in Long Melford. For the ceremonies a small shrine-like cupboard would have been placed in the recess to represent the grave within the tomb. It is probably the making or refurbishing of this that is recorded in 1536 when timber was bought, a joiner paid for working the timber 'in the sepulcer' and payment also made to 'Thomas Grene for payntyng the sepulcer'.

On the south wall of the chancel are the arched recesses of the sedilia and double piscina. Both these and the Easter Sepulchre are early fourteenth century in style but have been heavily restored. They were probably cut back to the wall surface when the chancel walls were panelled in wood in 1663 (see below). The present height of all these recesses indicates that the floor level has been raised by a couple of feet. The sedilia would have been at a comfortable sitting height for the priest, deacon and sub-deacon at the celebration of high mass. If the nave floor was originally below that of the chancel, as was usual, the original proportions of the nave were even more lofty and spacious than is at present apparent.

Although none of the original glass survives, nor even much documentary evidence of it, the church was certainly provided with stained glass in some or all of its windows. In 1503 Henry Veysey, apothecary, left money to make a window for the south aisle depicting the life of St Edward the Confessor. As with the masons, so with the glass: connections with King's College were very strong. One of the king's glaziers, James Nicholson, is known to have worked on the glazing of Great St Mary's in 1518. His work at King's is in a style which has been described as displaying 'outstanding vigour and virtuosity'. Other of the college glaziers probably also worked on the church, providing glass that would have looked in style very similar to that surviving in the college chapel. Concerning the content of the glass no further evidence seems to have survived. Very likely it would have contained typological themes and, since the church is dedicated to the Virgin, some windows with scenes from the apocryphal stories of Mary's life and miracles. The glass in the near contemporary church at Fairford, Gloucestershire, also dedicated to the Virgin, gives some idea of what such glass would have looked like in a parish church.

The church would have been full of imagery – statues, paintings, carvings – most of which have long since been destroyed. Many of the images would have been associated with the chapels; each chapel was dedicated to a saint, whose image would be placed above the altar. Those which have survived, for instance the Pelican and St Michael, are out of easy reach on the roof and hardly visible now that they are a uniform brown colour.

More colour was provided by the rich vestments and cloths, of which one precious survivor remains. This is the pall of Henry VII, now kept under glass cover in the north aisle. Because it has faded few people realise what a sumptuous object it is. Made of a Florentine fabric of the highest quality, it consists of cloth of gold with a design in cut-velvet. A cross of wine-coloured velvet divides the pall into equal parts. At the centre of this cross are the arms of England and France, with a dragon and a greyhound as supporters. The arms of this cross are charged alternately with roses and portcullises crowned, the Tudor badges.

In 1504 an Indenture was sealed, by which the University of Cambridge was to be paid £10 a year for ever to celebrate an annual

requiem in the church, on 11 February during the king's lifetime and
thereafter on the date of his burial. During this service a catafalque,
covered with the pall, was to be set up. A similar Indenture was drawn up
with the University of Oxford and a similar pall survives in the
Ashmolean Museum. It has been suggested that the Cambridge pall
might have been given by Bishop John Fisher. Its survival seems to have
been due to its being used as a canopy, carried over Queen Elizabeth
when she visited King's College in 1564. From this usage it acquired
royal rather than 'superstitious' connotations. The commemoration of
Henry VII was by no means the only service of its kind regularly held in
the church; about twenty annual dirges are recorded at various times.
After the Reformation this form of anniversary was replaced by the
endowment of annual sermons, such as the Chevin sermon which is still
preached.

The nave was partly or wholly pewed; it is possible that the ends of the
backless benches that still survive in the church date from this time.
Pews, or benches, began to be provided in English churches from the late
fourteenth century, in response to the increase in preaching. Before this
time, congregations stood, knelt or moved about during the service;
some would have brought their own folding stools. But reasonably comfortable seating would have been more conducive to the extended con-
centration required by a sermon; it would also keep the congregation
immobile, thus providing fewer distractions for the preacher. The
churchwardens' accounts of 1510–11 itemise money collected from
various parishioners for 'the Stolyng of the Chirche' and 'the Stoles in
the Body of the Chirche', both of which indicate the provision of some
seating in the nave. This was made by William White in 1511–12. Not so
far away, in the Norfolk fens, the two village churches of Wiggenhall St
Mary the Virgin and Wiggenhall St Germans were given finely carved
sets of pews at about this time. Parishioners' pews were rented from as
early as 1537: 'Item Resceyved for the Incumbe of a Seate in the Chirche
– 16d'. Pew rents formed an important part of the parish income until
they were abolished in the nineteenth century.

In 1488 Bishop Alcock preached a sermon on behalf of the fabric fund.
I like to think that the pulpit from which he preached was similar to some
still surviving in other parts of East Anglia, painted with images of the
four Latin Doctors. Highly appropriate for the university church, these
were the great theologians of early western Christendom: St Jerome,
whose Latin translation was the standard version of the Bible for more
than a millennium; St Gregory the Great, pope and reputed compiler of

the corpus of liturgical chant still known by his name; St Ambrose the hymnographer and his disciple St Augustine of Hippo, most influential of theologians. It was believed, alas with little evidence, that the Te Deum was composed antiphonally by Ambrose and Augustine in a fit of ecstasy and it is thus that they were usually portrayed, facing each other in the very act. In those churches with such pulpits where the screen paintings have also survived, such as Castle Acre, the twelve Apostles are shown on the screen. These, the authoritative source of the Christian tradition and thought between them to have composed the Apostles' Creed, would also have been highly appropriate for the university church. Those painted pulpits which survive in East Anglia are mostly fifteenth century. By the time of the furnishing of the new St Mary's fashion had changed and what was then provided was probably more like the pulpit surviving in nearby St Edward's church, a simple wooden structure carved with linenfold panelling.

The first stone of the tower was laid in 1491, perhaps, as suggested above, using the foundations of the previous tower. Work was still continuing on it through the 1520s and 1530s, as is evidenced by accounts for stone, wood and other building materials. The base of the tower is unusual in having a transverse vault abutting an east screen, not unlike the pulpitum of a cathedral or monastic church. As seen from the interior of the nave, the screen has three doorways. The central doorway leads into the base of the tower; that to the south gives access to the tower spiral staircase; the northern door opens on to a small, secure, vaulted space probably intended as a muniment room or treasury. Since the walls to north and south of the side arches of the tower are decorated as if intended to be seen, it seems that the original design was for the aisles to finish at the east end of the tower, with an open passage beneath it. The church in Dedham, Essex, has such a tower similarly detailed, perhaps designed by the same mason.

The original use of the aisle extensions is somewhat mysterious. They are continuous with the aisles to the full height of the roof in an east–west direction but open to the base of the tower through rather small arches. On the north arch surviving ironwork suggests that a door was at some time hung there. W. D. Bushell suggests that there were chapels here. It may be that the design was changed at an early stage to provide space for guild chapels which would not impinge upon the central part of the nave, regularly supplied with staging for the university Commencement ceremonies. On the other hand, the west door would have been the main ceremonial entrance for university processions. Before the Senate House was built there was nowhere closer than the Old Schools in which members of the university could robe and the procession form. It is possible that the spaces to either side of the tower were provided for such use. Above the screen wall was an open platform, probably provided with a balustrade in much the same place as the present early-nineteenth-century gallery front. The full height of the west window, now blocked up behind the organ gallery, was intended to be visible from and to throw light into the nave.

Frequent mentions of sedge in the accounts are a reminder that building ceased for the winter months, the incomplete work being provided with a temporary covering of thatch to protect it from frost damage. Two long pieces of wood were obtained at Stourbridge fair in 1527, presumably the main beams for the temporary structure which was to house the bells until 1596. In 1536 the west window was glazed, but the work, which had reached to just above that window, soon stopped. After a long hiatus probably due to the uncertainties and expenses of the imminent religious changes, the tower was finally brought to completion in the early 1600s. A spire was originally intended to cap the structure; it seems likely that this idea was abandoned because of the difficulties encountered in completing the tower itself. The original state of, and complex changes that have taken place in, the lower stages of the tower still await detailed archeological investigation.

Sixteenth- and seventeenth-century upheavals

The importance of Cambridge as a centre of ideas and education ensured careful royal and episcopal scrutiny. When the Reformation got under way Cambridge would have rapidly experienced its effects. Remote rural parishes may have dragged their feet and resisted change. At Great St Mary's the alterations required in church decoration and furnishings were probably carried out swiftly and thoroughly, whether or not the parishioners and university agreed with the theological rationale of the changes.

Recorded destruction starts with Henry VIII's break with the papacy: in 1541 Roger Young received 4d 'for taking down the Bishop of Rome's head'. This was probably an image of St Gregory who was usually portrayed wearing the papal triple crown. Then in 1547 the great silver cross and two silver censers were sold off by the churchwardens, together with other less valuable furnishings, the proceeds of twenty-two shillings being given to the poor. In this year also the church was whitewashed and a Bible bought. In 1549–50 the churchwardens met together to weigh the remaining plate and produce an inventory of the church's goods for King Edward VI's commissioners. In 1552 they delivered the plate to the king's officials in London. Just a year later, after the accession of Queen Mary, they were buying furnishings, vestments and imagery again.

In Edward's time, and again in Elizabeth's, all painted imagery would have been whitewashed over and replaced with texts from the Bible. Remains of such texts survive at nearby Willingham, on one layer of that church's fascinating palimpsest of pre- and post-Reformation wall-paintings. In addition, the Creed, Lord's Prayer and Ten Commandments were painted on boards which hung in the nave over the chancel arch or on the east wall of the chancel, where previously there would have been a reredos painted with the images of saints or scenes from the life of Christ. Coton church has a table painted with the Ten Commandments in the sixteenth century and repainted in the early seventeenth. At St Mary's such tables were bought in 1562, 1578, 1610 and 1660. That bought in 1562 is recorded as having been set over the altar. The crucifix above the chancel screen was removed, together with its attendant figures of the Virgin Mary and St John and other sculpted images throughout the church. Stone altars were destroyed and replaced by a single wooden communion table. This seems to have happened by 1540–1, when the churchwardens' accounts mention 'Goddes borde', a form of words most likely referring to a wooden table.

In Queen Mary's reign stone altars were required, only to be removed again very soon after the accession of Queen Elizabeth. In 1559 2s 8d was paid to Thomas Swyngges 'for takyng down the Alteres' and 10d to John Bell and William Chapman 'for takyng down the tabernacle'. In that year a new communion table was bought for 6s and also a register. In 1568 payments were received for the sale of various items including censers, vestments and a 'crosse of Copper with Images of mari & John' which had probably been acquired for the restored popish ceremonial of Mary's reign and retained until it was clear that Elizabeth was settled on the throne.

As with altars, so also roods were put back in Mary's reign and removed in Elizabeth's. In 1555 the rood (?screen) was painted and repaired; in 1556 payments were made for the rood and statues of St Mary and St John, as well as to six men for pulling up the rood (presumably a new crucifix and attendant figures to replace those destroyed in the previous reign). Under Elizabeth in 1562 all churchwardens were ordered to remove rood lofts but the screen beneath was to remain ('Item for a book that was sent to us for the pulling down of the Rood loft – 1d').

At Great St Mary's the rood itself was removed but the loft was only partially dismantled. Repaired in 1566, it was finally pulled down only in 1568. Damage to the stonework was made good in 1572, by stopping the holes where the beam which supported the loft was inserted into the chancel arch. This hesitation may have been due to uncertainty about the queen's religious policy and suggests that the wardens were attempting to be ready for anything. While the accounts in 1563 show money received for the sale of wood from the rood loft, in 1564 there is still an account for money 'in the hands of Richard Robinson for dirges and the rood light'; yet dirges and lights were very popish commodities. By 1568 most of the Marian acquisitions had been sold; but the church still retained a cope (of tissue, which usually means cloth-of-gold) and seems still to have marked the liturgical seasons with different coloured pulpit cloths, of red, blue and white.

In 1565 George Wythers of Corpus Christi College preached a sermon in the church urging the abolition of all superstitious painted windows 'whereupon followed a great destruction of them, and the danger of a greater by some zealots there'. Apparently Great St Mary's was very badly affected by this outburst, but there is no detailed record of the destructions. Some imagery must have remained because in 1567–8 certain of the windows were whitewashed as a cheap means of blotting out the offending imagery and in 1569 a glazier was paid 7s. 'for setting up the glass and repairing the same and putting out the images'. The following year 17s. 7d. was paid 'for new glass & for mending the old glass in divers places'. With such major expenses it is not surprising that during these years one of the chalices was in pawn in the university chest.

In 1620 the churchwardens were fined for not keeping their font in repair; it may have been carved with saints or images of the seven sacraments and defaced by iconoclasts. The old one was probably patched up to do service until in 1631 Francis Martin gave three pounds towards the cost of a new font. This was duly made in 1632 by George Thompson, 'according to direction from Dr Porter'; the date is carved on it. It is typical of the Laudian revival in blending Gothic and classical forms. The shape is that of a fifteenth-century octagonal font; its decoration is naively Renaissance in style. The wooden cover was provided in 1638. The accounts make it clear that the cover, and perhaps also the font itself, was painted, as were the church doors. It is not known what colours were used, but the contemporary font cover in St Botolph's church might give some idea of likely colouring.

In 1638 the churchwardens replied to Bishop Matthew Wren's visitation enquiries that at the three great feasts the communion table was brought into the body of the church by reason of the multitude of communicants. The implication of this is that on other occasions the table stood in the chancel; this would have been in accordance with Queen Elizabeth's Injunctions which allowed the table to be placed wherever was most convenient for the administering of communion but required that at other times it be kept in the chancel against the east wall. Wren's response was that they should receive at the rails. That is, the table should remain against the east wall of the chancel, with communion rails in front of it.

There is an account of a small sum paid in 1635 for 'cutting the Communion table'. It is unclear precisely what this signifies, but it could indicate that before this date a very long communion table had been kept in the central aisle of the nave. It may be that, in view of the hardening of episcopal attitudes towards the placing of the table, the parish thought it advisable to have this shortened. Thus it could fit against the east wall except when there were many communicants, so conforming to Elizabeth's Injunctions. There survives in Bottisham church an Elizabethan or Jacobean table which has been shortened by about a third of its original length, perhaps about this time. Wren's order went further than the Elizabethan requirements in not allowing the table to be moved from the east wall.

It is not known what arrangement was used in the church during the Commonwealth period but, so soon after the changes forced upon them by the bishop, they may have reverted to the earlier usage of a table in the nave, well suited to the large numbers of communicants and to a more 'puritan' understanding of the sacrament. The seventeenth-century table in the vestry may well be this communion table, which would have been placed lengthwise down the middle aisle.

The Laudian emphasis on having the table altar-wise at the east end of the chancel was an attempt to enforce respect for the table and the chancel. There were both practical and theological reasons for this. On the practical side was a perceived need to prevent disruption and protect the table. Not far away, in the Cambridgeshire village of Tadlow in 1638, the Christmas service had been seriously disrupted when, during the sermon, a dog ran off with the bread provided for the communion. Most likely this had been set out on the communion table in the centre of the open chancel. During the first part of the service the congregation would have been seated in the nave, with their attention on the preacher in the pulpit. At the offertory, when invited to 'draw near', those intending to communicate would move into the chancel and stand, kneel or sit around the table.

Because the table held the elements of bread and wine for the communion service it became the focus of different interpretations of that sacrament. The Laudians, who believed in the real presence of Christ in the consecrated elements, felt that the table which held those elements should be accorded respect; they also believed that the communion should be received kneeling, to signify obeisance to Christ, truly present in the sacrament. Puritans held that this view of the communion service smacked of popery and of the abhorrent romish doctrine of transubstantiation. They understood the communion as a commemoration of the Last Supper and considered sitting more suitable to those thus partaking of a communal meal. Considered similarly romish was the practice of men removing their hats in church, a practice which the Laudians encouraged as a sign of respect to the house of God.

The seventeenth-century pulpit at Orton Waterville, near Peterborough, is said to have come from Great St Mary's. There is little reason to doubt the truth of this claim. Although undated, it is stylistically of the 1630s and a sumptuous piece, suited to a proud town church. It is carved with female busts, similar to those on the pulpit in St Cuthbert's church in Wells, Somerset, which is dated 1636. When the aisle galleries were erected in the following century this pulpit would not only have been too low to enable the preacher to be seen by the upstairs congregation but also stylistically inappropriate for the new fashion in furnishing.

A gallery placed in the chancel in 1610, facing westwards, caused controversy because the university dignitaries sitting in it had their backs to the altar. James I, in 1616, gave instructions that it should be removed; the accounts of 1617 refer to money paid to 'four porters for removing the great timber that lay at the upper end of the chancel'. The remains of the medieval screen had probably been removed when this gallery was built. In 1640 a new chancel screen was erected. The moving force behind this was John Cosin, Master of Peterhouse, Vice-Chancellor of the University and a prominent High Church Laudian. A puritan reporter described the screen as having on top 'a great hollow pile of wainscot cast into the form of a pyramid' which could well be a reference to a Gothic tabernacle structure over its doors. It may have been similar in design to the screen in the church at Sedgefield, County Durham, dating from the 1630s. That screen is in a mixed Gothic style; Cole described the screen at Great St Mary's as having a canopy and spire-work, which suggests similarities with Sedgefield and with similar work at Brancepeth, where Cosin was incumbent. When, in 1663, the chancel walls were panelled with wood wainscoting as part of the Restoration refurbishing, that panelling was adorned with spirework, perhaps in an attempt to match the Cosin screen.

By 1640 the altar was at the east end and provided with rails. But in September 1641 the House of Commons issued an order for the removal of Communion tables from the east end and the destruction of their rails. The churchwardens, who seem to have been puritan in their sympathies, responded quickly but were temporarily prevented by the intervention of Dr Rowe, of Trinity College. Nevertheless, the accounts for 1641–2 itemise the removal of the rails and the step on which the table had been raised. In May 1644 a parliamentary ordinance instructed churches to remove vestments, fonts and organs. The font survived; whether it was removed to storage or continued in the church is not known.

The Restoration

The Restoration Settlement introduced into most churches a pattern of furnishing similar to that required by the Laudians. In the chancel a table stood altar-wise against the east wall, railed in. Seats for communicants were sometimes provided; otherwise the space was kept free and communicants knelt around. In 1660 at Great St Mary's 'mats and cricketts' were bought for communicants to kneel on, so presumably communion was no longer provided to those remaining in their seats; or perhaps both means of communicating were allowed. It seems that the new changes were quickly introduced. Other parishes reacted more slowly. Bishop Gardiner of Lincoln in his visitation charge of 1697 appealed to his clergy whether they did not 'find great inconveniencies in consecrating in so strait a place as an alley of the church and delivering the bread and wine in narrow seats and treading upon the feet of those that kneel?'. The old ways died hard, but in Cambridge the majority of parishioners and members of the university conformed. In the visitation records of 1685 three or four dissenters were given as having been excommunicated from Great St Mary's, a very small number.

The nave was set up for the services of morning and evening prayer. This generally meant the provision of a pulpit and desk for the minister with pews placed so as to face these, thus allowing the preacher to see and be seen by all. By the late seventeenth century the pulpit, desk and parish clerk's pew were being placed together in what is known as a 'triple-decker' arrangement. At the top the pulpit, in the middle the minister's seat from which he led the prayers, and below these the place from which the clerk led the congregation's responses. The parishioners sat in box pews, built high and provided with doors to protect from draughts. Already in 1636, in a report to Archbishop Laud, the church had been said to be overcrowded and the seats 'cooped up high with wainscot'.

A grand new organ, provided by the university in 1697, was placed at the west end of the church on a gallery. There is little surviving evidence of the form of this gallery, but the organ is known to have been placed further east than it is at present. The front, supported on two columns, probably looked similar to the contemporary organ gallery in the church of St Katherine Cree in London, which is likewise supported on two classical columns.

The eighteenth and early nineteenth centuries

In the eighteenth century the nave interior was transformed into a good preaching hall by the erection of the aisle galleries, money for which had been left in a bequest by William Wort. In 1733 the vestry gave the university leave to build galleries 'on condition of accepting responsibility for maintenance for ever'. These were built in 1735–6 and a tall pulpit was provided in the middle of the nave, facing east. Erection of the former was supervised by James Gibbs, architect of the Senate House and the Fellows' Buildings at King's College. Gibbs probably also designed them. The three-decker pulpit was carved by James Essex the elder, father of the architect of the same name. A new communion table had been acquired by 1734.

In 1737 the University Syndics agreed to pay the parish £100 towards new pewing in Norway oak. These parishioners' box pews were reconstructed in 1751 under the architect James Essex. Backless benches were placed in the middle of the nave (the pit) for the use of Masters of Arts. In 1754 the chancel also was transformed by the erection, under the supervision of the architect James Essex, of a gallery inside its western part with seats facing west. At this time the wainscot panelling around the chancel walls was replaced with lower, plain wainscot which is said to have had a pediment over the altar-table to serve as a reredos. The chancel itself would have remained otherwise empty, save for the communion rails. Those communicating at the monthly communion services would probably have knelt on the chancel floor, although seats may have been provided along the north and south walls, as in Peterhouse chapel. The erection of the aisle galleries had darkened the church by obscuring the medieval windows. In 1766 the window traceries were drastically simplified to allow more light into the nave.

An entry in the accounts for 1762 records a payment for a stand to be made for the curate to attend funerals in the churchyard. This was a structure like a sentry box, which could be taken from the church and placed at the graveside to protect the priest and his prayer book from the worst of the weather. One of these survives in the church of Walpole St Peter.

On the outside of the tower a circular plaque marks the position of the datum point cut in 1732 by Dr William Warren of Trinity Hall as the centre of Cambridge. From this point Warren measured three major roads out of Cambridge, setting up milestones many of which still survive. Warren was a fellow of Trinity Hall and the work was paid for out of a highways charity set up with bequests by two fellows of Trinity Hall and Gonville and Caius College. The Master and Fellows of Trinity Hall were trustees of this fund, which is why the milestones are marked with that college's arms. The original bequests were left by Dr Wlliam Mowse and Mr Robert Hare whose arms appear, respectively, on the first and last milestones of the Barkway route. Hare's arms are displayed above the inside of the south door of the church.

Overcrowding being still a problem, in 1819 another gallery was proposed for the west end of the nave, to extend across the westernmost bay. It was erected in 1837, at the same height as the aisle galleries and thus somewhat lower than the organ gallery. Until this date the organ had stood further forward. It was moved back, to the west of the tower arch, to provide more space for the new gallery. The pulpit was moved to the west end of the nave. The 1819 seating plan shows how the box pews were laid out.

The front of the west gallery, the organ gallery and the plaster vault above it were designed by William Wilkins, who copied the shape and tracery decoration of the sixteenth-century tower vault. He used the same motifs (and very likely the same workmen) for the gateway vaults of Trinity College's New Court and also for interior features of King's College's south range, both of which were under construction in the

1820s. The Ecclesiologists of a generation later thought it a poor, superficial job. But Wilkins evidently gave some thought to the task of blending his designs with both the medieval and eighteenth-century work. The surviving organ gallery front and vault blend quite successfully with the medieval nave and tower.

The Victorian restoration

The west doorway, which had been altered in the seventeenth century to a classical design, was a source of irritation to the new generations of medievalists. Various designs in Gothic style were sought, among them a couple from Edward Blore. But it was not until 1850 that it was at last rebuilt, to a design by George Gilbert Scott. Part of the north and east sides of the churchyard were ceded, in 1855, for the improvement of the market place. The chancel walls were discovered to be in poor repair and Trinity College undertook the work. Whewell, who was master at the time, took a personal interest in the details. The bursar's minutes record: 'The Master's idea is that the walls should, in the main, be rebuilt on the old foundation; + the style be made conformable to that of the better part of the church, viz, the clerestorey, which is good perpendicular work.' 'The Master will consult Mr Salvin on the restoration of the chancel walls, to correspond with the Architecture of the rest of the Church.' By 2 May 1857 Salvin's plans had been received and approved by the college. Three tenders were called for and that of Thomas Tomson, for £630, accepted. The east window was rebuilt in the Perpendicular style as part of this restoration and the battlements given a more ornamental form to mark the importance of the chancel.

Archdeacon Hare, in his Charge of 1840, had censured the arrangement of furnishings inside the church. Three years later in the Transactions of the Cambridge Camden Society, Venables referred to the eighteenth-century furnishings as 'an alteration so sadly characteristic of that dreariest period of English history'. Particular cause for complaint was the doctors' gallery and the placement of the font: 'when . . . the Lord's Table being already concealed by the Doctors' gallery, the font was pushed out of sight into an obscure corner beneath the staircase leading up to the same . . .' The font itself, however, met with a qualified approval: 'though of a decidedly debased character in detail, yet [it] partakes . . . of a catholick spirit and feeling, in its general conception . . .'

After much discussion a plan and designs were obtained from Scott. In the nave and aisles open pews, similar to surviving late-medieval East Anglian benches, faced east. The front desks had carvings of the four Evangelists: human figures with their beasts in front and below them. Stalls facing inwards were provided along both north and south walls of the chancel, reaching almost up to the east end. These had carved angels on their ends. The heads of colleges, professors and doctors, displaced from the chancel gallery, were to be seated there.

Some doubts were expressed by the Senate concerning Scott's arrangements for seating and pulpit. They asked whether he was 'of the opinion that the removal of the Pulpit to the North-Eastern Angle will be beneficial and satisfactory as a point from which all parts of the Church may be best reached by the voice of the Preacher'. Scott replied that he thought this proposed seating plan was the best, but only the members of the university could judge whether having some seats in the nave arranged choir-wise would better suit their purposes. He provided an alternative plan with seating for the heads of colleges in the front rows of the nave, facing inwards. 'As regards the Pulpit, I think the North-Eastern part of the Nave the most suitable position for it, and that the voice from that position would be heard throughout the Church.'

In 1862 the university petition for a Faculty explained the proposals:

> it would add very much to the beauty of the said church, and be of great advantage and convenience to the congregation attending Divine Service therein, if the alterations and the re-arrangement of the interior and of the sittings in the said Church hereinafter specified were carried into effect; that is to say:
> The Gallery called the Doctors' Gallery removed.
> The sittings in the Chancel and Body of the Church re-arranged so as to provide increased accommodation for persons *in statu pupillari*.
> The Church properly warmed.
> The Pulpit removed to the North Pier of the Chancel Arch, the Reading Desk also placed in a more convenient position, and the Font removed from its present site, and placed within the Body of the Church.
> The West Gallery removed altogether, and the North and South Galleries extended to the Western Tower.

Whewell was opposed to the removal of the doctors' gallery. In 1860 he wrote:

> The promotion of convenience which produced the erection of the gallery in 1751 was combined with a change in the style of architecture according to the taste of that time. Since then, our taste has altered, and many persons now appear to think Gothic architecture – some, one form of it, and some, another – essential to religion. It is probable that other changes of taste on this subject will take place; perhaps before long. I do not think it wise in the University, or in any public body, to lend itself to the impulses of caprice and fashion which produce these oscillations of taste . . .

Nevertheless, the Faculty was obtained and Scott's plan carried out. The furnishings were made by Rattee and Kett. But Scott's confidence in the placing of the pulpit proved to be mistaken. In August 1867 the vice-chancellor wrote informally asking him to suggest a solution to the problem:

> From many parts of the Church the Preacher cannot be seen at all; and of course, therefore, very imperfectly, as well as uncomfortably, heard. This is especially the case with a large portion of the Chancel, which is now assigned to the Heads of Colleges, Doctors and Professors. Several of the two latter classes have made a formal representation to that effect.

The solution of a movable pulpit, designed by Scott, was only reached after much debate and against the objections of the incumbent, H. R. Luard. It was installed in 1872. The university dignitaries moved from the chancel to the front pews of the nave, facing east. The panels of the eighteenth-century pulpit were inserted as screens in the west arches of the chancel chapels. When the parish built its own organ in the south chapel, now the vestry, the chancel stalls were taken over by the choir and the building had at last been converted from a preaching box into the Ecclesiologists' idea of a church.

Not all was perfect, however. The galleries were considered an indispensable eyesore. Luard wished to replace Salvin's Perpendicular east window with one in the Ecclesiologically approved Decorated style, to match the heavily restored, niches, sedilia and Easter Sepulchre. His opponents pointed out that the present window matched the rest of the architecture, especially the roof. A window in the Decorated style would have a much more steeply-pitched arch and would require a similar change in the roof to complement it. By 1869 Luard had admitted defeat, ordering the glass of the Nativity for the Salvin window from John Hardman & Co. of Birmingham. This company made much use of glass from the factory of William Chance, who was one of a number of mid-nineteenth-century researchers into the colouring techniques used by the best medieval glaziers. This will account for the silvery translucence of the background and the jewel-like intensity of the colours. Luard certainly contributed to the design. How much is unclear, but there is a scrap of evidence for his influence on the pattern of the south chancel window, also by Hardman, which illustrates the parable of the wise and foolish virgins. A letter from John Hardman survives in the university archives, containing the tantalising comment: 'Mr John H. Powell has made the alterations in the lamps, which you desired.'

Also designed by Scott, and given by J. B. Lightfoot, was a carved alabaster reredos on the east wall behind the high altar. This represented, in the centre, the Crucifixion, and on either side Samuel among the prophets and St Paul preaching at Athens, two scenes which, as Bushell notes, 'are well suited to a university church'. In addition, the two wall niches contained carvings of the sacrifice of Isaac and Moses lifting up the brazen serpent; both incidents considered to be antetypes of the death of Christ on the Cross. 1902–4 saw the clerestory windows filled with figured glass representing patriarchs, apostles, prophets and martyrs with phrases of the Te Deum. The glass is by James Powell to a design by William Cunningham.

The twentieth century

By the 1950s tastes had changed again. Alan Maycock wrote in 1965, looking back at changes that had been effected in the previous decade: 'the choir stalls and the seating in the nave and aisles are in the heaviest mid-Victorian manner and add to the somewhat sombre impression of the interior as a whole . . . However, the most recent alterations have done a great deal to bring back some much-needed light and colour into the building.'

In 1958, during the incumbency of Mervin Stockwood, major changes were made to the chancel. The Faculty petition listed eight of these: the removal of the Scott reredos and the sculptures in the two side niches; removal of three choir stalls from each side of the chancel east end; repaving of the floor; adaptation of the altar and provision of a pall-like cover embroidered with a depiction of the Last Supper; provision of a carved figure of Christ in Majesty; the altar to be brought forward on a curved step; removal of pews at the front and back of the nave; replacement of the north window of the chancel with a design by H. W. Harvey of York. The petition commented that since the reredos was 'unlikely to be acceptable to another church, so we intend to demolish it reverently'. It was further added that removing it intact would cost more than demolishing it. The total cost of these works, to the designs of George Pace, were estimated at £3,500. Pace considered that it would cost an extra £300 to remove the reredos intact. Moreover, there was no obvious place where it could be stored. The Diocese of Ely still has no provision for storage, pending re-use, of the high quality furnishings that continue to be removed from its churches.

No objection was raised by the university to the proposed changes. Trinity College Council declared unanimously in favour. The Diocesan Advisory Committee was less happy. Their report to the chancellor of the diocese signalled their agreement that more space was required in the chancel. But the members were 'disturbed about the proposal to discard the reredos' and felt that 'it is clear that if the scheme is carried out in its entirety it will entirely alter the present character of the chancel'. They were also 'a little doubtful whether something which was given to this church by so eminent a person as Dr Lightfoot should be lightly discarded'. It was suggested that perhaps the carved panels of the reredos could be saved. The architect's reply was totally uncompromising. He claimed that his design was 'a completely integrated work of architecture'. 'If one element or detail is rejected the architect's conscience could not do otherwise than work out a new design, also completely integrated.' His original design in essence can be seen today in the chancel: uncluttered and austere, some might say bare and unsympathetic; it is unquestionably a work of the 1950s.

Two rows of pews were removed from the front and back of the nave, providing necessary flexibility and room for movement. It is unfortunate that the front desks, with their carved Evangelist figures, were also removed. Perhaps no one noticed their significance as the only recognisably Christian imagery on the nave seating. They, with the other removed pews and choir stalls, are now at home in Linton parish church.

The altar cover with the Last Supper seems never to have been made. Instead a blue cover, with an appliquéd and embroidered gold and silver star, was made by Betty Gaskell and still graces the high altar on most days. It is difficult to imagine that the proposed Last Supper would have complemented the Majestas so well. The Majestas (properly *Majestas Christi*: the Majesty of Christ) was made by Alan Durst and dedicated in 1960 in memory of the Reverend Canon C. L. Hulbert-Powell and his wife. Its design, by Pace, incorporates imagery from the Revelation of St John. The figure of Christ in Majesty stands in front of the Cross as Tree of Life, flanked by the Evangelists' symbols and treading upon a dragon. Pace also designed the pendant light fittings in the nave, installed in 1968. In 1962 a small statue of the Virgin and Child, carved by Loughnan Pendred, was given to the church. The same artist made the processional crucifix and candles.

Since then practical facilities have been provided in the north-west and south-west corners of the church. Artistic enrichment has continued with the reordering in 1983 of St Andrew's chapel. The Risen Christ, sculpted by Gabriella Bollobas, hangs on the wall. It is complemented by a Cross, marked with the imprint of the body of Christ, made by Gordon Steele. The seating is by George Clarke and Tony Wolstenholmes and a tapestry, made by Alec Pearson, was given in 1984 in memory of Geoffrey Wood. In 1992, on completion of the new parish organ, a glazed screen was inserted in the upper east end of the south aisle, with an engraved design by David Peace.

Such changes both small and great will continue to be needed as the lively congregation of each generation, ministering to both town and gown, hands on the fabric and the tradition of Great St Mary's.

Bibliographical note

This chapter has been designed to complement the earlier historical essays which thus provide an essential background. Rather than duplicate the bibliographical material provided in those chapters I shall mention only books and articles of which I have made special use or which are not mentioned elsewhere.

I am grateful to Mr Philip Oswald for lending me Arthur Oswald's copy of Foster's edition of the churchwardens' accounts. The annotations in this copy have been most helpful in correcting the editor's misleading dating of some of the documents transcribed.

The City of Cambridge, The Royal Commission on the Historical Monuments of England (London, HMSO, 1959, repr. 1988), vol II, contains a detailed analysis of the building and furnishings, together with a ground-plan of the church and some illustrations.

John Harvey, *English Medieval Architects* (rev. edn 1984) has valuable information in the article on Wastell concerning the design of the church.

Illustrations of many of the other churches offered as examples for comparison with GSM in its original state can be found in Eamon Duffy, *The*

Stripping of the Altars: Traditional Religion in England 1400–1580 (New Haven and London, 1992). Plates 7–9 show Easter Sepulchres; plate 17 the pulpit with the Latin Doctors at Castle Acre; plate 29 the Apostles on the screen at Weston Longville; plates 26 and 27 the carved benches at Wiggenhall St Germans; plates 52 and 53 the Spring chantry chapel in Lavenham.

Some sense of what the original glazing may have looked like can be gleaned from Hilary Wayment, *King's College Chapel Cambridge, The Great Windows: Introduction and Guide* (Cambridge, 1992) where reference is made to the work of James Nicholson in the chapel and in GSM. Illustrations of surviving early sixteenth-century glass in a parish church can be found in *Life, Death and Art: The Medieval Stained Glass of Fairford Parish Church*, eds. Sarah Brown and Lindsay MacDonald (Stroud, 1997). Evidence of the sixteenth-century destruction of the glass is given in Graham Cheney, 'The Lost Stained Glass of Cambridge', *Proceedings of the Cambridge Antiquarian Society*, 79 (1990), 70–81.

Details of the Pall of Henry VII can be found in Hugh Tait, 'The Hearse-Cloth of Henry VII belonging to the University of Cambridge', *The Journal of the Courtauld and Warburg Institutes*, 19 (1956), 294–8. John Twigg, *The University of Cambridge and the English Revolution 1625–1688* (Woodbridge, 1990), has many references to happenings in Great St Mary's during the seventeenth century.

The story of the dog at Tadlow can be found in William Laud, *Works*, ed. William Scott (Oxford, 1853), vol. v, part 2, p. 367.

John Cosin was rector of Brancepeth, County Durham from 1626 until 1640. The woodwork put into Brancepeth church during Cosin's incumbency was destroyed in a fire in September 1998. Sedgefield has similar woodwork, inserted perhaps under Cosin's influence. Illustrations of the Sedgefield screen can be found in Nikolaus Pevsner, *County Durham, The Buildings of England* series, 1953, rev. Elizabeth Williamson, 1990, plate 63.

I am grateful to Trevor Cooper for allowing me to read the essay written by himself and Robert Walker on William Dowsing's visit to GSM. This is shortly to be published in Trevor Cooper (ed.), *The Journal of William Dowsing for Cambridgeshire and Suffolk: Iconoclasm in East Anglia during the English Civil War, 1643–1644* (forthcoming). The west (organ) gallery of St Katherine Cree is illustrated in Gerald Cobb, *The Old Churches of London* (London, 1941, 2nd rev. edn 1942–3), plate IV b.

Alan H. Nelson, *Early Cambridge Theatres: College, University, and Town Stages, 1464–1720* (Cambridge, 1994), gives detailed evidence of the staging set up in Great St Mary's Church for the university Commencement ceremonies from 1464 until the building of the Senate House gave the university a permanent place for its ceremonies. Various questions arise from this material concerning the nave seating, which must have been such as to allow room for the staging to be erected, it seems, between the piers of the arcade. This suggests that the central part of the nave was always free of fixed seating, as it continued to be for 'the pit' throughout the eighteenth century. Access to the staging was through doors to a staircase constructed in 1590–1 'on the North side of the Churche'. It may be that the ironwork on the northern arch of the tower indicates the placing of these doors.

The quotation from Bishop Gardiner is taken from W. M. Jacob, *Lay People and Religion in the Early Eighteenth Century* (Cambridge, 1996). Copies of various Faculty applications together with related correspondence can be found in the university archive volumes CUR.18.2 and 3. Vice-Chancellor Cartmell's correspondence file, Misc. Collect.47, contains a copy of his letter to Scott about the placing of the pulpit. Whewell's objections to removal of the chancel gallery were published in a pamphlet, a copy of which is in Cam.c. 860.36.

I am grateful to Mr Jonathan Smith, archivist of Trinity College, for his help in searching out documents relating to the college's involvement with GSM. The bursar's minute books have brief comments on restoration schemes for the chancels of many of the churches under their patronage throughout the 1850s, including GSM. They are a tribute to the college's sustained interest and generosity towards those parishes.

Further discussion of the fabric and furnishings of GSM can be found in my own and other articles in *Cambridgeshire Churches*, ed. Carola Hicks (Stamford, 1997).

Finally, special thanks are due to Mr Peter Meadows for help with the university archives, and to Professor Christopher Brooke for reading the draft and saving me from a number of errors.

9 Music: the organs and choirs

The organs of Great St Mary's

GRAHAM SUDBURY

The Church of St Mary the Great, Cambridge, has the distinction, shared with few other English churches, of having two organs. The university organ is at the west end of the church, built under the tower, and the parish organ is at the east end, to the south side of the chancel.

The first of the two organs was built at the initiative of the university. On 18 July 1697 the parishioners of St Mary the Great consented to a proposal from the vice-chancellor that an organ should be erected in the church 'at the only cost and charge of the University'. At this time, before the building of the Senate House, the church was used as an auditorium for university ceremonies (such as the conferring of degrees) as well as the weekly university sermon and the organ was required to assist at the performances which occurred on these occasions. It was built by Bernard 'Father' Smith, the king's organ maker, an immigrant from Holland but probably of German origin, and was complete by the end of 1698. Smith received £367 and his instrument stood on a wooden gallery at the west end of the church, in front of the tower arch. During the years that followed this organ was used to accompany both university and parish worship, but was maintained by the university alone. Various repairs and improvements were made. An echo organ was added by Henry Turner in 1713; the mechanism was reconstructed and new stops added in 1767 by Thomas Parker. Then a complete rebuilding took place in 1806, with pedals being added, by the organ builder John Avery. An important change took place in 1819 when the gallery was dismantled and a new stone loft was constructed for it, by Thomas Elliot, in the position in which it still remains. However, in spite of this succession of work the organ was all but unplayable by the 1860s.

Its condition was a cause of concern for the parishioners, and it is recorded in the minutes of a vestry meeting held on 2 April 1869 that it was decided to write to the vice-chancellor concerning the state of the organ, declaring that the parishioners wanted something done to improve it, as resort had been made to a harmonium for service

173

accompaniment. It was further stated that a subscription list had been opened for the parish to install their own organ in the chancel, but this action would be stopped if the university would take steps to repair the west end organ. The next documented evidence that can be traced comes from a memorandum circulated by the vice-chancellor to the Syndicate in October 1869 which reads as follows: 'The Syndicate . . . entered into communication with the Vicar and Churchwardens of Great St Mary's parish with the hope of obtaining their co-operation in rendering the organ adequate to the requirements of the University and the parishioners.' This attempt to obtain agreement did not succeed, 'the Parish having preferred to erect a new smaller organ for themselves at the east end of the Church'. So the shared use of the one organ by both university and parish came to an end.

The source from which this new parish organ was obtained is not recorded, but, as the Cambridge firm of A. T. Miller, organ builders, was founded in 1856, it would seem likely that Mr Miller was chosen to carry out this work. That it was indeed small is further borne out by a minute found later in university Syndicate records (when eventually considering the renovation of the university organ) which runs: 'There can be no doubt that the new organ in the Chancel, good as it is of its kind, is not on a scale sufficiently to satisfy our demands.' There are no further records of the parish organ until 1891. It would seem that in the twenty-one years of its existence, very little money had been spent on its maintenance, for in response to an assessment of the organ's condition, the university organist, Dr Garrett, wrote to the vicar on 25 February 1891:

> There can be no doubt that the condition of the Chancel organ is extremely unsatisfactory. The bellows is fairly sound, and large enough to warrant the suggested additions. The pedal stops are also in decent condition. But the scale and the plan of the organ . . . is so meagre and so small, that it is a wretched accompanying organ at best . . . I think the best thing you can do is to have the organ thoroughly rebuilt. I have gone over Mr A Miller's plans and have suggested some few modifications. If these can be carried into effect I think you will have an organ which will be at least serviceable for accompaniment. The proposed raising of the organ will be quite an easy matter, and it will be an immense advantage to the organist and the choir.

That same year the vicar issued an appeal for funds, estimating that £450 would be needed for the organ reconstruction. The work was completed the following year and a dedication service was held on 16

December 1892, taking in, as well as the work on the organ, the new chapel and screen, repairs to the tower and some stained glass windows. It is recorded that although the university contributed to some of these costs and improvements, the expenses connected with the organ were met by the parishioners.

Miller's cared for the instrument and made various improvements and extensions whilst Mr Albert Miller was the organist. A later, but undated specification drawn up by Miller's, shows that the great organ lost its Gamba and gained two more Open Diapasons and a Double Open Diapason of 16 feet. The pedal organ gained an Open Metal Diapason of 16 feet, an Octave of 8 feet and a Trombone of 16 feet (eighteen notes borrowed from the Choir Tromba). The Swell Organ lost the Gemshorn, gained a Celeste and the Twelfth became incorporated into the Mixture.

The Choir Organ became as follows:

1. Doppel Flute	8 ft.	5. Double Flute	4 ft.
2. Horn Diapason	8 ft.	6. Dulcet	4 ft.
3. Viola	8 ft.	7. Clarinet	8 ft.
4. Dolce	8 ft.	8. Tromba	8 ft.

In 1924 an electric blowing plant was installed, as the organist reported that 'he had refused to play some requirements, as the blowers stripped to the waist every Sunday, constantly grumbling, as impossible to keep the wind in, and I should not be surprised if they give up any time now'. Then in 1934 a move was made to have the organ renovated and the pitch lowered to standard 522 (C). A new pedal board was also installed.

Fourteen years later, in 1948, water penetrating the roof over the organ chamber did much damage to the instrument, rendering parts of it unplayable. Again, in 1953, another report was made on the deteriorating condition of the organ mechanism by the firm of E. J. Johnson, into whose hands the care of the instrument had passed in 1950. Still further damage was done to the organ by more water through the roof on the night of 5 November 1955. This steady deterioration finally led the parish to set in motion plans to renovate the instrument, but it was not until 1961 that the complete overhaul was carried out, including the installation of a new electro-pneumatic action, modernisation of stop jambs and a number of significant tonal alterations, especially to the choir organ.

In spite of this major work, the organ remained unsatisfactory. In 1964 the great organ soundboard – possibly one from the original parish organ

– had to be reconditioned, but, worse than this, the instrument began to show the damaging effect of central heating in the church, which had been installed in the mid-sixties, in the form of the slow but sure evaporation of the natural moisture content of the timber and other materials. This required the installation of a humidifier to counteract the drying out of the organ and, at the same time, some minor tonal improvements were made. In 1974 the Mixture Stop was added to the great organ.

Over the next thirty years, however, the 'action' seriously deteriorated, partly as a result of the central heating system. This situation coincided with a national trend to re-establish the nature of a more 'classical' style of instrument to do full justice to the wide range of the organ repertoire. After due deliberation the church council decided to replace the old organ with a completely new instrument. This was done in 1991 by the firm of Kenneth Jones and Associates in collaboration with the late Dr Peter le Huray, the then Diocesan Organs Advisor, and Christopher Moore, Organist at the time.

Meanwhile the university's organ was also repaired and improved on several occasions. After a protracted discussion, in which dons debated the relative merits of organs and scientific laboratories, the distinguished London firm of W. Hill and Son was commissioned to reconstruct the organ, retaining the case and most of the old pipework, but replacing virtually everything else. A minute inserted into the parochial church council's minutes on 25 May 1871, reads: 'Recorded that in 1870 the University enlarged and repaired the west end organ at a cost of £620, paid out of the University Chest.' With the completion of this work the organ assumed its present form. Some tonal alterations were made in 1963 when the instrument was renovated by Hill, Norman and Beard but, in general, the scheme was respectful of the organ's historical character at a period when such discrimination was rare. The most recent rebuilding was undertaken in 1995 by N. P. Mander Ltd of London. The intention was to restore the mechanism and structure of the organ, setting them up for another extended period of service and to make modest changes to the tonal scheme with the purpose of consolidating the Hill character of the instrument. The whole organ is again on tracker (mechanical) action, and the Swell reed chorus (proposed but not installed by Hill in 1870) has finally been completed. However, the pedal upperwork and the great cornet introduced in 1963 have been found useful, and these features have been retained. It was decided not to attempt to restore the case to its earlier appearance on this occasion, but the hope was retained that this might be undertaken in due course.

Specification of the university organ

Great organ		*Swell organ*	
Bourdon	16 M	Open Diapason	8
Open Diapason	8 S	Stopped Diapason	8
Stopped Diapason	8 S	Principal	4
Gamba	8	Fifteenth	2 M
Principal	4 S	Mixture	III
Nason Flute	4 S	Double Trumpet	16
Twelfth	2 2/3 S	Cornopean	8 M
Fifteenth	2 S	Oboe	8
Mixture	III S	Clarion	4
Trumpet	8		
Cornet (mid C)	IV M		
Choir organ		*Pedal organ*	
Stopped Diapason	8S	Open Diapason	16
Dulciana	8	Bourdon	16
Principal	4 S	Principal	8
Flute	4 S	Flute	8 M
Fifteenth	2 S	Fifteenth	4 M
Cremona	8	Mixture	II M
		Trombone	16

S: Smith pipework (1698)
M: Mander pipework (1995)

The unusual situation of a church with two organs arose out of a lack of agreement by the two bodies which used the church during the mid-nineteenth century. Each organ has undergone a succession of modifications and improvements, with the result that the church and its worshippers – both from the university and the city – benefit from two distinguished but different instruments. The university organ has historic importance, and subsequent work has respected its character. The pipework originally installed by 'Father' Smith can still be enjoyed. The parish organ, on the other hand, is a new instrument, with a tonal quality which complements the older organ. The combination of the two gives the church a rare and valuable musical resource.

Specification of the present parish organ

Great organ		Swell organ	
Double Diapason	16	Salicional	8
Open Diapason	8	Voix Celestes	8
Rohrflute	8	Stopped Diapason	8
Octave	4	Principal	4
Spitzflute	4	Nason Flute	4
Superoctave	2	Fifteenth	2
Mixture	II–III	Larigot	1 1/3
Cimbel	II	Sesquialtera	II
Trumpet	8	Mixture	II–IV
		Double Trumpet	16
		Cornopean	8
		Oboe	8

Solo organ		Pedal organ	
Double Diapason	16	Open Wood	16
Open Flute	8	Sub-bass	16
Wide Octave	4	Principal	8
Nazard	2 2/3	Trombone	16
Doublette	2		
Wald Flute	2		
Tierce	1 3/5		
Trumpet:	8		

Notes:

Swell to Great:	six combination pistons to each manual division
Solo to Great:	eight general pistons
Great to Pedal:	eight memory channels
Swell to Pedal:	balanced Swell Pedal
Solo to Peda:	tremulants to Swell and Great/Solo
Solo Octave to Pedal:	wind control

Source: Designed and built by Kenneth Jones and Associates, Bray, County Wicklow, Ireland.

Information on the university organ was supplied by Dr. Nicholas Thistlethwaite

The parish choir and the girls' choir

PETER MEADOWS

The parish choir came into existence in about 1870, when the present stalls were erected in the chancel and the parish organ was built in the south-east chapel. Previously the chancel had been obscured by the large university gallery facing west into the nave, and music was provided by the university organ at the west end. Until the twentieth century there was a university choir which sang from the west gallery during university services, but this dwindled until only a few boys chosen from the parish choir sufficed, and it came to an end finally in the 1940s.

The parish choir traditionally sang at the main services of mattins and evensong. For many years after the 1939–45 war it was directed by Dr Douglas Fox. Alan Tranah, who succeeded him as organist in 1963, recalls Douglas Fox:

> A man of great musical stature, sensitivity and ability, who, following the devastating tragedy of losing his right arm in World War One, went on to become nationally famous as a Public School Director of Music and an organ and pianoforte recitalist of note. It was unforgettable to watch him skilfully playing much of the standard organ repertoire, using his left hand, often stretched across two keyboards, with both feet simultaneously pedalling, making up for the lost limb, in his own masterly arrangement of the printed music so that aesthetically nothing was lost. I frequently turned pages or drew stops for him, but if not quickly enough for his liking he would do it himself with lightning grabs . . . He received the OBE for his years of distinguished achievement in the field of music.
>
> There were four services to play each Sunday during University Terms and a large choir of men and boys to train. Douglas was indefatigable, but needed assistance . . . he found the recruitment and training of city boys a new and arduous task. The boys – a mischievous breed anywhere – were unappreciative of Douglas' musical genius and saw only his eccentricities, of which he had many, thus making discipline difficult. A curate was always present to police the boys' practices, and many of the full ones too. My arrival eased the

problem and after a short time Douglas yielded the boys' practices
to me, which was a relief and a release for the clergy.

In 1960 Douglas had a severe and long attack of shingles which
nearly cost him his left eye. In 1961 he dislocated his good shoulder.
On both occasions he was in hospital for months, and I assumed full
duties as Director of Music. Douglas recovered from his setbacks
but retired in 1963.

Alan Tranah worked with three vicars, Joe Fison, Hugh Montefiore
and Stanley Booth-Clibborn. In Hugh Montefiore's time Series 2 and
then Series 3 Holy Communion services were introduced, and for both
rites Alan Tranah composed musical settings. Montefiore tried to
encourage a separate, mixed voluntary choir to sing at the parish communion, but newsletters of the time do not indicate any real success for
this venture. Gradually the parish choir assumed responsibility for
singing at this service also. Montefiore also, when the number of boys in
the parish choir fell, allowed a few ladies to join.

When King's College Chapel was closed for repairs and the reordering of the east end in 1968, the choir of King's College sang choral evensong in Great St Mary's for a month and a half, at 5.15 pm on weekdays
and 3.30 pm on Sundays.

Alan Tranah was succeeded by Graham Sudbury, who held the post
of Director of Music from 1975 to 1986. He also directed the music at
the Perse Senior School, the preparatory department of which was a
useful recruiting source of boys. In Graham Sudbury's time the parish
choir was first given an August break, with a voluntary congregational
choir supplying the music.

Graham Sudbury recalls:

> Choir festivals in King's College Chapel; the Bishop's Award for
> choristers and one of our boys gaining top marks; the Christmas
> carol services with scarcely room, or air, to breathe; many choirboy
> parents becoming and remaining involved with responsibilities in
> the church; some choir members moved on to the choirs of Eton
> College, Magdalen College Oxford, Lichfield Cathedral and others.

The first recording of the choir, 'The sounds of Great St Mary's', was
made in Graham Sudbury's time. He conducted a performance of Bach's
St Matthew Passion given in King's College Chapel by the combined
senior schools choirs and Great St Mary's parish choir: some of the gentlemen sang solo parts, and Gordon Steele, verger and bass, was a notable
Christus.

Christopher Moore was Director of Music from 1986 to 1992. He had been teaching music at Hurstpierpoint College in Sussex. The parish choir was at that time at a rather low ebb, with four or five boys, three girls, two lady sopranos, two lady altos and a number of men. Christopher Moore was determined to build the choir up again, and succeeded to the extent that there were seventeen boys by the end of his first year. He took the somewhat controversial decision to remove the girls from the parish choir and to encourage the formation of a separate girls' choir. The idea was some time in taking shape, but in 1989 a girls' choir was formed under the direction of Jan Payne. Rosie Midgley, one of the first members of the choir, recalls:

> The idea for a Girls' Choir at Great St Mary's came from Christopher Moore. He was my piano teacher and when he mentioned it to me I thought it would be an interesting thing to do. So on a chilly evening in the autumn of 1989, Sarah Haworth, Elspeth Knight and I met in the choir vestry. Our teacher was Jan Payne. The first piece of music we sang that night was John Rutter's setting of 'All things bright and beautiful' – a piece we have sung innumerable times since then.
>
> We decided to meet every week, and to invite our friends to join as well. For the first few weeks it was a bit uncertain, but the atmosphere was relaxed, and we quickly found which were our favourite pieces, mostly simple music at least to begin with. After about three months the choir began to grow, and when there were fifteen of us we started to sing in church.
>
> Reactions to us were mixed. People were so used to the idea that church music had to be sung by boys – especially in Cambridge with the famous boys' choirs. At times I fear that we were not very good, and after one especially disastrous service we were banned from Mattins for a year. Since then the choir has grown a lot, and there are now over a hundred girls who are officially members, although some do not come often. We sing at all services regularly, and visit other churches in the area. We have often sung at concerts in Cambridge and other places. The high point was our visit to Paris in October 1994. It was a festival of English music abroad, and we were the only children's choir to be invited.
>
> Jan was the Director of the Choir. She started it and put lots of time into making it work well. Then a year or so later she was joined by Elaine Brown, who had sung church music regularly while at Bristol University. It was a real shock in 1995 when Jan told us that she was leaving. But then Michael Haynes took over, and since he is the Director of the Parish Choir as well the two choirs now work much more closely together and sing together for big occasions.

Christopher Moore was faced not only with the task of reviving the parish choir but also of replacing the parish organ. The instrument of 1870 had reached the end of its useful life, despite periodic overhaul and repairs. It was, furthermore, badly positioned in the south chapel over the stalls, and the organist played from a loft without a clear view of the choir and conductor below. In 1990 an appeal was launched, the amount was raised, and the new organ was built in 1991. It was dedicated by Lord Runcie on 13 October 1991 and the inaugural recital was given by Simon Preston. The new instrument, by Kenneth Jones of Bray in Ireland, was placed in the south chapel and its elegant carved case, in light oak, fills the arch opening into the chancel, and (with the loss of two choir stalls) a console was created at chancel level. The new organ was so designed that behind it, at first-floor level, a new vestry room for the verger could be created. While the work in building the new organ progressed, the church was permitted to use the university organ for all services, and the choir sang from the north gallery.

During Christopher Moore's time, the sung Sunday services were the eucharist, according to ASB Rite A (for which Christopher introduced some new settings) and mattins according to the Book of Common Prayer. Evensong was very occasional, being sung at Easter and in July. Christopher Moore increased the number of cathedral visits (where choral evensong was of course sung). The parish choir sang at Ely, York, Canterbury, Norwich, Lincoln and Coventry, and (perhaps the high point) Westminster Abbey in April 1991, where Michael Mayne was then Dean. The parish choir made two recordings in Christopher Moore's time, music for Easter Day mattins, and a selection of Christmas music.

Christopher Moore also initiated the Great St Mary's Singers, a group of ladies and gentlemen who did not want the heavy commitment of singing weekly in church. The Singers performed occasionally (and still perform), usually on Sunday evenings, when a programme of sacred music might be offered as an alternative to evensong.

Christopher Moore resigned at the end of 1991 to return to full-time teaching. His successor, Jonathan Gregory, had been organ scholar of Clare College, and came to Great St Mary's from Northern Ireland where he had been organist of Belfast Cathedral, and later of St Anne's, Belfast. During his time a wide musical repertoire was maintained. His wife Yoshimi was Japanese, and Jonathan Gregory started the Anglo-Japan choir, in which members of the parish choir were encouraged to sing with Japanese living and working in England. A notable early performance of the Anglo-Japan Choir was Handel's Messiah, sung on one night in St George's, Hanover Square, London (a church where Handel played the organ), and on the following evening in Great St Mary's.

The university evening service had by now been discontinued, and Jonathan Gregory agreed to David Conner's request for regular choral evensong. Thus the choirs were able to perform the other great treasure-store of Anglican music, the settings of the Magnificat and Nunc Dimittis, by composers from William Byrd to Herbert Howells.

Jonathan Gregory was appointed organist of Leicester Cathedral in 1994. His successor, Michael Haynes, a graduate of the Birmingham Conservatoire, came to Great St Mary's from St Peter's, Bexhill-on-Sea. There he had maintained a men-and-boys choir on traditional lines, so he was well used to the situation which he found at Great St Mary's. Early in his time Jan Payne resigned the direction of the girls' choir, and Michael Haynes assumed the direction of both choirs. His monthly choir diaries and music lists are a feat of coordination! The parish choir and the girls' choir continue to sing separately, sometimes joining forces for big occasions. Occasionally smaller groups sing music not necessarily well suited for the massed ranks of the full choirs, as for example when singers from the choirs sang in a live broadcast of BBC Radio 4's Daily Service in 1997. Cathedral visits have continued, to new venues, such as Llandaff Cathedral, and Southwell Minster, and an overseas link has been formed with the Lutheran church of St Lamberti in Hildesheim, Germany, resulting in singing visits to them and return visits of the German choir to Cambridge.

10 Bells and ringers

GARETH DAVIES

Bellringing in the English style is an art that requires a unique combination of hands, head and heart. Hands for the physical effort of controlling a swinging bell weighing many hundreds of kilograms. Head to cope with the mathematical intricacies that turn the formless jangling of chimed bells into the precise combinations of change-ringing. Heart to promote the contribution that the bells make to church worship. Over the centuries the ringers at Great St Mary's have shown no lack of skill with their hands and heads, though they have at times been more fickle with their hearts.

There were bells at Great St Mary's even before the building of the present tower. For a time they hung in a detached wooden tower in the churchyard. Construction of their current home began in 1491, the first stone being laid at 'a quarter before seven in the evening'. Progress was painfully slow. Even though the four bells were hauled up into the new structure in 1515, the tower had still only reached half its final height by 1550. This should have made it impossible for the bells to be rung, but such practical considerations were of little concern to Elizabethan civil authorities and the church was fined 2s. 2d. in 1564 for failing to ring while the Queen was visiting Cambridge.

The tower was not completed until 1610. However, enough work had been done by 1595 to allow the bells to find their intended resting place. The churchwardens recorded that 'in this yere the great bell was sett up & Runge & never before'. A year later 'all our bells are rung out and was never before 1596'. We do not know who the ringers were at this date. We cannot be sure how and what they rang. If all the bells were rung together it is likely that the ringers were practising an early form of the, largely recreational, activity that was to develop throughout the following century into English change-ringing. Indeed, the widespread use of bells for recreation may have been one of the factors that had led them to escape the general dispersal of church property that followed Henry VIII's break with Rome. By contrast, the usual custom for church

185

services and some civic events was to chime a single bell, often with particular bells signifying specific services. In fact, various commentators railed against the practice of ringing more than one bell on a Sunday on the grounds that it broke the Fourth Commandment.

These two strands, ringing for pleasure and for service, were to diverge widely over the next three centuries. They were pushed further apart in May 1643 when, under Puritan influence, Parliament passed an Act forbidding, amongst other Sunday pastimes – such as dancing, masques and wrestling matches – the ringing of bells for pleasure on the Lord's Day. This drove the ringers to practise their art on other days of the week. The already tenuous link between change-ringing and the service of the church was strained to breaking point.

Across the country, this event marked the beginning of a period of great progress in the art of bellringing. So it was, too, at Great St Mary's. The records that we have for the church in the seventeenth century suggest that improvements made to the bells were mainly to enhance secular pursuits.

In 1611 the original four bells had been augmented by a fifth, and then a sixth in 1622. In 1668 a further two bells were added to complete the octave. This allowed yet more possible complexity in the mathematical combinations on which change-ringing is based (40,320 different changes rather than the 720 available with only 6 bells).

Even during these developments, the connection between church service and the bells was not entirely forgotten, unless the inscription on the new treble bell was intended merely as a commentary on the quality of the sermons! 'Cum sono, si non vis venire, numquam ad preces cupies ire.' (If my sound does not make you want to go to the service, nothing will.) But, even if single bells were still calling parishioners to worship, it was on change-ringing that the ringers were concentrating.

1668 saw the publication of *Tintinnalogia*, the first book on change-ringing. In it Richard Duckworth suggested that the art originated about the year 1610, and this and other evidence placed its origins in the Bedfordshire and East Anglian area. He also included details of various methods that were rung at the time. Interestingly, one of the first to be dealt with is 'Cambridge forty-eight' rung on five bells. Whilst there is no documentary evidence to suggest that this method was rung in the town, it is suggestive, given that bellringers have a continuing penchant for naming new methods after the places where they were first rung. Duckworth himself had no apparent connections with Cambridge, being an Oxford man. However, his collaborator in the publication of *Tintinnalogia* was Fabian Stedman, the 'Father of Change-ringing', who has become renowned for his Cambridge connections, though with the church and bells of St Bene't rather than Great St Mary's. Stedman's associations with St Bene't's have been widely celebrated and in 1931 the bells there were restored to celebrate the tercentenary of his birth. Unfortunately, recent research reveals no contemporary record of any connection between Fabian Stedman and either Cambridge in general or St Bene't's in particular.

However, in 1677 when Stedman published *Campanalogia*, his own book on change-ringing, he gave us the name of one ringer at least whom we can assume did practise the art in Cambridge and, very likely, at Great St Mary's. He appears as the author of *'Seventeen Peals composed at Cambridge, by Mr. S. S'*. This is Samuel Scattergood, scholar at Trinity College from 1664 and Fellow from 1669 until 1678 when he took holy orders and entered his first living, as Vicar of St Mary's, Lichfield.

There are two ways in which bells may, over time, become unringable – neglect and extensive use. In view of the developments through the century the bells at Great St Mary's were clearly not neglected. More likely, then, there was a thriving band of ringers, including Scattergood, who put them to regular use. Enough use that by the beginning of the eighteenth century the state of the bells and their fittings was causing concern. The churchwardens' audit book entry for 5 May 1707 records that: 'It is agreed at a general meeting of the Parishioners . . . that the Churchwardens . . . procure proposals for the new running of the bells and that they do cause a new clock to be put up in place of the old one.'

As with the building of the tower, the arrangements were not made quickly. Not until 1722 were the old bells lowered from the tower to be melted down and replaced with a new ring of ten bells from Richard Phelps of the Whitechapel Bell Foundry.

Although Phelps gave the church four years to pay the £600 or so his work cost, he clearly became nervous. On 5 June 1724 he challenged the election of the new churchwardens until he was given security for the £71.12s.0d cost of providing the two additional bells. As an alternative he offered the opportunity to clear the slate by a payment of £63.0s.6d. within a week. The security was quickly found!

Installation of the new bells provided the impetus for reforming and formalising the status of the bellringers' society and in 1724 the Society of Cambridge Youths came into being. Its financial and other records, now deposited in the Cambridgeshire County Record Office, run continuously from that date and provide much of the evidence for subsequent developments.

A particular feature of these records is that they contain not only the names of the members, but their occupations. They reveal that it was perfectly possible for the proverbial eighteenth-century cat to sit down, if not with an eighteenth-century king, at least with a good cross-section of the middle classes. They show an egalitarianism based, presumably, on aptitude for ringing, rather than an hierarchy based on birth or education. Thus, at its formation, the Society of Cambridge Youths comprised by their own descriptions, a whitesmith, a sawyer, three gentlemen, a watchmaker, a joiner, a peruke-maker, a baker, a bricklayer, the verger of Trinity College and, that most important person in bellringing circles, an inn-keeper. As if to emphasise not only the range of occupations but the lack of division between town and gown, they were joined in 1725 by Charles Mason, Doctor of Divinity, Fellow of Trinity College and Woodwardian Professor of Geology, and in 1726 by John Bell, gardener, who signed the register only with his mark. Nor was physical impediment a bar, as is testified by the membership from 1767 of 'John Incarsole, Gentleman (totally blind, but an excellent Ringer)'. Indeed he must have been. Bellringing is generally regarded as difficult and dangerous enough for the fully sighted.

What was it that brought this disparate group together in this rather esoteric and largely recreational pursuit? A clue may be gained from the Articles of Agreement that were drawn up by the Society to regulate its activities. These were (and still are) regularly revised. The version settled on in 1788 gives a typical flavour. There are twelve articles. Ten of them mention money. One mentions beer. One deals with voting. Most of those mentioning money do so in the context of fines for a variety of misdemeanours – being late or absent; refusing to look after the tower keys; failing to pay off previous fines. They also explain the procedure for becoming a member, including the payment of at least five shillings on joining, and losing a further five shillings on leaving. Fines were also the means of dealing with occasional anti-social behaviour. Thus, in June 1746 'Bennet is punish't Sixpence for pocketing the Cucumber and one Shilling for Blotting the Book.' Unfortunately, even sophisticated forensic equipment has been unable to reveal the explanation for this curious offence that is undoubtedly hidden beneath the blot.

The financial motif is understandable when one looks at the Society's accounts in detail. The ringers were paid for ringing on a range of occasions and by a variety of organisations and individuals. Responsibility for these funds devolved to the 'steward', who was elected each month from the membership. His job was to keep the accounts and keep safe the club 'box' in which the money was kept. At each monthly club night he would account for his stewardship and, if the funds justified it, a dividend, usually of a guinea, was paid to each member. The records show that between 1726 and 1803 the members of the Society shared between them some £1,441, while just one monthly dividend in May 1807 amounted to some 30 guineas. These club nights were always held in an inn, hence the importance of having an innkeeper as a member, though this was also a reflection of the physical effort involved in ringing, before the invention of ball bearings made it less thirsty work.

There were a number of fixed ringing days during the year, among them the anniversary of the monarch's accession, royal birthdays and the election of new churchwardens. On these and other such occasions, payments were made variously by the university, by the mayor and corporation or by the church itself . For such events it was agreed by a majority of the Society in 1729 'to meet at the Steeple on a Ringing Morning the Summer half year at 4 o'Clock and in the Winter at six upon the forfeit of 4d'. The ringing clearly lasted some time as 'Jno Bell is allow'd half an hour after each time.' As well as these 'high days and holy days' it became commonplace during the eighteenth century for the ringers to be paid to ring for special events. Numerous payments were made by proud and wealthy parents to celebrate their sons receiving their degrees. Parliamentary candidates asked for the bells to support their campaigns. Though these regular dividends were no doubt welcomed by the members of the Society, they do not entirely explain their involvement. The ringing itself was the thing. To further its development, at least as much money again was ploughed back into the doings of the Society.

Outings were popular. As today, the ringers were anxious to practise their skills not only on their own bells, but to sample the delights offered by other churches. Thus, in 1767 two guineas was spent on visiting Cottenham. A similar amount was paid for a trip to Saffron Walden the following year, and double that amount to go to St Ives in 1769. Because the Great St Mary's band had a good reputation locally, other trips were made by invitation, often to open newly installed rings of bells. There was also a steady stream of visitors the other way. Over £3 was spent on entertaining the Norwich ringers in 1776.

Ringing also had its competitive side. There were, and still are, formal competitions, but there was also an informal rivalry between ringers from different towers and different parts of the country. When news came that Cambridge was to be visited by ringers from London, the Society resolved in 1789 that it would meet every Monday for a year to practise ringing something reasonably difficult for the time – Treble Bob on twelve bells. It is not clear how successful they were, but by the time of the College Youths visit they felt sufficiently generous to spend over £12 on entertainment for the occasion. At the same time they had agreed to forego their monthly dividends with the aim of saving for an excursion to Oxford; an event that duly took place in 1790 at a cost of somewhat over £88.

That the ringers could practise Treble Bob on twelve was due to the addition of the two further bells that had taken place in 1770 (raising the possible number of different changes to 479,001,600 – about 33 years continuous ringing!). This augmentation largely happened at the instigation of two of the ringers who collected subscriptions to pay for the work. However, the opportunity had probably arisen because in 1769, while the tenor bell weighing over a tonne was being rehung, the workmen dropped and broke it. This necessitated the metal shards being sent back to the foundry for recasting.

Further improvements were also made by the ringers to the ringing room. A chandelier was purchased in 1780. This helped make sense of earlier cryptic entries in the accounts such as 'Woman for the month ls. 8d.' which prove to refer to payments made for the supply of candles and maintenance of the tower. An even more significant purchase was made in 1782 when the ringers acquired and had installed a quantity of sixteenth-century linen-fold panelling.

The other feature noticeable of the ringing room is the collection of peal boards affixed to the wall. A 'peal' in this context is the continuous ringing of at least 5,000 different changes in a predetermined order. It is a test of both mental and physical stamina. At Great St Mary's such a peal will take at least three hours and fifteen minutes to complete. Certainly the eighteenth-century ringers felt that such performances were worthy of note and the boards record their efforts and those of more recent exponents. They were not always content with the minimum requirement and a number of the boards record 'long lengths'. There were 6,000 changes of Oxford Treble Bob Royal (10 bells) in 1790, 6,600 changes of Plain Bob Maximus (12 bells) in 1788, and 7,002 changes of

Grandsire Caters (10 bells) in 1791. Each of these performances lasted more than four hours.

By the end of the eighteenth century, ringing at Great St Mary's had reached a peak that compared very favourably with developments elsewhere in the country. However, the momentum was not to be sustained. By comparison the nineteenth century was to be a somewhat disappointing tale of stagnation.

In 1847 John Carr, later 'Leader of the Cambridge Company', published an idiosyncratic 'Narrative of Various Peals in Change Ringing and Interesting Cricket Matches', which described visits to Great St Mary's and other Cambridgeshire towers in 1843 and 1844. The picture it paints shows that while the ringers were holding their own they were not building on the achievements of earlier years. Partly this was due to a failure or an unwillingness to attract new members, a situation that was not to be solved for over a hundred years.

The situation worsened in 1879 when the Cambridge University Guild of Change Ringers was founded and for the first time there was a formal split between town and gown. Henceforth, it was unusual, if not positively frowned on, for an undergraduate to be elected to the Society of Cambridge Youths. The University Guild held its own practices and the available talent was split between the companies.

The formation of the University Guild, many of its members destined for ordination, was a symptom of a major change that was generally affecting bellringing. For decades the clergy had had little interest and even less control over what happened in the towers of their churches. The bellringers had been left to their own devices. Abuses, such as drunkenness, were not uncommon. In the second half of the nineteenth century there was a strong movement for belfry reform, which meant not only the clergy reclaiming the most far-flung parts of their churches, but the formation of diocesan associations of bellringers with overt clerical control. Though beer was certainly drunk by the ringers at Great St Mary's, as in most churches, there is no evidence that they were, themselves, particularly badly behaved. Nevertheless, there was no escaping the general trend.

Until 1724 the bells had been rung from ground level at the foot of the tower. The recasting and augmentation of the bells in that year gave an opportunity to construct a ringing room much higher up the tower, only some ten metres below the bells themselves. The shorter ropes needed gave much greater control over the swinging bells. But the climb to this room, up the circular tower staircase, meant that the ringers were, and remain to this day, out of sight, if not out of earshot. In the 1860s it was proposed that this situation should once more be reversed and the bells rung from the foot of the tower. Fortunately for the quality of the ringing, nothing came of this proposal.

The Great St Mary's ringers were, in any case, themselves involved in moves to re-establish the link between the ringing of bells for pleasure and in the service of the church. At the end of the century the Ely Diocesan Association of Change Ringers was founded, its inaugural meeting presided over by the Vicar of Great St Mary's and with some of the Society as founder members. Amongst its aims were 'the promotion of Change Ringing and Belfry Reform'.

If the ringers during the nineteenth century left little imprint on history, this was more than made up for by the bells themselves, or at least the clock chimes which struck on them. The clock installed in 1724 did not have chimes. However, it was in its turn replaced in 1793 and Joseph Jowett, Regius Professor of Civil Law, was asked to produce a suitable tune. Various traditions have it that he was helped in this by either Dr Randall, Professor of Music, or by his student, William Crotch, and that the tune is based on variations of an extract from Handel's 'I know that My Redeemer liveth'. Whatever the truth, the chime, which makes use of the third, fourth, fifth, eighth and tenor bells, sounded out uneventfully over Cambridge every quarter of an hour until 1859 when it was adopted for the newly installed clock and bells at the Houses of Parliament. As the Westminster chimes from Big Ben (though strictly speaking this is the name just of the tenor bell), the tune then became famous throughout the world.

Ties between the church and the ringers were strengthened further before the Great War with the appointment of the Reverend Anchitel Harry Fletcher Boughey as the church's first ringing vicar. But it was in 1928 that the knot was pulled tight when the ringers substantially revised the rules of the Society. For the first time, ringing for Sunday service became an official aim and the post of president was created, a role that has been filled ever since by the incumbent vicar. However, old habits die hard and in 1929 the secretary of the Society was still suggesting that 'an attempt should be made to put [the rules] in a form that speaks less of profit and more of service to the church'.

It also proved more difficult than expected to provide ringers for even a limited number of Sunday services before the war. So many men in those days were employed in shift and other Sunday duties. The imme-

diate post-war period also proved rather difficult. It was even feared that
there was a danger of ringing dying out in Cambridge and an attempt was
made to recruit new ringers through press advertisements. However, by
1950 matters had improved and the Society was ringing for services
almost every Sunday.

In 1952 it was decided to rehang the bells in a new, steel frame and, for
the first time, in the more usual clockwise order. Up until then the ringers
had been used to the bell ropes falling in a circle such that the next heaviest bell was to the right rather than to the left. The bells rang out again
after rededication in April 1954, but the Society's fortunes continued to
give concern over the next twenty years, even though the range of possible recruits had been extended by a decision that same year to admit
lady members to the Society.

In 1974 the 250th anniversary of the Cambridge Youths was marked
by a peal of 5,007 Stedman Cinques. It proved to be another turning
point in the fortunes of the Society. Since that date it has gone from
strength to strength, in terms of numbers, in terms of quality and complexity of the methods that have been rung and in its service to the
church. Membership of the Society has regularly stood well over the
thirty-mark. Many of the leading lights have been university undergraduates who have stayed on to work in Cambridge as it has become a centre
of technological excellence. Others have been attracted to the city for
similar reasons as the population at large has become more mobile. There
has thus been no shortage of fully fledged ringers, though the Society has
also taken on the training of a number of raw recruits.

The Society's progress has been reflected in its success in the National
Twelve Bell Ringing Competition, which it has won three times in recent
years against very stiff competition, allowing Great St Mary's to claim,
if only briefly, on each occasion that it had the best Sunday service band
in the country. But such successes and other activities are built on the
solid foundations of service to the church. Since 1975 the Society has
been committed to ringing for Sunday morning service throughout the
year and for the 9.30 service out of term (the University Guild meeting
that obligation during term). Indeed, voting membership of the Society
is now dependent on a minimum number of Sunday ringing attendances.

In 1991 the Society celebrated the 500th anniversary of the start of
work on the tower, by meeting at 'a quarter before seven in the evening'.
Those present recorded their names and occupations. A time-travelling
eighteenth-century member would have wondered, no doubt, at the
precise roles of computer, electronics and engineering consultants,

physicists, meteorologists, and agronomists and been astonished at the presence of several women and even a baby. However, he would have felt very comfortable with his physical surroundings. The candles would have gone but he would recognise the panelling and the peal boards. His money would still be placed in the 'box'. And above all he would still be able to take a rope and join in the ringing with his twentieth-century counterparts.

Conclusion

Inevitably, the end of a book such as this leads us to look ahead into the future. This is especially so when it has been produced in moments snatched from the life of a busy and fast-moving church community, full of hopes and plans for the future.

We are conscious that Cambridge is changing and that these changes form the context in which Great St Mary's will live and minister. The corporate and communal ideals which – as has been noted – characterised student life in the fifties and sixties have given way to the more individualistic ethic which has come in the harsher economic climate of the eighties and nineties. For the time being the commitments which shaped the post-war ministry of Great St Mary's are unlikely to command great enthusiasm among the students of the university. Big university services are likely to remain a feature of the past.

The city is changing too. New roads and a faster rail service – as well as quick air connections between Cambridge airport and Amsterdam – have connected Cambridge more intimately with other parts of England and with continental Europe. Commercial activity is expanding, and Cambridge has more high-tech industries than any other city in Europe. The city centre is noisy and crowded, and there is a new international character to its users. The city and county councils have a strategy to drastically reduce the number of cars which enter the city centre. This will have an effect on the churches of the city centre, which will probably become less local congregations and more centres for specialised activities and programmes.

At the start of this book we noted that the church of Great St Mary's is defined by two sets of relationships – with the university since it is the university church and with the city since it also the parish church of St Mary the Great. These relationships point towards the two characteristics of the life of the church which have evolved through its long history.

The first is the quality of its church and congregational life. This is shown in the continuing pattern of worship, on Sundays, through the week and on major festivals. This draws an extraordinary variety of people, which can be relied on to surprise and fascinate. In addition there is a costly and committed pastoral care, offered to both regular members and to visitors who want somebody to talk to.

The second is the concern for theological, political and social issues. Great St Mary's situation as the university church requires that this dimension of its life be attended to with care, and programmes of study and reflection are an integral part of its life.

The real question as to whether Great St Mary's has a future is bound up with the question of whether and how these two features can be maintained.

The future of Great St Mary's – and of its magnificent but under-used sister church of St Michael – depends upon its ability to discern and to plan for a ministry in a changing community. It will have to work closely in partnership with other churches, student bodies and community groups. It will respect the needs, questions and experiences of all those who come, and will be open to explore with them what faith might mean. It will discover what mission might be when it is carried out among an international and in large part un-Christian constituency of users.

In exciting times, fidelity to a regular cycle of worship, priority for pastoral care, and readiness to discuss and to debate, will ensure that the qualities of the past are continued into the future.

Index